Investigating *Heroes*

Investigating *Heroes*

Essays on Truth, Justice and Quality TV

Edited by DAVID SIMMONS

McFarland & Company, Inc., Publishers
Jefferson, North Carolina, and London

LIBRARY OF CONGRESS CATALOGUING-IN-PUBLICATION DATA

Investigating Heroes : essays on truth, justice and quality tv / edited by David Simmons.
    p.   cm.
Includes bibliographical references and index.
Includes filmography.

   ISBN 978-0-7864-5936-0
   softcover : acid free paper ∞

   1. Heroes (Television program)   I. Simmons, David.
PN1992.77.H47I58 2012
791.45'72 — dc23   2011044678

BRITISH LIBRARY CATALOGUING DATA ARE AVAILABLE

© 2012 David Simmons. All rights reserved

No part of this book may be reproduced or transmitted in any form or by any means, electronic or mechanical, including photocopying or recording, or by any information storage and retrieval system, without permission in writing from the publisher.

Front cover: cast of *Heroes*, season 1, 2006 (NBC/Photofest)

Manufactured in the United States of America

McFarland & Company, Inc., Publishers
  Box 611, Jefferson, North Carolina 28640
    www.mcfarlandpub.com

To Nicola Allen,
my very own Wonder Woman.

Table of Contents

Acknowledgments ... ix

Introduction
    DAVID SIMMONS ... 1

Part 1: Heroes and Villains

The Redemption of HRG
    LYNNETTE PORTER ... 7

"I'm Different ... Special": The Body of the Superhero
    BRONWEN CALVERT ... 19

Elective Affinities: *Heroes* and the Contemporary Conception of the Family
    STAN BEELER ... 30

"Last in My Class, Last on the Sports Field, I'm Not a Loser Anymore": Centralizing the "Geek" in Quality Television
    DAVID SIMMONS ... 41

Part 2: Borrowings and Intertexts

Naturalizing the Fantastic: Comics Archetypes
    JULIA ROUND ... 51

Superpowers and Super-Insight: How Back Story and Motivation Emerge through the *Heroes* Graphic Novels
    KRISTIN M. BARTON ... 66

"Niki's Not Here Right Now": Fragmented Identity in NBC's *Heroes*
    LAURA HILTON ... 78

Science Fiction and the Uncanny Realism of *Heroes*
    DAVID HIPPLE ... 90

Super Style: Notes for a Stylistic Analysis
    SÉRGIO DIAS BRANCO 109

Part 3: Ideas and Concepts

Heroes, Control, and Regulation
    LORNA JOWETT 119

"You're Broken. I Can Fix You": Negotiating Concepts of
U.S. Ideology
    TORSTEN CAENERS 130

Heroes' Internationalism: Toward a Cosmopolitical Ethics in
Mainstream American Television
    KENNETH CHAN 144

"This Power, It's Bigger Than Me": Time Travel as Narrative
Device and Catalyst for Character Exposition
    KEVIN LEE ROBINSON 156

Filmography 169
About the Contributors 171
Index 175

Acknowledgments

The process of bringing this book to completion has been a long and rewarding one. I would like to thank all of the contributors whose continued efforts have made this collection a pleasure to compile and to read. The strength of this book lies in their expertise and enthusiasm. I would also like to thank Stacey Abbott; her help and guidance in the early stages of this project was much appreciated. Further thanks go out to Lorna Jowett for all the many conversations we had discussing contemporary genre TV (go *Primeval*!), the staff and students at Northampton University including Stephen Keane and Kevin Robinson for their collegial excellence, and to Lawrence Phillips for funding some of this work (in a roundabout sort of way). This work would not have been possible without the tireless support of my family, my mum and dad Marlene and David, and my two brothers Brian and Paul. Finally, I must express my love for my partner Nicola Allen, whose support, both emotional and intellectual, has proven to be an invaluable source of strength throughout the course of bringing this collection to fruition. I thank you.

Introduction

David Simmons

Bounding on to the scene in September 2006, NBC's *Heroes* (2006–2010) was an immediate hit both commercially and critically. With its first season of 23 45-minute episodes, *Heroes* regularly picked up over 10 million viewers in the USA, while its terrestrial UK broadcast on BBC 2 averaged 4 million viewers an episode. The show's success saw it broadcast in foreign territories including Australia, France, Germany, and Hong Kong, where it aired to further commercial success. Critically, the show was both nominated for, and went on to win, a range of notable awards in genre and mainstream fields. In 2006 the American Film Institute named *Heroes* as one its ten best television programs of the year while the Writers Guild of America nominated the program for best new series of 2007; the show was nominated for a prestigious Golden Globe Award for best television drama, and one of the central actors, Masi Oka, was nominated for Best Supporting Actor on a Television Series. In 2007 the Academy of Television Arts and Sciences nominated *Heroes* in eight categories, while the Academy of Science Fiction Fantasy and Horror Films nominated the show for five Saturn Awards in the same year.

For those not in the know, over four seasons *Heroes* follows a group of interrelated characters that discover who they have superhuman powers, telling the story of how they react to and use these powers for good or for evil. Part of the show's appeal seems to have lain in its ability to mediate between the demands of genre and mainstream audiences by employing superhero/comic book trappings in an ostensibly realistic milieu. Indeed, to put it simply, comic book fans could recognize and appreciate the references and self-referential nature of the show while a more mainstream audience was able to engage with the broader concept of "ordinary" people dealing with the extraordinary circumstances depicted over the show's four seasons. As Ben Strickland notes in *Saving the World: A Guide to Heroes* (2007): "Audiences can watch *Heroes* to see how ordinary people learn to use their extraordinary powers....

This format speaks directly to viewers living in an uncertain, unsteady world by presenting individual, local, national, and global issues through a reassuring lens of romantic wish fulfilment" (Strickland 103). The depiction of the heroes in the show as fallible, "normal" people who experience some of the same problems that the audience conceivably might (Claire's teenage angst about fitting in with her peers, Hiro's anxieties over appeasing his parents' wishes) lent the show a hybridized quality that appealed to two different audiences. Indeed, in its ability to successfully mediate between the inherent grandiose spectacle of seeing superhuman individuals utilize their often visually spectacular powers and a desire on the part of the audience to be able to relate to these characters on a more human level, it is possible to situate *Heroes* in an emergent tradition of contemporary tele-fantasy — including the *X-Files* (1993–2002), *Buffy the Vampire Slayer* (1997–2003) and, more recently, *Lost* (2004–2010) — which transcend the potential limitations of their genre in terms of audience demographics to become cult shows that receive both high ratings and critical genre acclaim.

Borrowing many of the ideological concerns introduced by comics such as *Watchmen* (1986–87) and the *X-Men* series (1963–present) *Heroes*' appeal may have been equally attributable to its exploration of what it means to be a hero and what role such individuals should play within society. In foregrounding its super-powered characters' continual struggles to fit in with a "normal" world that harbors an inherent distrust of such figures (embodied in organizations such as Primatech and the Company), "*Heroes* explores the question of who should (or even can) act heroically, even as it illustrates the reality that being a hero may be a risky proposition on many levels" (Porter, Lavery & Robson 7). This more psychologically realistic reading of the superhero speaks to a contemporary era in which notions of heroism are being questioned yet remain relevant, at least on an ideological level, as Kring suggests in his explanation of the show's origins:

> I started thinking about what would connect with an audience ... with things like global warming, diminishing resources, terrorism.... I started thinking about a show that sort of dealt with that in a way by populating the planet with various people that may be coming along to actually do something about these larger issues [Weiland].

Given that it only aired for four seasons, *Heroes* was able to attract a large hardcore audience in a relatively short amount of time, partly due to its subject matter appropriating some of the fandom surrounding its comic book leanings, but perhaps also as a result of its creator's concerted attempts to utilize a range of multimedia formats (websites, webisodes, podcasts and graphic novels) to disseminate and reward interested viewers who wanted to engage with the show's world and characters in a manner that went beyond the confines of the weekly episodes. In this manner, *Heroes* can be seen as being at the forefront of contemporary attempts to create genre shows which allow for the creation of a range of interrelated products across a selection of salient different media. Though a proposed mini-series to be entitled *Heroes: Origins* never saw the light of day, other spin-off ventures proved to be successful — such as the best-selling graphic novel series — demonstrating the level of interest and support that the show managed to retain right up until its end.

Yet, as any avid fan of the program will know, *Heroes* was cancelled at the end of its fourth season and has yet to be re-commissioned by any of NBC's rival networks. A number of reasons have been given in the popular press for the show's failure to win a fifth season including its declining quality, poor writing, and the show's dwindling audience figures from season two onwards. *Heroes* creator Tim Kring stated:

> It's hard to sustain something that's a zeitgeist phenomenon. Things burn bright and short these days. We did an awful lot of episodes — 24 a season — which is difficult to do. A little less of it might have gone a longer way. People talked about the first season because it was new. Once the initial premise has been explored and the characters come to terms with what's happening to them, once those questions have been answered, the questions that are asked after that are less interesting [Anderton].

Yet while Kring's comments seem to imply that the show's initial success was partly a stroke of luck, perhaps the result of an audience impressed by the novelty of a superhero-inflected television show, there is evidence to suggest that *Heroes*' audience were still tuning in in large numbers (albeit through DVR time shift recordings and illegal bittorent trackers) and that season four marked the beginnings of a return to form with several critics agreeing that it showed "an improvement on what came before it" (Canning) and in retrospect can be considered "a worthy farewell to what deserves to be remembered as one of TV's most enjoyable shows" (Whitley). In its ostensibly premature cancellation, *Heroes* is emblematic of larger issues facing contemporary U.S. television shows which find themselves having to prove their success by means of the increasingly outdated Nielsen system.

This book seeks to explore the important issues surrounding *Heroes*, in terms of its content, marketing and reception. This collection investigates the show's fusion of "cultish" and mainstream trappings into a cohesive and successful whole. It looks at how *Heroes* managed to combine supposedly "lowbrow" elements (comic books, superheroes) with a "quality" television form that prizes characteristics such as moral ambiguity, depth of characterization and liberalism.

The book is divided into three parts. Part 1 looks at some of the more interesting and popular characters from *Heroes*' four-season run, examining the relationships between them, and their resonance with contemporary television audiences. In "The Redemption of HRG," author Lynette Porter discusses the "apparently mild-mannered employee and average family man" Noah Bennet. Porter examines the show's depiction of Bennet as an ambiguous character whose sometimes morally dubious attempts to balance a difficult home life with the increasing demands of his job complicate notions of what constitutes heroism in the contemporary era, and reverberate with a sector of the show's audience who might also be attempting to juggle the different elements of their lives. Bronwen Calvert's chapter "'I'm Different ... Special': The Body of the Superhero" examines the presentation of some of the show's central characters, exploring how they serve to destabilize, subvert and disrupt some of the conventional notions of the hero figure found in superhero texts. Calvert particularly focuses on the implications the show's characters have in terms of gender and the superhero, analyzing Niki, Tracy and Claire and the male characters of Peter and Hiro, to suggest that *Heroes* is engaged in an ongoing interrogation of established models. In his chapter "Elective Affinities: *Heroes* and the Contemporary Conception of the Family," Stan Beeler argues that the equivocal representation of familial relationships in *Heroes* was a crucial part of the show's initial success and later failure. Beeler examines the utilization of tropes drawn from the slasher film alongside the show's decidedly more complex and mature depiction of familial relationships in the form of Niki and Micah (among others) to suggest that *Heroes*' attempts to appeal to a diverse range of audiences may have contributed to its downfall. In the final chapter of Part 1, I discuss the representation of the "geek" in contemporary genre television, analyzing the popular character of Hiro in order to suggest that recent trends have worked to centralize the fan on screen, reconfiguring their specialist genre knowledge from a niche preserve into a recognizably postmodern and culturally reassuring act.

The chapters in Part 2 explore *Heroes*' utilization of narrative and aesthetic elements from other art forms. In "Naturalizing the Fantastic: Comics Archetypes" Julia Round charts the show's debt to superhero comic books. However, in a move that testifies to the innovation of *Heroes*, Round surveys the ways in which many of the tropes and mechanisms drawn from the comics' medium are used to normalize rather than emphasize the fantastic events in the show. Round's chapter goes on to propose that because these tropes were not developed as the series continued, they became diluted (through combination with a television aesthetic) or were repeated until what once seemed fresh and original stagnated into cliché. In her chapter "Superpowers and

Super-Insight: How Back Story and Motivation Emerge through the *Heroes* Graphic Novels," Kristin M. Barton takes a detailed look at the graphic novel spinoffs from the show. Barton proposes that the creators of the show went beyond a simple utilization of the sequential narrative form (perhaps as an additional revenue stream) and instead attempted to position the content available online as an integral part of the *Heroes* "meta-text" providing valuable insight into the televised show's characters and narrative.

Laura Hilton's chapter "'Niki's Not Here Right Now': Fragmented Identity in NBC's *Heroes*" analyzes the character of Niki as an example of the Gothic archetype of the doppelganger or double. Hilton contends that the trope of doubling has long held a central place in the superhero genre in the form of the alter ego, with figures such as the Hulk drawing upon earlier literary precedents including *The Strange Case of Dr. Jekyll and Mr. Hyde* (1886) and concludes that Niki represents an important staging post on the way to situating the female double as a relevant counterpart to her more established male equivalent. "Science Fiction and the Uncanny Realism of *Heroes*" sees David Hipple consider *Heroes* in a more holistic fashion, situating the show in terms of its science fiction and fantasy leanings. In particular, Hipple argues for a rereading of the show as "*mature* SF" proposing that in its consistent refusal to emphasise the visually spectacular aspects of its construction, *Heroes* rejects many of the popular conventions of science fiction on screen in favor of focusing on the human elements of the genre. In contrast to both Round and Hipple, Sérgio Dias Branco contends that the visual effects in *Heroes* distinguish the show from many of its televisual contemporaries. In "Super Style: Notes for a Stylistic Analysis" Branco provides a detailed examination of the use of special effects in the show and how these contribute to an aesthetic that is noticeably drawn from superhero comics.

In Part 3 of the book some of the more interesting and significant ideas that lie behind *Heroes* are discussed. Lorna Jowett's chapter "*Heroes*, Control, and Regulation" examines the complex view of power/lessness embodied in two of the central female characters in the show, Claire Bennet and Niki Sanders. Jowett uses these characters to explore *Heroes'* engagement with heroism and femininity, proposing that while both are defined in different ways by physicality and excess, each adhere to patriarchal gender models which suggest that their power needs to be regulated and controlled. In "'You're Broken. I Can Fix You': Negotiating Concepts of U.S. Ideology," Torsten Caeners examines the relevance of selected U.S. ideological concepts in *Heroes*. Caeners charts the application of concepts such as "the city on the hill," "the melting pot" and "Manifest Destiny," and concludes that *Heroes* offers its audience a contemporary reworking of these ideological precepts. In contrast to Caeners'

U.S. focus, in his chapter "*Heroes*' Internationalism: Toward a Cosmopolitical Ethics in Mainstream American Television," Kenneth Chan argues, through a close exploration of the character of Hiro Nakamura, that *Heroes* is significant for its attempt to present television audiences with a cast of characters who are both truly international and cosmopolitan in nature. Indeed, Chan believes that *Heroes*' internationalism may signal a critical shift in mainstream U.S. thinking about its role in global affairs, moving away from the strident nationalism and religious and ideological fundamentalism of the Bush era. In the last chapter, "'This Power, It's Bigger Than Me': Time Travel as Narrative Device and Catalyst for Character Exposition," Kevin Lee Robinson explores *Heroes*' utilization of time travel. Considering the show alongside other notable genre examples that contain time travel, Robinson suggests that *Heroes* is unusual in the realm of television because the concept of time travel and indeed time itself is an intrinsic part of the show's format. Past and future events underpin character motivation and development, and the fluidity and fatalistic nature of time are consistently utilized throughout the show. Like many of the scholars in this volume, Robinson suggests that time travel serves to call attention to the characters in *Heroes*, demonstrating the human focus of the show and its foregrounding of the relationships that drive their actions.

Works Cited

Anderton, Ethan. "Tim Kring Talks Downfall of HEROES; Thinks Future of TV Lies in Shorter Seasons." *Collider.com*. 6 Jan. 2011. 14 Jan. 2011. http://collider.com/tim-kring-heroes/68585/

Canning, Robert. "Heroes: Season 4 Review." *IGN*. 16 Feb. 2010. 2 Jan. 2011. <http://uk.tv.ign.com/articles/106/1069339p1.html>

Weiland, Jonah. "1— on —1: Talking with Heroes Creator Tim Kring." *CBR*. 21 September 2006. 14 Jan. 2011. <http://www.comicbookresources.com/?page=article&id=8146>

Whitely, Julian. "Heroes Season 4 DVD Review." *Den of Geek*. Unknown. 10 Jan. 2011. <http://www.denofgeek.com/Reviews/612201/heroes_season_4_dvd_review.html>

Porter, Lynette, David Lavery & Hillary Robson. *Saving the World: A Guide to Heroes*. Toronto: ECW Press, 2007.

Part 1: Heroes and Villains

The Redemption of HRG

Lynnette Porter

When *Heroes* first began, in 2006, one of its creepiest villains, Noah Bennet, aka HRG (so named by fans because of his horn-rimmed glasses), didn't have a power and seemed highly ordinary. An apparently mild-mannered employee and average family man seems trustworthy and innocuous, perhaps the perfect cover for a devious operative keeping an eye on anyone identified as having a power. His villainy predates the series' greatest villain, Sylar, and is all the more striking because Bennet is very much a social "insider"—a company man with a typical middle-class family: a wife, two children, and a dog.

Just how much of a company man Bennet really is becomes clear almost immediately in the series. In fact, the first season's "Company Man" (1:17) not only pays tribute to the character's popularity (as one of those characters *Heroes*' fans love to hate) but provides a backstory about, strangely enough, a character who not only isn't a hero but isn't a "special." Most other episodes during that wildly popular, critically acclaimed first season focused on the emerging powers of the series' budding heroes, such as Nathan and Peter Petrelli, Hiro Nakamura, Niki Sanders, and, quite fortuitously, Noah's daughter, Claire Bennet.

Nevertheless, HRG proves to be special in his own right because of his double life and carefully crafted dual personalities. In contrast, *Heroes* characters like Niki or Sylar, who also lead double lives because they have an "evil twin" persona, usually lack control of this alternate personality. Niki's evil twin takes over her mind, leaving her with no memory of the horrors committed while her double is in charge (e.g., massacred men in her garage; "Genesis," 1:1). Sylar works as a watch repairman by day (at least early in the series) but becomes a serial killer as he learns more about his power and craves the powers of other "specials." Toward the end of the first season, for example, he visits his adoptive mother and begs for her to accept him. When she becomes afraid and tells him to leave, a frustrated Sylar tries to force her to listen. During a scuffle, he "accidentally" stabs her with scissors, killing her ("The Hard Part" 1:21). His tears as he holds her cooling body are as much for himself as for her, but the "good son" aspect of Sylar's personality loses control of the killer within. This murderous persona takes charge and becomes more calculating as the series progresses, but during the first season, Sylar often seems to be unable to control his special abilities as well as his desire for violence.

Thus, from the beginning, HRG is emphasized as in a class by himself. Not only is he a different type of villain, as well as dual personality, but also a key catalyst to *Heroes*' main plot each season. Among all *Heroes*' recurring or guest characters over the years, HRG/Noah Bennet is unique. During season one he shows the greatest understanding of the history and nature of people with special powers. The most intriguing revelations take place in his scenes, which are often flashbacks to an earlier time, such as his job interview with the Company ("Company Man" 1:17) or the late-series shocker that his first family was killed by a "special" ("The Wall" 4:18). The story of these heroes and villains discovering who and why they are special is told through a series of revelations about and by Noah Bennet/HRG.

Although the role initially was envisioned as a temporary character, the chemistry between actors Jack Coleman (HRG) and Hayden Panettiere (Claire), plus fan love for the enigmatic character, quickly led to the senior Bennet becoming an important element in each episode (Jensen). As such, he becomes the character who evolves the most, from strict Company man to the "reborn" Noah Bennet, parent of an independent daughter and a tabula rasa for any future adventures taking place after the regular TV series ended. Because of his importance to the story, he also is one of the few characters introduced in the first episode who survives until the final scene of NBC's 2010 series' finale.

HRG's personal struggles with good and evil make his role representative of adults' frustration with society, but the ironically hopeful nature of his job and his belief in his ability to change the world increase his complexity as a character and make him seem worth redeeming even at his most villainous moments. More than the heroes who populate this series and also veer between their better and worse natures, HRG is an important character because he is "one of us"—those without special powers who find it increasingly difficult to deal successfully and humanely with employers, the government, and family members. His likelihood of redemption is, in many ways, also ours.

HRG as a Symbol of Modern Humanity

Symbolically, HRG/Noah can represent the dichotomies that many career-oriented adults in Western societies feel they must maintain in order to be successful, even if the events he experiences are larger than those in real life. His shadowy line of work requires him to be heartless and calculating; his role as Claire's father encourages him to show warmth and love while he (over) protects his special little girl. As befitting a live-action drama mimicking a comic book, *Heroes*' dramas and dichotomies are exaggerated. As a "villain," HRG emotionlessly meddles in the lives of "specials" by monitoring, kidnapping, imprisoning, and drugging them, among other dastardly deeds. When he feels the situation at home requires this level of intervention, he shows no hesitation in having his wife's memory wiped, weaving an intricate web of lies around his family, and threatening (also with a side order of memory loss) the teenage boy who attacked Claire ("Hiros" 1:5). HRG's dark side is indeed very dark, as well as cold, unrelenting, and practical, qualities needed to be good at his job.

At home, Noah must be convincing as a doting father and indulgent husband. He brings his daughter stuffed animals to add to her collection and has heart-to-heart chats with "Claire bear." He heads the table and tries to keep up with his family's daily activities when they sit down to dinner. In many ways he is a throwback to *Father Knows Best* (1954–1960). The family's "hero" seems to be doing his best to provide for his family. This exaggerated dichotomy between work and family personas invites audiences to ask which personality is real, because these roles seem too disparate to be contained within one character who is in control of his mind (unlike Niki or Sylar) and who accepts both roles as equally important in his life.

Despite his "normal" middle-class life and "typical" work/family issues (e.g., overtime, required business travel, an unrelenting boss), most *Heroes* fans wouldn't choose HRG as the character with whom they identify. The Noah personality, introduced first, invites identification (and even sympathy). The HRG personality, however, is revealed to viewers only gradually and mirrors audiences' darkest fears about Big Brother. During the first season, HRG is the shadowy man trailing the series' heroes; at first, viewers don't even know that Claire's father is the dark figure lurking in the background. In fact, the first revelation about HRG is that he does indeed have a name—Noah Bennet ("Company Man" 1:17; "How to Stop an Exploding Man" 1:23). By the end of the first season, audiences have become well acquainted with both sides of the HRG/Noah character, each revealed independently, and at last know his complete name (his first name is revealed only during the season finale), further humanizing him and making him a complete, if complex, character.

In his four-season struggle between two disparate lives, HRG/Noah represents the average middle-class career person with a family. Although most career-minded parents don't face quite as many or as complicated dilemmas as Noah does, the desire to balance home and family coupled with the harsh inability to "have it all" is certainly a modern dilemma faced by most adult viewers. Noah's difficulty in finding balance in his life, and the resulting consequences of favoring job over family to get ahead, make even HRG a more sympathetic, understandable character.

During season four, Noah finally understands just how much the HRG persona has cost him. With the breakup of his marriage and estrangement from Claire, Noah at last recognizes the consequences to his family of his obsession with work. Even in a subsequent romantic relationship with former Company employee, Lauren Gilmore, Noah has difficulty with the concept of dating. Instead, their best moments as a tentative couple occur when they work together to hunt villainous "specials" in order to protect Claire. The final scene of the series brings together Noah and Lauren and suggests that, with his recent understanding of the need to form loving, rather than purely work-related relationships, Noah might at last be able to create a future with Lauren.

HRG as the Epitome of the Modern Employee

As a worker, Noah is identified as the epitome of a company man, as the title of his most important backstory episode identifies him. Even his "Company" persona is split into two parts: his cover job as a middle manager at Primatech Paper and his covert job as a mid-level spy and tracker who takes care of problem "specials." Unlike jobs in those *Father Knows Best* days, when Dad left for work in the morning, clocked in and did his job for eight hours, then returned home in time for dinner and family time, modern employers expect a lot more from their workers. Employees feel the desire to succeed in their career, but they also, quite practically, have to survive layoffs and outsourcing. Like most mid-level employees who still want to move up the corporate ladder into higher (and more secure) levels of management before they become too old or otherwise obsolete, HRG is determined to work harder and to be more dedicated than any other employee. (His desire for vengeance against "specials" isn't revealed until season four, which makes HRG's dedication to the Company seem much more like a normal desire to get ahead on the job during most of the series.)

HRG invests his soul in his job, to the extent that his family becomes an extension of his work life. He is given baby Claire to "adopt" (i.e., rear, monitor, and control) as part of his job. Being a good employee, he reluctantly accepts this task. Ironically, the very test of how good a Company man he is — taking on the immense responsibility of a "special" child who likely will create trouble for him down the line — is the very act that eventually forces him to re-evaluate his dedication to the Company, change his values, and lose his identity as a Company man. Almost from the moment she is born, Claire begins to lead her pragmatic adoptive parent toward his ultimate redemption as loving father Noah, the antithesis of HRG.

Until *Heroes*' last season, the idea of not being a Company man (even when the Company is gone and HRG works for the government) is abhorrent to HRG. He futilely tries to maintain some semblance of balance between his Company life and his family life, but because they are intertwined with the concept of "work," he eventually has to choose one side or the other. Equality or balance isn't a possibility — one life must be sacrificed for the sake of the other, yet both "work" and "family" are necessary. Thus, HRG/Noah Bennet faces the same dilemma as other adults, particularly those reaching or at middle age: Success or survival in a career (not just a job) *or* immersion in family life before it's too late. "Having it all" isn't an option any longer. At some point, deliberately or by default, every head of a household must face this decision and accept the fallout.

When Noah Bennet is viewed as a "typical" adult struggling with the same societal roles and problems as everyone else, he is no longer a true "villain." His actions may lead to extreme outcomes, including illegal or immoral activities, but he automatically becomes "one of us" in a way that Sylar or other one-sided, one-lived, one-dimensional villains never can.

In fact, a villain like season four's carnival-owner Samuel Sullivan seems evil not just because his extended family is a farce, to be used only for personal gain and as pawns in his scheme, but because he doesn't understand the concept of love and only has a "Company" mentality. The actions he mimics as loving are clearly revealed to be false and purely manipulative — whether he is encouraging Claire to join his family and thus mimicking a benevolent, understanding father or trying to woo a former lover by mimicking the actions of a suitor in love. Samuel can't maintain either façade for long; he is immersed in his villainous "work" life to the exclusion of all else.

Similarly, Angela Petrelli, an original member of the Company, also loses the capacity to love her sons for who they are, not what she wants them to become. Both Nathan and Peter become so frustrated and wary of their mother's "love" that their attempts alternately to please her (and thus win her love) or thwart her (as a perceived villain) can never redeem her. Although Angela mourns the loss of her elder son, she goes to the extreme of scheming a horrific way to bring him back from the dead because of her conviction that Nathan can still play an important political role. In many ways, both Samuel and Angela indicate what Noah Bennet might have ultimately become — a man unable to love his daughter — without Claire's redeeming influence and unconditional yet tough-love interactions with her father.

Until Claire matures and can express both her love for Noah and her fear and disgust of HRG, he tries his best to be a Company man and, indeed, viewers find out in the final season, has a good reason for wanting to believe in the Company's values. His pregnant first wife is accidentally killed by a villain with a special power, and Noah wants revenge for the loss of his family ("The Wall" 4:18). The Company not only gives him an outlet to control and sometimes punish anyone with a special power, but it eventually gives him a family by presenting him with baby Claire, thus mending his crumbling marriage and, it is implied, helping lead to his second wife's pregnancy with their son. The Company allows Noah an outlet for grief and thwarted love and later rewards his dedication with a new family. HRG becomes even more indebted to the Company that "saved" him and makes him into a superficially successful modern adult, one with a respectable (and, to his and the Company's mind, socially crucial) job and the ideal family. Perhaps HRG believes that the Company "redeemed" him from his unsuccessful life as a used car salesman-cum-vigilante, eventually giving him everything he wanted. Noah only realizes how much he has sold out to the Company when Claire is old enough to see the cracks in that "perfect family" façade and begin to ferret out the truth behind her father's lives.

Disillusion with and Dissolution of the Company Man

Only when Claire grows up — and realizes that she has the ability to self-heal, making her virtually indestructible — does she also realize that her father leads a double life, one that makes her "happy family" a sham. In a similar epiphany during season four, Noah realizes that his work life has become a sham, and in favoring it over his family, he has lost almost everything. Claire and Noah react to these epiphanies in opposite ways — Claire wants to confront change and let everyone know who and what she is; Noah likes to hide from change and try to control/stop it, but when he can't, he doesn't know who or what he is. As with other aspects of the father-daughter redemptive relationship, Claire has to guide Noah to an understanding of his better nature, hidden deep beneath layers of duplicity and self-delusion.

One of the first father-daughter conflicts arises from Claire choosing to rebel when her father wants to protect her. Claire feels compelled to attend her high school's football Homecoming, not only as a cheerleader but as Homecoming queen. Noah feels equally compelled to "save the cheerleader" by grounding her, even though Claire becomes angry with him for this decision; HRG doesn't explain why Claire needs to stay away from Homecoming — he keeps work-related information about heroes, villain Sylar, and prophesies about cheerleaders to himself. When Claire escapes the house to attend Homecoming ("Seven Minutes to Midnight" 1:8; "Homecoming" 1:9), she sets into motion the first in a series of confrontations that eventually break down the dividing wall between the HRG and Noah Bennet personas, allowing work and home lives quite literally to bleed into each other.

The more Claire (and the audience) learns about the Company and HRG, the more she questions her place in the family and confronts her father about his actions regarding "specials." As one of those her father hunts, Claire forces HRG to see life from the perspective of a "special," a quite different viewpoint than he has either as her father or a Company man. Claire becomes disillusioned with her beloved father and anticipates the future dissolution of her "typical" family life. At this point, Noah has to decide which "life" to save — that of HRG the Company man or Claire's dad.

At first he tries to maintain both, allowing Claire to know what he does for the Company but promising to protect her. She is the exception to his job — he needs to know what the Company plans to do so that he can continue to save her from his employer. By keeping his job, he can keep Claire. That plan, however great in theory, backfires spectacularly. Like many teens struggling to find her adult identity, Claire doesn't want to be protected by her father. She wants to live honestly — which means that the world should know how "special" she is. Noah understands how dangerous a proposition that can be, as do most parents who want to protect their children from people who will misunderstand, use or abuse them, or, at the very least, not value their special gifts. Like a typical teen, Claire has to rebel against this authority, not only against her father, but also the Company (and later, the government) he represents. That his personal and professional lives have become so entwined makes her rejection of HRG also a rejection of Noah.

The simple "moral to the modern story" as far as *Heroes* is concerned is that, at least for most people, work needs to be separate from family. Either work needs to take priority and be allowed to dominate one's values and time, or family becomes the priority at the expense of the ultimate career. Believing that balance between the two can be achieved over a lifetime is a lie, and either choice will lead to some regret about the road not taken.

HRG ultimately is sacrificed so that Noah can emerge, but his many years as a Company man leave his family life decimated. Throughout the final season, Noah tries to rebuild personal relationships, but it is too late to reconstruct his family. The "villain" who ends up destroying his family is himself—a product of loyalty first to the Company and later to the government's homeland security operation in which he has a similar job of tracking "specials." No matter how much HRG believes that his job-related choices will help protect his family, no one protects his family from him. Ironically, this decimation of his personal life leads to Noah's affirmation of his core values— primarily, to love Claire and help (but not control) her.

Individuals Can Change the World

For all that HRG's job seems morally reprehensible to those who don't share the Company's philosophy for living in a morally gray world, one of HRG's core beliefs is rather hopeful. No matter how many times Noah complains that he can't buck the Company because it is too large and far-reaching to evade, his actions belie his words. His schemes and deeds illustrate that he believes one person *can* change the world. His fear that one "special" may have the power to destroy humanity is matched by his belief that a determined Company man like himself can make a difference in fighting this threat.

As a hardcore Company employee, HRG believes in his duty to track down and monitor "specials." When paired with "special" partner Claude, HRG resists, not only because he dislikes all people with a power but because he believes that he can do the job better alone. When he falls in love with baby Claire despite his initial resistance, he shows that he believes he can make a difference in her life and, furthermore, she can make a difference in the way the Company views potentially "special" children. His little girl isn't the threat that the Company believes she may become. Even when her power manifests itself, Claire's dad believes that she can be protected and can live a full, free life as a "special"—as long as no one knows what she can do. Ironically, Claire succeeds in changing the Company's view of "specials" by convincing the ultimate Company man that his job will destroy who she is.

Noah's hubris is the result of his belief in the power of the one. Even when he no longer works for the Company or their successor, he believes that he is the only one who can protect Claire. He alone can control the government's plan to capture and persecute "specials" during Nathan Petrelli's political regime. He alone can control Claire and thus keep her special ability secret. When these plans fail and Noah and Claire become further estranged, he believes that he alone can make amends for the dissolution of his family and regain college-student Claire's trust. Throughout the series, Noah believes so much in the power of one person to change the course of modern (or familial) history that he often believes, to his detriment, that no one else but he is capable of effecting that change.

Perhaps this value is so ingrained that he inadvertently instills it equally deeply in Claire, much to his final regret. The series' finale concludes with Claire committing a deadly act, just as she used to do back home in Texas as a cheerleader. She once again documents her self-mutilation, knowing that she will survive to heal in a matter of moments. In the final scene, however, she performs this feat in front of "the world" — a crowd of journalists with cameras. Noah can only look on in horror as Claire climbs atop a Ferris wheel and plunges to the ground, only to stand up, self-heal, and face the group documenting her action.

Claire believes that she should never live a lie — and by hiding her special ability to self-heal, she is doing just that. She wants to prove to the world that "specials" can be trusted and valued, not feared and hunted. Whether she succeeds may be left to any future stories beyond the original TV series, but in the final moments of the finale, viewers see the world that Noah Bennet has helped create.

In many ways, his role proves that one person can tip the balance to instigate a society-changing course of action. That belief, however, doesn't mean that one person always can control the outcome of his or her action or must work for the greater good. HRG would be horrified that his life's work has been ruined — Claire is "outed" as a special, and he no longer can protect her. Noah may be worried for his daughter, but she — not the Company or his job — is the focus of his anxiety. At some level he must realize that Claire embodies the positive aspects of her upbringing (e.g., standing up for what one believes in, taking the power of one person very seriously) rather than simply defying her father because of teenaged rebellion or mistrust.

Death, Redemption, and Rebirth

In a 2007 interview, Coleman anticipated the significance of his character in the overall *Heroes* story:

> I suspect the relationship between Claire and HRG is one of the core values of the show and as twisted as the relationship is, they've said so many lies to each other, but ultimately, I think they really do love each other and there is a tremendous bond there, and I think it's one of the bedrocks that they will build story on. It's much more of a domestic issue than some sort of superhero issue [Chan].

This explanation would prove prophetic. The Noah-Claire dynamic in many ways drives the plot of the entire series. It also makes a superhero story relevant to viewers dealing with their own parent-child and work-home conflicts.

Even in early episodes, Claire's dad is willing to sacrifice his body — not just his career or reputation — in order to protect his daughter. He becomes a more sympathetic character during season one when, charged with handing over Claire to the Company, he instead helps her escape and fakes an attack in which he is really shot ("Company Man" 1:17). Of course, Noah knows how to get shot so that he won't die, but his pain from the injury and abandonment of his daughter (not to mention forced memory loss in order to protect her) is very real.

Part of HRG dies with this self-sacrifice for Claire. The Company man lies and deceives his boss in order to free his daughter. He fails to complete his assignment and risks the Company's wrath. The Noah persona also makes a difficult sacrifice — he loses memories of Claire. With this episode HRG becomes less of a villain when his daughter takes precedence over his job and when he is shown to be willing to suffer for his past actions. HRG/Noah pays the price of being a Company man and, in the process, is on his way to being redeemed from villainy. However, he still has a long way to go before he completely leaves the "villain" category, as defined by Claire and the viewers.

Throughout the many volumes of the *Heroes* saga, Noah is willing to die for his daughter; his willingness to sacrifice his body to protect her is never questioned. Unfortunately, the HRG persona is more difficult to kill until season four, when HRG's work-related persona finally is sacrificed once and for all. Until that point, whether HRG works for the Company, the government, or himself, he still retains aspects of his shadowy persona and performs morally questionable acts.

In the last story arc on *Heroes*, this theme of sacrifice, loss, and death leading to redemption is replayed with the real possibility that this time Noah will actually die, rather than simply be injured or suffer loss. Noah and Claire are buried in a carnival trailer far below the surface. Claire can survive being crushed by the weight of the earth or deprived of oxygen; her body will keep regenerating. Noah doesn't have that option. As he gasps for air, he forces Claire to admit that she should leave him to save herself. By staying with her father, she risks any chance of escape. She needs to be free, once and for all, of her dad before she can lead her own life ("Brave New World" 4:19). This scene also becomes symbolic for the coming-of-age Claire, who must finally establish her own adult identity as an independent woman — which she does by the end of the episode.

HRG has to "die" as a Company man attempting to control "specials" (especially Claire) before Noah can be "reborn" as a better man and father. The HRG persona has been dismantled one piece at a time with each sacrifice he makes to regain Claire's trust and to be reunited with her. The broken, vulnerable Noah of season four has lost his home, marriage, family, job, and reputation. He more sincerely wants to help "specials" and ensure that Claire is safe. He focuses not on what he wants (or what he wants because it will make him a better Company man) but rather on Claire's needs. In doing so, he puts himself in harm's way and inadvertently ends up buried in a trailer.

Although Noah often has tried to win back Claire's attention and favor, only to betray her trust in his ongoing efforts to protect her and make decisions for her, he finally succeeds through what he believes are his dying words. He encourages Claire to leave him, when throughout the series his efforts, even when physically separating him from his daughter, have been to bind her to him. When he believes he is doomed to die buried alive, he accepts his impending death and encourages Claire to make the choice to leave him. He doesn't decide for her this time but uses the last of his breath to convince her to save herself. Throughout the series, Noah-as-dad has sacrificed himself to save his cheerleader daughter — being shot to allow Claire to escape the Company's clutches, pushing her toward her biological father and grandmother, creating a new ID for her in another state, working as a double agent (even with Sylar) to control events that he believes ultimately will keep his daughter's secret hidden from the public. This time Noah can't control the outcome and has no ulterior motive; he simply wants Claire to survive and lead her own life. When discussing this scene with *TV Guide*, Coleman noted,

> In the finale there are some pretty sweet scenes between the two of them that should be pretty touching. Even though there's been strain throughout the season, it never got to the point of "I hate you and never want to see you again." It was always mitigated by a sense of love, and the two of them have always been able to overcome their issues [Bryant].

Despite their many conflicting ideas, Claire always comes "home" to Noah, whether to berate, challenge, or forgive him. When she tearfully breaks down and fears to leave him (i.e., lose him to death), Noah finally understands that he will always be important to his daughter. For all that he loves Claire, the

HRG persona often kept Noah from loving unconditionally. Becoming the beneficiary of Claire's unconditional love, despite his many failings as a father, redeems him. With this realization, Noah understands that none of his past deeds has truly separated him from Claire; thus, death can't either. This final father-daughter emotional moment brings Noah's story full circle and finally lays to rest the HRG persona.

Although a deus ex machina in the form of "special" Tracy, who has the power to control water, manages to float Claire and Noah to safety, nevertheless, the last remnant of his control over Claire "dies" during his time underground. The water metaphorically washes away Noah's sins; his "rebirth" after being buried is a symbolic resurrection. When Noah arises from HRG's "grave," he is reborn into a new world, facing new challenges as Claire's father, not her keeper.

"Brave New World" ends this volume of the *Heroes'* saga, as well as concludes NBC's TV series, but it also closes the stories leading to Noah's redemption and Claire's coming-of-age. By the conclusion of this episode, father and daughter truly are entering a brave new world as characters now freed from their past. They have dealt with their issues, including those of HRG as "villain" and Claire as "hero," and can move forward stripped of past pretense and self-delusion. As a modern parable for the redemption of an average modern man, Noah Bennet's story, more than those of superheroes, becomes the most symbolic and empowering in the series.

Works Cited

Bryant, Adam. "Heroes Finale Preview: Showdown at the Carnival." *TV Guide*. 7 Feb 2010, http://www.tvguide.com/News/Heroes-Finale-Preview-1014769.aspx.

Chan, Elizabeth. "The Man Behind HRG on Heroes." *TV Squad*. 27 Feb 2007, http://www.tvsquad.com/2007/02/26/the-man-behind-hrg-on-heroes/.

"Heroes' Jack Coleman Discusses H.R.G." *MovieWeb*. 10 Nov 2006, http://www.movieweb.com/news/NE2oS267Az6Z54.

Jensen, Jeff. "Jack Coleman: Father Figure." *Entertainment Weekly*. 15 Oct 2007, http://www.ew.com/ew/article/0,,20036782_20037403_20152506,00.html.

"I'm Different ... Special":
The Body of the Superhero

Bronwen Calvert

The "classic" representation of the superhero — the "archetypal visions of the good guy" who "[fought] crime in the name of perfect justice" (Hughes 546) — has mutated over time. Alternative, more recent portrayals of superheroes from comics/graphic novels like *The Uncanny X-Men* (1963–present) or *Watchmen* (1986–1987), from films like *Superman Returns* (2006) or *Batman Begins* (2005), and from television shows like *Smallville* (2001–2011), *Heroes* (2006–2010) or *Misfits* (2009–present) share a common thread, a focus on "deconstructions of mythology and the superhero" (Hoppenstand 521). In *Heroes*, much of this focus rests on an exploration of the embodiment of the superhero, which takes place through internal exploration of character as well as external representation of these "different" and "special" bodies — which is constantly undercut by their utterly ordinary appearance. The body of the superhero allows, and even encourages, the destabilization, subversion and disruption of conventional notions of "the hero" and of the "heroic" body, so that we see the collapse of the classic "wimp/warrior ... duality" (Brown 32).

Within the "superhero" narrative in comics/graphic novels, film and television what is most commonly emphasized is the visual *spectacle* of the superhero body. The viewer is invited to engage with this presentation and display of the superbody, which "continue[s] to be a site of spectacle" (Taylor 345). Through this, the viewer also encounters the "paradox of spectatorship" (Johnson 10), which poses different issues for male and for female viewers, and places different emphases upon the bodies of male and female characters. In recognizing that the question of "visual pleasure" (originally posed by Laura Mulvey, and tackled by Tania Modleski, Merri Lisa Johnson, Yvonne Tasker and others) can be far more complex for both male and female viewers, as well as for characters within the narrative, space is opened up for different interpretations of the connections between bodies on display and the viewers observing them.

In general critical terms, the superhero body is "mysterious, invested with magical abilities and a metamorphic pliability" (Bukatman 49); it is "malleable, plastic, and subject to all kinds of wild reconfigurations and metamorphoses" (Taylor 347). It is open to observation and analysis by other characters within the narrative, as well as by viewers/spectators outside it. The individuals of *Heroes*, whatever their special abilities, are physically marked by their emerging powers. These abilities may also "mark" their experience of embodiment: for example, where those powers directly affect the appearance of or the capabilities of bodies that are otherwise presented as "normal."

These "superhero" bodies are marked in various ways; for example, by race and class. The narrative includes characters of color, some of whom have leading roles (Mohinder, Hiro and Ando), and others who recur for one or several seasons (D.L., Micah, the Haitian). Class operates to mark the superhero characters, too: for example, Niki as stripper/exotic dancer; Nathan and Tracy as individuals who have status and power in the political world; Matt and Peter as lower status, blue-collar workers (police officer and nurse/paramedic respectively). Their status as superheroes, while a "private" one, nevertheless means that some of these social and cultural markings are overturned. The individuals form loose, shifting alliances and connect with others (both with and without special abilities), cutting across many of the boundaries that would ordinarily separate them.

The superhero bodies are literally "marked" with scars, wounds and tattoos, which transform their bodies into "the blank page on which engraving, graffiti, tattooing, or inscription can take place" (Grosz 141). Several characters have the mark of two parallel lines somewhere on their necks, signifying that at some point they have been abducted, injected and categorized by the Company (see, for instance, Matt and Isaac). This mark, which is initially a fearful sign of coercion and loss of control, becomes a means by which those with special abilities can recognize each other; thus, a positive sign that connects individuals. Future versions of Peter Petrelli are marked by a scar on the face, which acts as a physical emblem of the passing of time, and of the transformation of Peter's own embodied self into a more troubled, compromised and fractured identity — one that could more easily be defined as villain (see "Five Years Gone" 1:20; "The Second Coming" 3:1). Tattoos as marks play a role in the narrative, too. The tattoo of the helix symbol marks Jessica and this, as with Future Peter's scar, allows characters and viewers to recognize Jessica over her alter ego Niki. The helix tattoo, like the parallel line scar, additionally marks Jessica as a person with abilities.

Marking further includes elements of performance, masquerade and costuming. Scott Bukatman notes that a superhero body is both secretly and publicly marked (54). The superhero masquerade produced by masks and costumes is paralleled by the masquerade of the civilian identity, and these parallel identities both display *and* disguise or camouflage the superhero body (Weltzien 241). In *Heroes* it is notable that, while the superhero characters are fairly consistent in their attempts to keep their abilities secret, few try to create any kind of secret identity. Instead, we more often see the rejection of any secret, specifically superhero identity. Ando refuses Hiro's attempt to turn him into a superhero with a (ridiculous) costume, logo and "Ando-cycle" (though he does ride away on the motorcycle; "A Clear and Present Danger" 3:14). However, this and the duo's "Dial a Hero" business ("Dial-A-Hero. How may we save you today?" "Acceptance" 4:4) is regularly played for comedy, along with a knowing intertextual nod at the classic comic/graphic novel sources on which Hiro relies for guidance. Micah as "Rebel" is arguably one of three characters with abilities who does create a successful secret superhero identity, one that succeeds in outwitting the authorities. However, this identity is in name only; Micah does not wear a costume or a mask, unless that costume is the disguise of a school-age child. A second more-or-less successful superhero identity, that of Niki and her alter ego, Jessica, is more problematic. It is certainly possible to view Jessica as Niki's secret identity. However, Niki and Jessica are not, in the conventional sense, two sides of a single superhero, both engaged in performance and masquerade in order to maintain the separation of secret and public identity. Rather, Niki and Jessica are split and separate identities struggling for power and agency within the same superhero body; the narrative constantly overturns and destabilizes the sense that one of these is the real or fixed identity.

A further example of a successful superhero identity in this narrative is Sylar. He does rename himself once he is aware of his special abilities, and throughout the narrative clear distinctions are made between his Sylar and Gabriel identities. In the glimpse of the future in season three, his attempt to live a normal life with his son is under the name Gabriel, and he actively rejects the name Sylar ("The Second Coming"). Thus, we do have a consistent separation of civilian and superhero, which is further complicated by the positioning of Sylar as the troubled villain of the series. It is worth noting that once Peter rehabilitates Sylar in season four, Sylar still retains his superhero name and this suggests that his secret identity will also be maintained through his transformation from villain to possible hero.

The aspects of performance and disguise connect with a pervading theme of superhero narratives, "the ... theme of duality" (Brown 32). But in the case of *Heroes*, this theme is also subverted and overturned. While the majority of those with special abilities do not create specific superhero identities, elements of performance and disguise are brought into play in relation to characters' civilian or public identities. These identities often *do* involve wearing a costume: for example, cheerleader (Claire), taxi driver (Mohinder), policeman (Matt), nurse (Peter), and politician (Nathan). A further duality is evident in the gap between what is expected of the superheroes — or what they expect of themselves — and what they manage to achieve. The clearest articulation of this is Claire's declaration in relation to the flawed Nathan: "You can fly. You're supposed to be Superman" ("Turn and Face the Strange" 3:22).

Superheroes are also marked by gender, and here malleability, reconfiguration and fragmentation all work to complicate gendered representations of the comic book superhero (Taylor 347–348). The destabilization, subversion or disruption of the heroic body has already been observed in recent fantasy television narratives, with special reference to the female action hero. While some critics question whether female action heroes in television are just "sex symbols developed primarily for a male audience ... how much is their power lessened by making them appear feminine and beautiful?" (Inness 9), others examine ways in which such narratives offer the subversion of some of the more "traditional" ways of conceptualizing female bodies. Dawn Heinecken sums this up with a nod to work by Iris Marion Young, Susan Bordo, and Carole Spitzack, all of whom have investigated ways in which women are encouraged to "make their bodies small and to take up less space" (Heinecken 3). In shows like *Buffy the Vampire Slayer* (1997–2003), *Dark Angel* (2000–2002), *Alias* (2001–2006) and *Dollhouse* (2009–2010), audiences are presented with female bodies that are small and may take up less space, but are also strong and powerful. Where a fantasy element is present, such narratives generally succeed in presenting female action heroes in this way; the narratives provide reasons for these heroes' abnormal abilities (for instance, Max in *Dark Angel* is genetically engineered, Buffy is helped by demonic power) so that audiences can accept physical feats carried out by small, slight female bodies. In Jason Middleton's definition of the "cult heroine" we see a combination of "signifiers of feminine sexuality with conventionally masculine action-hero powers. [The cult heroine's] body is in effect rendered superhuman" (Middleton 163). This is literally true in the case of women with special abilities in *Heroes*.

Still, much of this critical comment appears to assume that the presentation of the *male* action hero is more uncomplicated than that of the female. In *Heroes*, however, this is not the case. In this narrative, characters of both genders are shown to have problematic connections with their embodied existence, to struggle with aspects of the monstrous, and to present alternative versions of the hyper-muscled superhero. Their embodied representation undercuts the depiction of comic book superheroes; the male characters, no matter what their ability, are always embodied in realistically masculine ways. Both male and female bodies are subject to transformation, mutation, penetration and dissolution. Male bodies are not represented as impossibly powerful and strong, but as problematic sites of struggle, and while some male bodies follow a classic, tall and muscled version of masculinity, others represent maleness in different ways. Indeed, the male bodies in *Heroes* tend to demonstrate more differences than do the female bodies, which are all small, slight, usually white, and often blonde (see, for instance, Claire, Daphne, Niki and Tracy).

For the female superheroes of this narrative, the representation of special abilities is frequently problematic. Although the abilities they possess transform their bodies, they do not give all of the female superheroes additional force or strength; indeed, few of the female characters have such powers (Niki and Tracy are notable exceptions). Claire's healing ability demonstrates the continual regeneration of all parts of her body, but she has no control over her regeneration and it does not enhance the capabilities of her body (for example, if she jumps from a high structure she is not able to survive injury or even death, even though her body subsequently regenerates). Similarly, Daphne's ability of tremendous speed does not give her any additional strength; furthermore, without her ability she needs leg braces and crutches in order to walk at all ("The Eclipse, Part 1" 3:10). Claire's ability is further problematized and compromised because she is so often cast in the role of heroine needing rescue; in season one she is the cheerleader who must be saved; in "The Eclipse, Part 2" she is helpless and hospitalized without her healing ability (3:11). Daphne, too, is cast in this role, as, for example, when Matt, Peter and Mohinder join forces to "save" her from Building 26 ("Exposed" 3:18), and when Matt attempts to cushion her death by imposing visions of alternative futures upon her mind ("Cold Snap" 3:20). So with both Claire and Daphne, the female character cast in the role of helpless heroine is diminished as a superhero figure; meanwhile, heroic behavior is transferred to those — often male — characters who are engaged in rescue.

In comparison to Claire's and Daphne's abilities, Niki/Jessica's and Tracy's enable them not only to use their bodies in unexpected ways, but to affect the bodies of others. Niki/Jessica's enhanced strength allows her to fight and defeat larger (male) bodies, despite her petite appearance (which aligns her with the "cult heroine"). However, Niki's strength and superhero ability is externalized by means of her split personality, Jessica; for Niki, the person with the strength is not her, but another person entirely. Tracy's ability, however, is an acknowledged part of her, with which she struggles throughout the seasons in which she appears. From her introduction in season three, the narrative invites the viewer to sympathize with her: her freezing ability manifests suddenly; she cannot control it; she kills someone but does so involuntarily; she feels guilt for what she has done ("The Butterfly Effect" 3:2). Audience sympathy is further invoked when she is captured by the government agents and incarcerated in the mysterious Building 26 ("Clear and Present Danger"). The scene of capture is an abrupt and shocking incursion into the narrative. Tracy, barefoot and in a short dressing gown, is counterposed against several armed men in head-to-toe black, their faces concealed, brandishing guns, who have broken in to her apartment; this is a demonstration of power and force against which Tracy, despite her special ability, has no hope of winning. Further uncomfortable scenes follow in which Tracy is shown in a prison cell with her arms shackled to a pole behind her back, shot in the glare of red light from the heat lamps that prevent her from using her freezing powers ("Building 26" 3:16).

Tracy's ability mutates or progresses so that what begins as an ability that is uncontrolled and external — directed against attackers, for example — becomes an ability that transforms her experience of embodiment and the way that her body exists in the world. This is evident in her complete transformation at the end of "Cold Snap." This transformation is undertaken with decision and control, and it is premeditated — she asks Micah to turn on the sprinkler system and warns him in advance to "stay ahead of the ice." The transformation process comprehensively slows down the narrative: while Tracy's action to freeze her surroundings occurs instantaneously, the scene is extended with flowing shots of both Tracy and the soldiers frozen and immobile. In a reversal of the apartment scene, Tracy's ability is predominant; she faces down the approaching soldiers, and like them she is dressed in dark clothes. Finally, an extreme close-up of her eye impossibly covered with ice crystals emphasizes the otherness of her embodiment; this is reinforced and (apparently) concluded when Danko shoots her at very close range, shattering her body into pieces in an opposition and counterpoint to her ice formation. Her eye once again takes the focus, emitting a single tear and suggesting that her freezing process may be reversed, which does occur when she reforms her solid physical body from water flowing out of a tap ("Orientation" 4:1). So, as her ability develops, she is able to exist in both solid and liquid states and to move her body through otherwise impenetrable materials (the storm drain, the kitchen cold tap). From a helpless individual unable to rein in her dangerous power, she becomes a figure emphatically in control of her special abilities.

For the male superhero bodies in the narrative, there are also instances of troubled representation. Overturning the classic representation of the superhero, *Heroes* tends to present its male characters as compromised and imperfect. This narrative stresses the everyman hero, and shows us bodies which may possess special abilities, but are not particularly tall or muscled, which occasionally are small, or even slightly overweight (for instance, Matt Parkman). Some instances of more traditional versions of superhero masculinity—Nathan and Sylar, for instance, who are both tall, apparently strong, dark-haired men—are undercut by their representation as villains: fallible, morally compromised, or, in Sylar's case, simply evil. In terms of the everyman hero, however, Hiro Nakamura and Peter Petrelli are both characters with whom the viewer is encouraged to follow and identify. These two characters appear throughout all four seasons of *Heroes*; Peter is in its first shot and so guides the viewer into the narrative ("Genesis" 1:1). Neither character fits the template of the classic superhero nor the muscled action hero; both are played by actors who are small and wiry rather than muscled or obviously strong. They also have low or everyman status in terms of employment at the series' beginning: Hiro the "salaryman" or office worker and Peter the hospice nurse. Peter, in particular, is presented as a character who has not fulfilled his potential and is overshadowed by his politically ambitious brother Nathan. Both Nathan and their mother Angela criticize Peter's work as a nurse; Nathan, for example, taunts him with, "watching old people die, now there's a career" ("Genesis"). Indeed, Peter's work is in a job that is typically coded as female, and therefore tends to be regarded as of lower status.

However, Peter and Hiro are among the most powerful characters in the series in superhero terms. Their special abilities are constantly used in the narrative to help to avert disasters and to control others whose abilities are a threat. In the future scenario in "Five Years Gone," Future Hiro tells Ando there is "only one person who's powerful enough to get us through—Peter Petrelli." Their powers transform their experience of embodiment. Hiro's ability with time and space threatens to overwhelm his body, and this is manifest in his brain tumor ("Orientation"). Peter's ability means that he is constantly taking on and using new powers, and as season two progresses, his multiple powers must be contained within his body, which occasionally appears to struggle to control them ("Angels and Monsters" 3:5). After his ability is replicated with the synthetic vaccine, he is still able to access different abilities that continue to transform his body in various ways (for example, with enhanced speed and agility, or the ability to fly). Both Peter and Hiro speak of their destiny as heroes and believe that their powers give them a purpose and a duty. In this way, and in their wish to use their special abilities to help others, they connect with the image of the classic superhero.

The exploration of the superhero's destiny persists into the fourth season, where both Peter and Tracy struggle to reconcile their abilities with their wish to "help people who can't help themselves" ("Acceptance"). These two characters in particular appear to be successful in taking on a superhero identity to achieve their desire to do good. At the beginning of season four, Peter combines his special abilities with his job as a paramedic to be first on the scenes of accidents; while his hero identity is undercut ("Are you that hero?" asks a process server presenting him with a lawsuit from one of those he tried to help, "Ink" 4:3), his paramedic's uniform becomes a costume or disguise that enables him to perform his good deeds without being observed. Tracy's struggle can be read in parallel to Peter's. At the beginning of season four, she tries to return to her old life as nominal aide and actual mistress to the governor of New York. The opening scene of "Acceptance" sees her dressing — choosing her costume for the identity that she attempts to recreate. However, the slinky *femme fatale* identity that worked so well in her old life does not fit with her new wish to do good with her special abilities. Tracy's refusal of the old version of herself means that she can embrace her superhero identity more fully, and begin to use her powers to help others. The culmination of this desire is manifested in the series finale, when she uses her water transformation to free Noah and Claire from a buried caravan ("Brave New World" 4:19).

Tracy's mutations and transformations code her body as unpredictable and monstrous, and link her superhero body to the bodies of Mohinder, Peter and Sylar, which also adapt, morph and change in monstrous ways. While it could be said that anyone with special abilities has the potential to be coded as monstrous (and this occurs with, for example, the government plan to incarcerate *all* those with special abilities), this is particularly so for those whose abilities may overwhelm the body and spill out, whether inadvertently or deliberately, to threaten others. This is seen in various episodes, such as in the case of Stephen Canfield, who can create vortexes ("Angels and Monsters"), or Flint, who shoots fire from his hands ("The Butterfly Effect"). Throughout the narrative it is regularly demonstrated that "where once superheroes guaranteed social stability, they now threaten to disrupt it" (Bukatman 70). This is reflected in the overt Guantanamo parallel of season three, in which Nathan plays an instrumental role in "round[ing] them up and put[ting] them in a facility where they won't be a danger to anyone" ("Dual" 3:13). The Guantanamo-type orange jumpsuit and hood that the superheroes are dressed in introduces another costume or disguise that confers meaning upon the wearer. In this case, the jumpsuit and hood identify them according to government policy as dangerous potential terrorists, while they also disguise them so that it is impossible to distinguish one superhero from another.

The disruption of "social stability" is most strongly demonstrated in the way the superheroes themselves, or more specifically, their *bodies*, threaten the world with oblivion. In a reversal of the classic superhero narrative, here the superheroes become the very thing that the world must be protected from: Peter is the exploding man who threatens Manhattan at the end of season one ("How to Stop an Exploding Man" 1:23); Sylar explodes and destroys the town of Costa Verde in one possible future ("I Am Become Death" 3:4). In this way, the ordinary person must be protected *from*, not *by*, the superhero, and the superhero body is the monstrous means by which the normal world is threatened.

Mohinder turns himself into a monstrous body with the help of the synthetic vaccine. Though he declares that he is "completely the same in every way — just different" ("The Butterfly Effect"), it is clear that his is a particularly troubling transformation. In scenes that recall Cronenberg's film *The Fly* (1986), Mohinder's body emits slime and grows scales, and Mohinder's alienation from his own body is evident in scenes in which he struggles to glimpse these changes by peering at his back in a mirror ("The Butterfly Effect"). His superhero body is a body out of control, and his monstrosity threatens other bodies when he is compelled to encase them in cocoons for an unexplained and unnatural purpose. Initially, his body cannot maintain its transformation, and appears to undergo a kind of hibernation in a cocoon of its own; but his transformation is complete once his body has absorbed some of the synthetic vaccine that he has developed for the Primatech labs ("Dual"). After this, though he retains his strength, he has lost the overtly monstrous aspects of his body, its slime, scales and cocooning ability; and so he can be returned to the order of the good heroes with a new alliance with Matt and Peter.

Sylar is the character most consistently represented as monstrous, yet he also possesses similarities to Peter, who is equally consistently shown as good and heroic. This is particularly notable in their multiplication of abilities; indeed, it is from Sylar that Peter gains "the hunger" to acquire additional abilities ("I Am Become Death"/"Angels and Monsters"). For Sylar, those acquired abilities transform his body in different ways. He gains abilities that allow his body to transcend usual limitations (enhanced strength and speed, for instance); this is magnified in the case of Claire's and James Martin's abilities. By taking Claire's ability, Sylar's body is able to heal itself and regenerate, to the point of immortality: as Sylar tells Claire, "you'll never die, and now neither will I" ("The Second Coming"). And with Martin's ability his body can alter its appearance, shape shifting into the guise of any other person. This can be maintained for long periods, as we see after "An Invisible Thread" (3:25) when Sylar is persuaded that he "is" Nathan Petrelli, and lives as Nathan for a period of time. Sylar's core ability, however, is "how things work," his understanding of the mechanics of things, which he extends to the human brain. It is the transgressive act of opening up the body, turning it inside out, that allows Sylar to undertake a transformation of embodiment which gives rise to the additional powers contained in his own body. The parallels between Sylar's "knowledge" of the inner workings of the brain of different superheroes, and his understanding of the mechanisms of clocks, reveal a vision of the body as a machine. Through Sylar, the body of the superhero is mechanized, and becomes a site of horror as it is turned inside out, its workings revealed to police officers, coroners, and the employees of the Company — and, of course, to the viewer of the television series.

It is notable that the overtly monstrous superheroes are drawn back onto the side of good by the series four finale. Peter's influence draws Sylar into an alliance that the two maintain until the end of "Brave New World," and through several instances in which Sylar could kill but does not, there is a sense that his superhero identity is one that is no longer a threat to others. Similarly, Tracy's and Mohinder's monstrous transformations appear to be under control and they are able to use their abilities to help others in the classic superhero manner. While these examples suggest closure, the series finale also raises questions that leave the narrative open to further development. Claire's demonstration of her special ability means that the presence of superheroes has been announced successfully (to a live television audience) and suggests a possibility for change in the way the heroes exist in the world. However, since previous attempts to reveal the special powers have not met with success, the need for masquerade and disguise may persist. The body of the superhero, in this as in other narratives, will certainly remain different, special and monstrous.

Works Cited

Brown, Jeffrey A. "Comic Book Masculinity and the New Black Superhero." *African American Review* 33.1 (1999): 25–42.
Bukatman, Scott. *Matters of Gravity: Special Effects and Supermen in the 20th Century.* Durham, NC: Duke University Press, 2003.
Grosz, Elizabeth. *Volatile Bodies: Toward a Corporeal Feminism.* Bloomington: Indiana University Press, 1994.
Heinecken, Dawn. *The Warrior Women of Television: A Feminist Cultural Analysis of the New Female Body in Popular Media.* Intersections in Communications and Culture, Vol 7. New York: Peter Lang, 2003.
Heroes: Complete Seasons 1–4. USA: Universal Pictures, 2010.
Hoppenstand, Gary. "Not Your Parents' Comics, or Maybe They Are." *Journal of Popular Culture* 39.4 (2006): 521–522.
Hughes, Jamie A. "'Who Watches the Watchmen?': Ideology and Real World 'Superheroes.'" *Journal of Popular Culture* 39.4 (2006): 546–557.
Inness, Sherrie. "Boxing Gloves and Bustiers": New Images of Tough Women" [introduction]. *Action Chicks: New Images of Tough Women in Popular Culture*, edited by Sherrie Inness. 1–20. London: Palgrave, 2004.

Johnson, Merri Lisa. *Third Wave Feminism and Television: Jane Puts It in a Box.* London: Tauris, 2007.
Middleton, Jason. "Buffy as *Femme Fatale*: The Cult Heroine and the Male Spectator." *Undead TV: Essays on* Buffy the Vampire Slayer, edited by Elana Levine and Lisa Parks. 145–167. Durham and London: Duke University Press, 2007.
Mulvey, Laura, "Visual Pleasure and Narrative Cinema." *Visual and Other Pleasures.* Reprint. 14–26. Basingstoke: Macmillan, 1989.
Tasker, Yvonne. *Spectacular Bodies: Gender, Genre and the Action Cinema.* London: Routledge, 1993
_____. *Working Girls: Gender and Sexuality in Popular Cinema.* London: Routledge, 1998.
Taylor, Aaron. "'He's Gotta Be Strong, and He's Gotta Be Fast, and He's Gotta Be Larger Than Life': Investigating the Engendered Superhero Body." *Journal of Popular Culture* 40.2 (2007): 344–360.
Trushell, John M. "American Dreams of Mutants: The X-Men 'Pulp' Fiction, Science Fiction, and Superheroes." *Journal of Popular Culture* 38.1 (2004): 149–169.
Weltzien, Friedrich. "Masque-ulinities: Changing Dress as a Display of Masculinity in the Superhero Genre." *Fashion Theory* 9.2 (2005): 229–250.

Elective Affinities: *Heroes* and the Contemporary Conception of the Family

Stan Beeler

In 1809 Johann Wolfgang von Goethe published the novel *Elective Affinities* (*Die Wahlverwandshaften*) in which he explored the notion that human relationships are governed by scientific principles of chemical attraction. In our contemporary society the quest for understanding of the scientific underpinnings of the basic principles of human association continues — albeit in a somewhat different form. Current notions of inherited traits would suggest that we should have a natural affinity for those who share our genetic heritage. *Heroes* presents its audience with an interesting new take on this underlying trust in the laws of inheritance through its representation of a host of characters with genetic mutations that provide them with superpowers. Indeed, many of the characters who appear in the series are related to each other not only through this somewhat random genetic similarity, but also through a bewildering network of familial connections. Occasionally these family relations are helpful for the characters of *Heroes*, but more often than not, a character's natural family can do more harm than good. Claire Bennet (Hayden Panettiere), Hiro Nakamura (Masi Oka), Peter Petrelli (Milo Ventimiglia), Micah Sanders (Noah Gray-Cabey), Mohinder Suresh (Sendhil Ramamurthy) and Matt Parkman (Greg Grunberg), among others, all have equivocal relationships with their families. Although families — by birth, by adoption, or by marriage — are central to the complex plot structures of *Heroes* and can, upon occasion, provide unexpected assistance, the protagonists are never sure if their relatives can be trusted. At times it appears to the protagonists that the genetic mutation will serve as a tribal marker, enabling characters with superpowers to identify a trusted group, but this belief in a natural affinity is quickly disabused when they realize that mutants are just as likely to kill, capture or cheat each other as anyone else. In the diegesis of *Heroes* there appears to be no automatic affinity based upon family or genetic similarity. The characters must, through a gradual and often painful process of experimentation, discover who can help them and, of course, who is a danger. In the world of *Heroes*, family, whether it is based on genetics or socially constructed, is never a certain recourse. Although this rather prominent thematic tendency would appear to be a significant anomaly for contemporary broadcast television series, the equivocal representation of families is a trope that *Heroes* shares with many contemporary horror films.

> In mainstream fiction, and especially in romance, the happy nuclear family is often presented as a goal to be achieved rather than a reality to be lived.... The model of mother, father, and children living happily together persists in American culture. Americans are told that this model is, despite mountains of evidence to the contrary, the only acceptable way to achieve a healthy, happy, moral life. According to this view, anything else is not a family, and anything else is subversive [Benefiel 263].

Contemporary popular film, like television, is often used as a means of gauging society's collective psyche. Observers feel that by analyzing common elements in popular media we may ascertain the cause and effects of social trends for a given time and place. Although it is clear that there are aspects of popular media that can highlight trends that are of significant importance to society, it would seem that divining the cause of these wounds upon the Zeitgeist from the evidence in film or television is not a straightforward task. Indeed, Pat Gill precisely identifies contemporary anxieties concerning the family as reflected in the branch of contemporary horror known as teen slasher films as follows:

> Teen slasher films both resolutely mock and yearn for the middleclass American dream, the promised comfort and contentment of a loving, supportive bourgeois family.... What is striking about most of these films is the notable uselessness of parents, their absence, physically and emotionally, from their children's lives [17].

However, when Gill seeks to identify the cause of this popular culture phenomenon the assessment is somewhat less transparent. In Gill's argument the disruption of the ideal family life in suburbia and the concomitant anxieties are attributed to the steep rise in the U.S. divorce rate after 1960. Teenagers, the target audience for and the primary protagonists of slasher films, are dealing with parents who are "absent, either physically or emotionally" (18). I believe that it is too facile to simply assume that a higher divorce rate is the single cause of the breakdown of the North American family unit. It is quite possible that the divorce rate may be a symptom of underlying social and economic changes that have expressed themselves in myriad ways, including a sense of distrust in the social mechanisms of the family. While the increased divorce rate may or may not be the underlying cause for the negative representation of the family in teen slasher/horror films, my own interest is focused on the fact that rejection of the familial is one of the most important plot mechanisms for *Heroes*. Teen slasher films are aimed at a specific demographic that, as Gill suggests, would be greatly affected by the disruption of the family caused by divorce or separation of the family unit. However, the disruption of the family as reflected in *Heroes* is not restricted to the anxieties of a strictly teenaged audience. Like most broadcast television, *Heroes* is aimed a broader demographic — both male and female viewers from ages 18 to 49 (Carter) — than the teen slasher film and, therefore, has a deep resonance with a wider spectrum of audiences. In fact, the entire range of parent-child disruptions possible for an audience ranging from their early teens to established citizens in their 30s and 40s is represented in *Heroes*. The series represents parent-child conflicts from grade school — Micah Sanders and his debt-ridden mother — to the adult fear that parents may suffer from age-related dementia as is the case with Angela Petrelli. In "Genesis" (1:1) Angela is arrested for shoplifting socks despite the fact that she is obviously quite wealthy. It also structures plots around sibling rivalry that extends as far as fratricide between brothers in their forties (Samuel and Joseph Sullivan), The one common element in all these representations of families is that parents and children or brothers and sisters have a great deal of difficulty in dealing with their relations.

While it is obvious that *Heroes* does not owe all of its heritage to the slasher film, the series does play upon many of the tropes — both visual and narrative — that are used to identify the filmic genre and this is especially true when the subject material of an episode or plot thread deals with a teenaged protagonist. As Andrew Gordon points out in a discussion of the closely related genres of fantasy and science-fiction films:

> These films reaffirm the ambivalence of the adolescent, who is torn between childhood and adulthood, between needing parents and hating them, between clinging to home and desiring to destroy it or escape from it. To grow up means to break away, to separate from the safe family nest and establish a life of one's own; this can rarely be accomplished without both inner and outer conflict [187].

Claire Bennet — the cheerleader — and her struggle to grow up in small-town Texas provides the teen segment of the audience with a striking case for identification. In one of the nested plotlines that dominates the first episode of the series, Claire's exploration of her newly discovered, remarkable ability to heal is an essential component of the — at times baroque — plot structure of the series. Claire and her schoolmates serve as a focus for the teenage demographic even though, as is common with television, there are a number of somewhat sympathetic characters from other age groups in this plotline whose function is to attract a wider range of audiences.

Claire's near invulnerability provides the series' creators with ample opportunity to present graphic images of violence and injury while still maintaining a level of safety that is appropriate for prime-time broadcast television. In fact, in the pilot episode, Claire's home-video recordings of her suicidal experiments with the boundaries of her healing incorporate more than one aspect of the slasher film. As the young girl is repeatedly injured in horrific fashion, the scenes are presented to the audience in hand-held-camera POV shots that are a signature of slasher film cinematography. The visceral impact of this documentary-style footage adds to the episode's visual similarity to a horror film. John Carpenter's technique of filming acts of violence with a hand-held camera as if through the eyes (and mask) of Michael Myers in *Halloween* (1978) may be seen as a one of the paradigms for this aspect of the show. Although Claire — unlike the victims in slasher films — suffers no permanent injury, the stylistic concordance of the situations serves to give the audience a sense of unsettling familiarity. Yet, in deference to broadcast standards, Claire is always shown immediately healing from her injuries. The horrific impact is greatly decreased and *Heroes* opens up its demographic spectrum to both younger and older audiences who are less likely to revel in the bloodthirsty milieu of the slasher film.

Claire's situation, as represented in the series, is the most obvious reference to difficult parental relationships, although it has significant differences from situations presented in slasher films. If presented in a slasher film, Claire's relationship with her parents and sibling would be more definitively focused upon her isolation and alienation and there would be fewer attempts at reconciliation. Gill describes a detailed example from *A Nightmare on Elm Street 4: The Dream Master* (1988) in which Freddy Kruger's victim's "final fatal encounter with Freddy is the direct result of her mother's actions" (28). In *Heroes*, the manner in which Claire interacts with her family is open enough to allow for a more parent-friendly interpretation. For example, in the first scene in which we are introduced to Claire's adoptive mother Sandra (Ashley Crow) and brother Lyle (Randall Bentley), the dysfunctional nature of her home life is graphically presented in a manner that is visually patterned upon a pivotal segment of Sam Mendes' *American Beauty* (1999). As Lyle, Sandra, and Claire sit for a meal in a perfectly symmetrical shot which is intended to reveal the rigid mindset of the family traditions, it is clear that there is no real communication going on between Claire, her brother, and her mother. As Sandra chats about her dog Mr. Muggles (perhaps a sly reference to the term for normal human beings from the Harry Potter series), Lyle wonders why his father is not home. Claire finally loses patience with their inability to recognize the momentous changes going on in her life and blurts out the truth about her adventures in a burning building. After a moment of shocked silence, Lyle reacts with disdain — "God, you're so crazy sometimes" (1:1) — while his mother interprets Claire's statement as a metaphor. From the teenaged girl's perspective this simply confirms her impression that no one in her family understands her. On the other hand, parents in the audience may observe the same interaction and think that young people seem to be incapable of reporting their personal problems in a comprehensible fashion. Later in the same episode, while Sandra attempts to bond with Claire with talk of shopping and movies, Claire accidentally amputates the fingers of her right hand in the sink's garbage disposal unit. Again we have a slightly modified version of a horror film trope. If a garbage disposal unit is turned on in a horror film — like the pistol in the famous Chekov quotation — it must be used to injure someone before the end of the film. Although Claire holds up the bloody, wounded hand in good horror-film fashion, her mother does not notice and the digits quickly regenerate. In a horror film, the effect of violence upon the audience is usually exacerbated by the reaction of on-screen characters. Blood rarely spurts in the diegetic world of the slasher film without accompanying screams and futile attempts to provide first aid. In this instance, no one but Claire — and the audience — is aware of the injury and the impact of the scene is substantially reduced by her blasé reaction as her fingers grow back. While her family's lack of awareness in this scene can be interpreted as a validation of Claire's alienation from her mother, it is also possible for a more mature audience segment to see Sandra's reaction as a genuine attempt to share with her rather secretive and oblique daughter.

As the series progresses we come to realize that while Sandra is an ineffectual mother, apparently more obsessed with her dog than with her children, Claire's adoptive father, Noah Bennet (Jack Coleman), is a classic example of a distanced, yet controlling parent:

> Some parents [in slasher films] are well meaning, but inept and insufficiently attentive, making a show of interest while failing to grant the seriousness of their children's worries and fears. Other parents are exacting, abrupt and impatient.... They may constrain their children, but never teach them [Gill 19].

Later we learn that Noah has adopted Claire at the behest of his employers, but seeks to keep her out of the reality of mutant-control that is his day-to-day business. We do not doubt that Noah comes to genuinely love his daughter, but he has great difficulty in effectively helping her to accommodate her new powers. Like many parents in more normal situations he seeks to ignore the transition of his daughter from dependent child to a powerful, self-actuating adult. The fact that he uses the mind control of the Haitian (Jimmy Jean-Louis) to erase his wife's memory so many times that she begins to have serious health problems is completely consistent with the pattern of negative adulthood established in slasher films. However, the consistently positive representation of his affection and concern for his daughter bespeaks a message more in tune with an older demographic group. As the series progresses, Noah's character becomes more sympathetic and by the final season of *Heroes* he is perceived as more supportive of his daughter than her mother. Yet, the pattern of separation and divorce of the teen parents is remarkably similar to the situation one would expect in a teen slasher film.

The inadequacy of both adoptive and natural families is confirmed in season one as Claire's dissatisfaction with Noah and Sandra leads her to seek her birth parents. This does not result in the happy reunion that one might expect from a simpler form of broadcast television like the forensic science drama *Bones* (2005–present) or the spy show *Chuck* (2007–present). When she finally finds her birth mother Meredith Gordon (Jessalyn Gilsig), Claire realizes that this woman is even less likely to provide the comforting nuclear family that she seeks. Meredith is a frightened yet dangerous woman with pyromantic powers who hides from the world in a trailer park. When her meeting with Meredith leads to Claire discovering her birth father, Nathan Petrelli, she is horrified to find that he is afraid that her existence could interfere with his political aspirations. Claire's meeting with Meredith and her subsequent introduction to her birth father make it clear that her birth parents are no closer to an idyllic suburban family than her adoptive parents. As in a teen slasher film, the social expectations of a white, middle-class teenager are repeatedly disappointed. Claire's introduction to grandmother Angela reinforces her lack of confidence in the myth of the trustworthy circle of relations. The one mitigating instance in this round of disappointment is her uncle, Peter Petrelli (Milo Ventimiglia). Peter's efforts to save Claire from the implacable, nearly invincible villain, Sylar (another slasher film trope), prove that some family members are deserving of trust.

In the framework of a teen slasher movie, affinities and protective groups are almost always developed by age group rather than familial relationships. The elective affinity aspect of the teen slasher/horror film pattern is mirrored in *Heroes* with Claire's attempt to develop a pseudo-family to replace the inadequacies of her two "real" families. In season four Claire more or less gives up on both her adopted family and her real father, mother and grandmother when she goes off to attend college. Her first attempt at bonding is with her roommate Gretchen Berg (Madeline Zima). While this relationship seems to fit within the framework of a teen coming-of-age experience, it is never really developed in the series narrative and the eighteen-year-old demographic segment is disappointed in their expectations. In "Hysterical Blindness" (4:5) *Heroes* had the option of developing an edgier profile with Gretchen serving as a gay love interest (she kisses Claire), but it is quickly passed over. Yet, Claire does manage to find another group that is an archetypal representation of a more conservative family-by-choice. The Sullivan Brothers Carnival, a collection of mutants who choose to associate in a familial group, are more than eager to have Claire join them. Unfortunately, the relationship is dangerous as it is based upon manipulation by Samuel Sullivan (Robert Knepper). It is no surprise to the audience to discover that Samuel is a fratricidal svengali who is willing to abuse the trust of his followers to wreak his vengeance upon the society of normal people. Claire's brief association with the Sullivan Brothers Carnival is not completely consistent with the patterns established by slasher films as the attempted association is not based upon a sympathetic age group and therefore disappoints the central interests of the teenaged audience. Yet the Carnival is clearly an example of the slasher film's paradigm of false security followed by horrified realization of betrayal. When she accepts Samuel as a surrogate for Noah, Claire presents the danger of accepting support from either family or fellow mutants. Claire's story is, perhaps, the most obvious example of the series' use of an ensemble cast to cover as many of the demographic bases as possible. *Heroes* attempts to attract as wide a swath of viewers as possible, within the lucrative target audience of viewers between the ages of 18 to 49. Incidentally, this is the target demographic of the series' home network, NBC. Using tropes from teen slasher films in a show that covers a broader spectrum is a somewhat precarious tactic as it risks alienating a more mature spectatorship, if too shocking, and boring the teen audience, if it seems too tame.

Sylar is another example of a slasher film trope that has been modified to fit within the parameters of broadcast television. When Gabriel Gray/Sylar (Zachary Quinto) is introduced, we are presented with a character who has direct references to the classic horror film, Alfred Hitchcock's *Psycho* (1960). Like Norman Bates before him, Sylar has serious mother issues and in "The Hard Part" (1:21) he inadvertently kills his stepmother when she attacks him with a pair of scissors because he has frightened her with his powers. This scene is quite similar in content to Brian De Palma's classic horror film *Carrie* (1976) as Gabriel's stepmother assumes there is a demonic source to her son's superhuman abilities. In this case the horrific, yet accidental, murder has diegetic witnesses — Hiro and Ando — who sympathize with the plight of the soon-to-be villain. Although Sylar serves much the same function as Freddy Kruger in the Nightmare on Elm Street franchise, his psychological situation is presented in greater detail than the antagonists in most slasher or horror films. Sylar, like Claire, also discovers that he has been the subject of a rather sordid and mercenary adoption situation. His birth father has sold him to his adopted parents and then killed his real mother. In an epic, Oedipal battle between Sylar and his father in "Six Shades of Gray" (3:19) Samson Gray, a cancer-ridden taxidermist, at first demonstrates a cavalier attitude towards life and death. When Sylar finally tracks him down he openly invites his son to kill him and end the misery of his slow, wasting disease. However, when he sees that Sylar has acquired the gift of healing from Claire, Samson tries to kill his son and steal the power for himself. Sylar demonstrates the violent tendencies of Norman Bates as well as an extreme version of Bates' multiple personality. He acquires the ability to shape-shift from one of his victims, James Martin, in the episode entitled "Into Asylum" (3:8) and later, with the help of the Petrelli family, begins to doubt his own true identity. Sylar serves as the nearly unkillable stalking monster that is so common in horror films. He is the older, implacable, threatening presence that makes the teens run in slasher films, and in *Heroes* he tracks down and executes his fellow mutants in order to gain their powers. In scene after scene we see reflections of the horror film as Syler first befriends his victims and then kills them with a signature methodology that is as recognizable as Freddy Kruger's finger-knives. First Sylar pins his prey against a wall, then slowly and implacably he removes the top of the skull using his finger as an invisible knife. There is no question that Sylar's motivation for his career of stalking and killing is associated with his uncomfortable relationship with his family, both real and adoptive, and because it is represented in great detail over the course of the entire series, it is impossible for the audience to be completely emotionally divorced from his situation. Gabriel Gray, as a man, is worthy of our sympathy, but in his persona of Sylar the killing machine, the audience fears him. At times this equivocal representation works, but occasionally the audience has some difficulty in accepting that the abused young man could become so horrible. The problem may stem from the inherent narrative differences between film and serial television. In a horror film we are given a brief summary of the reasons for Freddy Kruger's bloodlust, while in the extended format of a television show there is time to become really acquainted with Sylar's personal angst and it is much more difficult to simply dismiss him as a monster.

While Claire provides us with an example of an audience focus for teenagers, *Heroes* provides its audience with instances of dysfunctional families from a broad spectrum of age demographics. Most of the children represented in the series — be they young or grown up — have a difficult relationship with their parents and this extends for generations. In the first few seasons of the show, Micah Sanders (Noah Gray-Cabey), who is still in grade school, must deal with a mother who makes her living as an Internet porn star. Micah's mutant talent is not particularly spectacular (an almost magical affinity with machines) because he is presented as a passive agent in the parental struggle that is the heart of this narrative line. Although it would seem logical that since Niki Sanders (Ali Larter) and her son Micah are both mutants they would develop a bond based upon their familial relationship as well as shared experience of special powers, this is not the case. In fact, Niki's power at times seems nothing more than a veiled reference to multiple-personality disorder that makes her relationship with her son extremely difficult. She is, in fact, very close to the damaged parent that features so prominently in slasher films although the fact that her son is substantially younger than the typical protagonist in a slasher film changes the audience interpretation of events and, concomitantly, the demographic who would be interested in his story line. The audience does not identify with Micah so much as sympathize with his situation. When Niki's power manifests, it is in classic horror film fashion; she blacks out and wakes up in a room full of bodies. Although Micah's affection for his mother is unquestionable, the fact that they are constantly on the run from loan sharks or mutant-control agents makes it easy to categorize this as another one of those difficult familial relationships that are so common in the series. When we finally are introduced to Micah's father, D.L. Hawkins (Leonard Roberts), we discover that he has been in prison for a crime he did not commit and has escaped using his own mutant powers. Micah is placed in the unenviable position of serving as a point of contention between his very powerful and frightening parents. In "Better Halves" (1:6) while attempting to reconcile with his wife and son, D.L. discovers Niki's dual personality problems when, in a scene highly reminiscent of a horror film, he comes upon the dismembered bodies of some mob enforcers. Niki has the money from the robbery for which D.L. was incarcerated. Micah walks in while his parents are fighting using their mutant powers and evokes a suitably sympathetic response from an audience segment with children of their own. After knocking his wife unconscious, D.L. abducts Micah for his own protection. While on the run in "Nothing to Hide" (1:7), Micah slips away from his father and phones his mother. This scene is particularly poignant as it highlights the unenviable position of this child who is forced to choose between loyalty to his mother or father. Later, in "Homecoming" (1:9) Micah makes an impassioned plea with his father to return to his wife and help her deal with the sickness that manifests itself as Niki's alter ego. Still in her alternate form Niki/Jessica hunts down D.L. three episodes later in "Fallout" (1:11) and shoots him in the shoulder. In a moment of lucidity Niki realizes that she is a danger to her son and turns herself in. This plot arc, which is drawn out over six episodes of the first season, uses tropes of both fantasy and horror films to depict the suffering of a child who cannot trust his violently inclined parents. Even though D.L. seems the more rational of the two, the writers of the series make some attempt to morally justify Niki/Jessica's behavior through the provision of a traumatic back story. In "Six Months Ago" (1:10), Niki's father, Hal Sanders, appears and we discover that he was responsible for Niki's sister Jessica's death and that Niki attributes the violent, superhuman personality that takes over her body to her dead sister. Micah's dysfunctional family covers all of his known relations. Although D.L. appears to be the more rational, both parents seem more caught up in their struggle with each other than with the welfare of their son. Micah is unable to trust his parents in their normal roles as caregivers or in their extended function as fellow mutants. When we consider the number of episodes that are used to present this story arc, one of the fundamental flaws of the series narrative structure becomes obvious. Because the spread of the demographic target is so broad, the interweaving of plot structures that focus upon different segments dilutes the interest of audiences who are interested in a particular group of characters.

One thing that is clear from this discussion of the broad spectrum of familial disruptions presented in the show is that the writers were constantly struggling to reach one audience without alienating another. The thematic unity provided by a general distrust of family may have held the series together at first, but as the show progressed, it could not maintain the balance required to keep everyone in the overly broad target group watching. *Heroes* lost its market share because it split the market too far. As Barbara Selznick indicates:

> The splintered audience has diminished the possibility of any television show finding a mass audience. Instead the goal of today's television executives is to create programmes that draw loyal viewers with desirable demographic and psychographic characteristics who will follow texts across media while they spend money in ancillary markets and attract advertisers to networks. The terms "narrowcasting," "niche markets" and "target audiences" are central in this fragmented viewing environment [179].

Heroes ignores this sage advice and works too hard at trying to be everything to everybody. Claire is an alienated teenager, but instead of climbing on board with her justifiable teenage resentment, we were encouraged to sympathize with her parents — two sets of them. Sylar is a good solid monster, but we were shown so much of his underlying familial trauma we could not wholeheartedly loathe the man. Although this chapter has only briefly touched upon the ways in which the trope of the unreliable family has been used in

Heroes, it has presented the folly of extending a metaphor that is most applicable to a teenaged audience across a wide range of potential viewers. In the end, the series may be said to have fell apart under the weight of its own attempts at diversity.

WORKS CITED

Benefiel, Candace R. "Blood Relations: The Gothic Perversion of the Nuclear Family in Anne Rice's Interview with the Vampire." *Journal of Popular Culture* 38.2 (2004): 261–273.
Carter, Bill. "NBC Hired a Hit Maker. It's Still Waiting." *The New York Times*. 16 May 2009, http://www.nytimes.com/2009/05/17/business/media/17silver.html (accessed 11 Nov 2010).
Gill, Pat. "The Monstrous Years: Teens, Slasher Films, and the Family." *Journal of Film & Video* 54.4 (2002): 16–30.
Gordon, Andrew. "You'll Never Get Out of Bedford Falls: The Inescapable Family in American Science Fiction and Fantasy Films" [cover story]. *Journal of Popular Film & Television* 20.2 (1992): 2.
Selznick, Barbara. "Branding the Future: Syfy in the Post-Network Era." *Science Fiction Film and Television* 2.2 (2009): 177–204.

"Last in My Class, Last on the Sports Field, I'm Not a Loser Anymore": Centralizing the "Geek" in Quality Television

David Simmons

This chapter takes Greg Taylor's assertion that "today, cultism is everywhere" (259) as its starting point and seeks to explore the contemporary cultural diffusion of cultism that is evident in *Heroes*' (2006–2010) incorporation of that which was once culturally marginalized. In particular, through a character-based approach, I will examine the manner in which quality TV has worked to centralize the figure of the geek, renegotiating the audience's relationship with definitions of the cultish. With the growing breakup of television viewers into various niche audiences in the 1990s, programs such as *The X-Files* (1993–2002), *Buffy the Vampire Slayer* (1997–2003), *Lost* (2004–present), *Heroes* (2006–2010), *Chuck* (2007–present), *Reaper* (2007–2009) and *The Big Bang Theory* (2007–present) have increasingly included central characters whose cultism is presented as an empathetic signifier in stark contrast to the more traditional depiction of the geek as a socially inept "loser" (e.g., the Comic Book Guy in *The Simpsons*, 1989–present). This chapter will attempt to interrogate these more favorable contemporary depictions, centering on the character of Hiro and the depiction of his fandom in *Heroes*, in order to evaluate the extent to which such characters serve to shore up the supposedly specialist knowledge of a culturally savvy audience, encourage their viewers to take pop cultural forms and works more seriously, or merely propagate an often ironically inflected set of aesthetic discriminations.

William Shatner's much quoted (scripted) exclamation, made as part of a *Saturday Night Live* (1975–present) sketch, that a group of hardcore *Star Trek* (1966–1969) fans should "Get a Life!" seems to epitomize the conventional view of genre fans that up until fairly recently dominated the cultural zeitgeist. Such an attitude positions fans as somehow Other to mainstream "normal" and socially acceptable culture, as "emotionally unstable, socially maladjusted, and dangerously out of sync with reality" (Jenkins 10). This negative perception of fans and fandom has been explored in some depth in a spate of recent scholarly work including Lisa A. Lewis' *Adoring Audiences: Fan Culture and Popular Media* (1992) and Henry Jenkins' influential study *Textual Poachers: Television Fandom and Participatory Culture* (1992). Indeed, discussing the widespread construction of fandom in the mass media, Jenkins notes the manner in which recent reports still "frequently characterize fans as psychopaths whose frustrated fantasies ... take violent and antisocial forms" (10).

In light of the apparently pervasive nature of these derogatory perceptions of fandom, it is interesting to note the suggestion that a great deal of the early success of *Heroes* can be attributed to the inclusion of the geeky "fanboy" character of Hiro Nakamura (played by Masi Oka); in an article entitled "Super Hiro: Japanese Nerd is Hit of 'Heroes'" Helen A. S. Popkin exemplifies this sentiment. Popkin eulogizes the character's significance on the pop culture landscape. Writing following Oka's failure to take home a Golden Globe for "Best Actor in a Supporting Role," and after only half of the first season of the show had aired, Popkin suggests, "Hiro is now one of the most popular characters on primetime TV," and commends Oka's performance as "a delight." Key to the adulation heaped on the character seems to have been Hiro's initially optimistic attitude to the events he encounters and the powers he finds he possesses, a factor that might have been sorely missing if we are to believe the anecdotal story that Kring only added the character on the recommendation of his "wife who saw that the pilot script lacked someone actually happy to have superpowers" (Popkin). Indeed, Hiro's embracing of his abilities stands in stark contrast to many of the other characters in the show who seem to reject or struggle with their newfound super heroic abilities, partly because it will impede them "fitting in" to the world around them. This perception of superpowers as a burden is most notable in the teenaged character of Claire Bennet, whose "ability makes her feel like a freak rather than a hero" (Porter et al. 136). Claire is initially depicted as a teenager who is eager to conform to the conventional patterns of behavior for a "normal" U.S. teenage girl and many of her storylines in the early part of the show concern her attempts to follow traditional models of being a teenager (being accepted by her peers at school, dating boys, etc).

In comparison to a figure like Claire, Hiro's acceptance and ready approval of his superpowers (note Hiro's affirmative catchphrase "*Yatta!*" ("I did it!") contribute to a perception of the character as someone who is comfortable, or at least already familiar with, being socially ostracized as a result of his interests and related activities: "His father thinks he's weird, and his sister laughingly calls him insane" (Porter et al. 122). Where Claire longs to become a part of the hegemonic systems of U.S. culture that state she should be like everybody else, Hiro is shown to want to escape from what he views as the homogenizing practices of mainstream Japanese society. In a heated discussion at the end of the first episode ("Genesis" 1:1), Ando is surprised by Hiro's lack of concern over his potential for being ostracized should it become known that he has special powers. Rejecting Ando's suggestion that his friend should just try to fit in, Hiro angrily exclaims, "Why do you want to be the same? ... I am special! ... I wanna boldly go where no man has gone before," proposing that they should break away from their previous lives as "homogenous yogurt" (1:1).

Interestingly, it is possible to read Hiro's desire to be an individual as partly being a rejection of his Japanese nationality; Ando exclaims, "We are not special. We are Japanese" in the first episode, while on the subway ride home Hiro uses a poster of the Statue of Liberty as a means of removing himself from the humdrum nature of his Japanese office-bound life in favor of the excitement and endless possibilities of New York City; witness the circular point-of-view tracking shot that re-introduces us to Hiro in "Don't Look Back" (1:2) and emphasizes the character's sheer joy at having escaped to the Big Apple: "I love New York!" Although Hiro chooses to decorate his office space with Japanese pop-culture artifacts such as a Godzilla toy, it is significant that Hiro is not initially presented as a Japanese pop-culture obsessive or Otaku. Rather, Hiro is a fan of many forms of popular culture—(*Star Trek*, *Quantum Leap* (1989–1993), *X-Men* comics, Sherlock Holmes)—espousing a love of a diverse and international range of texts that might help engender the character (and the show) to Western television audiences and reflect larger audience-based strategies; as Matt Hills suggests, "[*Heroes*] appears designed to 'travel' between and across international audiences, even while simultaneously retaining a strongly U.S. centric flavour" (71).

From the very outset of *Heroes*, we are led to perceive Hiro as a fan. As Lynnette Porter, David Lavery, and Hillary Robson propose in their enlightening *Saving the World: A Guide to Heroes* (2007), Hiro is "admittedly nerdy" and "reads comic books and loves to compare his abilities to those of his favourite television or movie heroes" (31), while in a later chapter devoted to the character, the authors suggest that we view Hiro as "a culture geek, who grew up with *Star Trek* and *Star Wars* and peppers conversation ... with popular culture references" (106). While several scholars have noted the show's concerted efforts to appeal to a range of demographics not traditionally thought to be interested in sci-fi or fantasy television, through the inclusion of high-quality production values, soap-like family-orientated storylines and characters such as the family man HRG or the mature and female Angela Petrelli, Hiro's appeal seems to be aimed squarely at a niche-genre-savvy viewership. Yet, interestingly, while Dick Fiddy points out that the wealth of recent genre shows whose creative staff were themselves fans of genre texts: "*Doctor Who, Life on Mars, Primeval, Torchwood, Spooks ... Alias, Buffy, Smallville, Chuck,* and the *X-Files* ... were all driven by showrunners who were self-confessed cult TV fans" (229), the creators of *Heroes* have frequently cited their lack of fanboy credentials. In his answer to an interview question about series creator Tim Kring's genre knowledge, writer and co-executive producer Jeph Loeb suggests that Kring is anything but a comic book geek:

> You'd think that Kring is a total geek, when he's not a comic book guy at all. Which shows to go ya what we've always known about comics — that it's CHARACTER that drives the narrative mixed with the cool of the visuals. Kring just got it [Loeb qtd in Porter et al. 50].

Though Loeb's comments about Kring's approach might ironically be interpreted as alluding to a deeper understanding of what makes comic books effective, they ostensibly work to distance the creative personnel behind the show from the model of the comic book fan. In spite of this refusal and perhaps as a result of the program makers' acute awareness of the power of the cult audience, Hiro seems designed to attract and appeal to "the cult viewer, the one you can rely on to tell his/her friends and family about the series, watch on a regular basis, spend money on licensed and unofficial merchandise, or develop a fan website" (Robson 218). Indeed, such comments by the show's creators, when coupled with the inclusion of Hiro as a central character, may testify to the ongoing tensions that exist in much of contemporary genre television, which often attempts to attain "mainstream cult" status (Hills 70), appealing to both a casual mainstream audience, drawn in by the promise of a strong narrative drive and ensemble soap-like storylines, and an arguably more dedicated niche viewership hungry for a complex hyperdiegetic world from which they can accumulate in-depth textual knowledge.

The show's audience is encouraged to identify with Hiro's love of everything geeky. In the opening episode of season one ("Genesis" 1:1), we meet Hiro in his small homogenous office cubicle at Yamagato Industries. Unable to bear the monotony that he feels as a result of the stifling conditions he works in, Hiro seemingly concentrates so hard that he manages to alter time by turning back the clock on his desk by one second. This act fills Hiro with joy and he proceeds to run through the office he works in, disrupting the other workers with his exclamations of happiness until he reaches the cubicle of his friend Ando, whereupon he discusses his newfound ability to alter the space-time continuum. Almost instantly, the two conceive of Hiro's abilities in genre terms, with Ando exclaiming (albeit sarcastically) that Hiro is like "Spock," the character from *Star Trek: The Original Series* (1967–1969). While this first evocation of popular genre culture might appear derogatory in nature, the rest of the episode works to validate Hiro's fanboy knowledge, positioning the character's love of cult texts as imbuing him with a recognizably moral sense of right and wrong. Discussing the possible uses of Hiro's newfound ability, Ando questions where his friend has learned so much about scientific attitudes towards time, to which Hiro replies "X-Men number 143, when Kitty Pryde time travels." Later, in the same conversation, Ando suggests that Hiro might be able to use his ability to get money, to which Hiro instantly states, "A superhero doesn't use his power for personal gain." Though such a declaration might mark Hiro out as naive, as someone who is living in an unrealistically innocent world derived from the overly simplistic narratives of comic books and genre television, this is not the case. Instead, and partly as a result of Oka's appealing portrayal, we are encouraged to sympathize and empathize with the character of Hiro as he goes about attempting to change the world around him for the better.

Hiro is also significant for being a character who is depicted as actively utilizing his knowledge of cult material (comic books, superheroes, popular culture) to help him make sense of the world around him, adhering to the model of "textual poaching" that fan scholar Henry Jenkins describes as involving "a type of cultural bricolage through which readers fragment texts and reassemble the broken shards according to their own blueprints, salvaging bits and pieces of the found material in making sense of their own social experience" (20). Following some of the ideas concerning popular reading laid down by French scholar Michael De Certeau, Jenkins suggests that fans are not passive viewers but active participants who, in addition to appreciating media texts, also actively seek to use such texts for their own means: "In the process, fans cease to be simply an audience for popular texts; instead, they become active participants in the construction and circulation of textual meanings" (16).

From "Don't Look Back" (1:2) onwards, Hiro is involved in a struggle to stop Claire Bennet from being killed by Sylar, a quest that he has discovered he must fulfill by reading Isaac Mendez's comic book which prophesizes that Hiro must help in saving the cheerleader in order to save the world. Hiro, then, is literally involved in enacting—or re-enacting—the narrative that he has encountered in the pop-cultural form that is the comic book *9th Wonders*. Mendez's comic book functions as a means of validating the "cultism" that Taylor mentions. In "Fallout" (1:11) it is the comic book artist Isaac Mendez's painting of Hiro fighting a huge dinosaur with a sword that convinces him to resurrect his quest to save the world as originally laid out in the comic (even though he is scared he might "step on a bug" and change history, in a nod to Ray Bradbury's short story "A Sound of Thunder" (1952). Consequently, in the last episode of the first season, "How to Stop an Exploding Man" (1:23), Hiro does kill Sylar (albeit temporarily), allowing Peter to be saved by his brother Nathan, effectively meaning that Hiro's love of and belief in the validity of comic books becomes an instrumental factor in saving the world.

Though often criticized as marking the beginning of the show's decline in quality, the second season of *Heroes* offers the viewer an interesting exploration of fandom and what it is to be a fan, albeit in a slightly more oblique fashion than was evident in the first season. "Volume Two: Generations" sees Hiro transported back to seventeenth-century Japan whereupon he encounters one of his childhood heroes, the fabled samurai Takezo Kensei. Supposedly "a wild savage with great power" ("Godsend" 1: 12), Hiro quickly discovers that Takezo is in fact a somewhat cowardly Englishman (later known as Adam Monroe) who tends to shy away from battle until Hiro shows him that he has the ability to heal himself from any wound ("Kindred" 2:3). Upon this discovery Kensei goes mad with power, eventually attempting to "cleanse" the world through the release of the Shanti virus in "Powerless" (2:11).

The majority of the second season sees Hiro occupied with trying to ensure that Takezo fulfills the stories that Hiro learned and loved as a small child; In "Four Months Later" (2:1), Hiro tries to get Takezo to save the village at Otsu, while in "Kindred" Hiro tries to get Takezo to fight the ninety angry Ronin. Hiro's desire to make sure that Takezo completes these tasks and thus remains true to the established narrative legends of Takezo Kensei sees him differ from the fans that Jenkins describes, who consider "the best [stories to be] those which not only conform to the fans' expectations about favorite characters but also contribute new insights into their personalities or motivations" (58). Rather than embrace the discovery that Takezo Kensei is not the grandiloquent hero figure that stories have made him out to be, Hiro initially tries to mold events so that they fit with the stories he has in his head. However, over the course of his time in seventeenth-century Japan, Hiro comes to learn that he cannot get the "real" Takezo to fulfill his role as "a great leader. A hero" ("Godsend" 1:12). Instead, after being betrayed in "The Line" (2:6), Hiro must turn against his childhood idol and defeat Takezo in battle, reclaiming control over the Kensei narrative by effectively assuming personal mastery over the narrative in a move that mirrors the process of writing fan fiction, which "builds upon the ... the collective meta-text as the base from which to generate a wide range of ... stories. Fans ... 'treat the program like silly putty,' stretching its boundaries to incorporate their concerns, remolding its characters to better suit their desires" (Jenkins 102). These fan narratives often then feed back into a collective overarching canonical narrative, altering and shaping it in subtle yet significant ways much as Hiro's actions contribute to the construction of the meta-text of Takezo Kensei.

Hiro as fan goes on to assume at least partial authorship of his own version of the narrative. In "Out of Time" (2:7) it is revealed that the story of Takezo is in fact the creation of Hiro. When Yaeko (a seventeenth-century princess that Hiro has had a romantic relationship with) finds out that Hiro will become separated from her as he takes up the mantle of Takezo to fulfill the character's last trial, she tells him she will tell his tale for as long as she can speak and thus suggests that the stories Hiro loved so much as a child were in fact based on his own actions: "Everything Kensei accomplished.... You did all these things. Not him. As sure as I live, you are Takezo Kensei" ("Out of Time" 2:7). This assertion of textual mastery by a fan is unusual in contemporary genre television, repositioning Hiro from a somewhat passive participant in a narrative that initially gives him pleasure and that is dependent on "the presence of a powerful author" (Jenkins 76) to a much more active role as a producer of that narrative, whose actions determine the direction the story of Takezo Kensei will take for both himself and those who also share knowledge of the legend (such as Isaac Mendez, who paints a picture of the battle between Hiro and Adam/Takezo seen in "The Eclipse, Part Two" 3:11). In this fashion, Hiro's storyline in much of season two serves to validate the role of fan as an individual whose familiarity and adoration of selected narratives is important.

As *Heroes* moves from season to season, it is noteworthy that Hiro's deployment of the pop cultural bricolage he is familiar with functions in a manner that is shown to be beneficial. In fact, in contrast to the model of fans that views their specialist knowledge as a negative trait; as confirmation of their "devot[ing] their lives to the cultivation of worthless knowledge" (Jenkins 13), *Heroes* works to present Hiro's enactment or utilization of knowledge gleaned from popular culture as beneficial, not only to himself, but also the wider social good. Hiro (and Ando) increasingly appear to enact this process in the world of the show. At the end of the first season, Ando tells his friend that "your whole life you talked about your favorite stories, *Star Wars*, *Star Trek*, Superman, Kensei ... all the heroes you wanted to be. One day people will tell the story of Hiro Nakamura" (1:23), echoing Jenkins' claim that "fans actively assert their mastery over the mass-produced texts which provide the raw materials for their own cultural productions and the basis for their social interactions" (16).

Hiro's utilization of his fan knowledge resembles a form of ostension (defined by Linda Dégh and Andrew Vázsonyi as "presentation as contrasted to representation" [qtd. in Tosenberger]), which is itself analogous to Jon Fiske's concept of enunciative productivity: an engagement with textual materials which transforms them into an active resource. This purposeful employment of everything Hiro has learned from popular culture is most evident in season four of *Heroes* in which Hiro and Ando set up a "Dial-A-Hero" agency offering to "help people in need, whatever the need may be" ("Orientation" 4:1).

Though initially unsuccessful in spite of Hiro's protestations that "my business model says we can't fail," Dial-A-Hero eventually manages to acquire a client, a little girl whose cat has got stuck on a rooftop. Following his use of his powers to stop time and thus prevent Ando from falling off the roof with the cat, Hiro discovers that he is dying. As a result of his condition, Hiro becomes "unstuck" in time and travels to his own past, meeting his younger self at a carnival he visited as a child. At the carnival Hiro is convinced to deviate from his heroic moral code and change his (and Ando's) destiny, altering the past so that Hiro never knocked into Ando, making him spill his slushy drink over Hiro's sister Kimiko. Upon returning to the present, Hiro finds out that his actions have made Ando much happier and as a result he decides that he must "go back and undo all the wrongs I have committed in my life."

In "Acceptance" (4:4) Dial-A-Hero gets another call, although this time it is rather more serious in nature. A man called Tadashi calls the agency from the rooftop of the same building Hiro and Ando are currently in, telling Hiro he is about to commit suicide by leaping to his death. Tadashi is contemplating suicide because he was recently fired for inappropriate behavior; to stop Tadashi from dying, Hiro vows to go back and change history for the better. Yet on returning to the present, Hiro finds that Tadashi still jumps. Tadashi's plight acts as a metaphor for Hiro's own desire not to tell his sister that he is dying and it is only by realizing, then articulating, this discovery to Tadashi that he can actually save him. The "epiphany" that Hiro has as a result of helping Tadashi helps to alleviate his own problems, encouraging him to share his condition with his sister. Similarly, in "Tabula Rasa" (4:6) Hiro is on his deathbed yet finds time to show Emma Coolidge (a deaf woman who sees sound as a form of colored light) how to control her powers. Hiro suggests that Emma should embrace [her] ability, rather than be afraid of it in order that she can "learn to use her powers to do good things in the world" (4:6).

Season four reinforces Hiro's moral code, which states that he shouldn't use his powers for selfish reasons but should instead focus only on helping others by presenting us with a kind of anti-hiro in the shape of Samuel Sullivan. Indeed, it is possible to read Samuel and his carnival's member's actions as illustrating the incorrect direction for fandom to take. For, though at first, the Carny's self-marginalization at the edges of mainstream society might appear to resemble the similar convening of fans at specialist conventions, with Samuel extolling messages of inclusion that seem to chime with the communal and non-judgmental nature of much genre fandom ("A family is more than blood. It's about trust, about love. About those who embrace you — the real you. Unconditionally." ["Shadowboxing" 4:9]), Samuel is not all that he seems. While espousing messages of unconditional love such as "We're family. Family accepts. Family forgives" (Tabula Rasa 4:6), Samuel is actually manipulating those around him, and becoming stronger through assembling and exploiting those he takes into his carnival. Samuel's ultimately self-serving actions distance him from the amateur, non-hierarchal and communal behavior of the "true" genre fan and more closely resemble the image of the Machiavellian studio executive who is blamed for "the more calculated positioning and reception of the of the modern nice-driven text" (Angelini and Booy 26), changing a minority passion into "just another element of the cultural logic of capitalism" (Pearson 17).

In the conclusion to *Textual Poachers*, Henry Jenkins suggests that his work has not been about the validity, or lack thereof, of particular pop-cultural texts but rather the affirmative processes that fans engage in when dealing with them: "I am not claiming that there is anything particularly empowering about the texts fans embrace. I am, however, claiming that there is something empowering about what fans do with those texts in the process of assimilating them to the particulars of their lives" (301). In a similar fashion, Hiro's active utilization of the pop-cultural texts he knows and loves seem to form the basis of many of his actions over the course of *Heroes*' four seasons; his self-confidence is gained, in part, through a belief in the validity of such texts. The sense of ideological right and wrong he finds therein leads him to save the world and genuinely help those around him on multiple occasions. Of course, Hiro's close resemblance to members of the show's intended audience might also signal a decidedly more cynical element to the character, positioning him as a concerted and calculated attempt to attract the "geek" or fanboy audience by presenting them with a character that they might hold up as their own; as Porter et al. note of one *Wired* writer's suggestion: "Hiro succeeds because of his interest in popular culture ... 'creating the cheeky conceit [of] the chubby nebbish Hiro as the central hero of *Heroes*'" (106). Yet, upon reflection, this seems to be an overly critical way of looking at a character whose journey can be seen concurrently not only as the story of a misfit character coming to terms with his superpowers (following Joseph Campbell's mono-myth of the hero as outlined by Porter et al.) but also as the narrative of a fan moving from a recognition to a positive acknowledgement of his status as fan (season one), then towards the utilization of his fan knowledge, first to gain textual mastery (season two) and finally to help others (season four).

WORKS CITED

Angelini, Sergio, and Miles Booy. "Members Only: Cult TV from Margins to Mainstream." *The Cult TV Book*, edited by Stacey Abbott. 19–27. London and New York: I. B. Taurus, 2010.
Bradbury, Ray. *A Sound of Thunder and Other Stories*. London: HarperCollins, 2005.
Fiddy, Dick. "The Cult of Cult TV?" *The Cult TV Book*, edited by Stacey Abbott. 225–231. London and New York: I. B. Taurus, 2010.
Fiske, John. *Understanding Popular Culture*. Boston: Unwin Hyman, 1989.
Hills, Matt. "Mainstream Cult." *The Cult TV Book*, edited by Stacey Abbott. 67–73. London and New York: I. B. Taurus, 2010.
Jenkins, Henry. *Textual Poachers: Television Fandom and Participatory Culture*. New York and London: Routledge, 1992.
Lewis, Lisa A. *Adoring Audiences: Fan Culture and Popular Media*. London and New York: Routledge, 1992.
Pearson, Roberta. "Observations on Cult TV." *The Cult TV Book*, edited by Stacey Abbott. 7–17. London and New York: I. B. Taurus, 2010.
Popkin, Helen A. "Super Hiro: Japanese Nerd is Hit of 'Heroes.'" *Today Television*. 16 Apr 2007. 16 Feb 2011, http://today.msnbc.msn.com/id/16756741.
Porter, Lynette, David Lavery, and Hillary Robson. *Saving the World: A Guide to Heroes*. Ontario: ECW, 2007.
Robson, Hillary. "Television and the Cult Audience: A Primer." *The Cult TV Book*, edited by Stacey Abbott. 209–220. London and New York: I. B. Taurus, 2010.
Taylor, Greg. "*Pure* Quidditas *or Geek Chic*? Cultism as Discernment." *Sleaze Artists: Cinema at the Margins of Taste, Style, and Politics*, edited by Jeffrey Sconce. 259–272. Durham, NC: Duke University Press, 2007.
Tosenberger, Catherine. "'Kinda like the folklore of its day': 'Supernatural,' Fairy Tales, and Ostension." *Transformative Works and Cultures* 4 (2010), http://dx.doi.org/10.3983/twc.2010.0174 (accessed 16 Feb 2011).

PART 2: BORROWINGS AND INTERTEXTS

Naturalizing the Fantastic: Comics Archetypes

Julia Round

When *Heroes* first aired back in 2006, audiences hailed it as "innovative and engrossing" (Doux 2010), celebrating its diversity, originality, and, most of all, realistic treatment of fantastic subject matter. As the series wore on, until its cancellation in 2010, this praise was replaced with accusations of contrived and unfinished plot lines, incoherent characterization, and repetition ("Every show seems like a reworded repeat of the week before. This is not television, this is a broken record" [DeNardo 2007]), a significant shift in reception. This article explores these reactions in the context of comics' history, arguing that many of the tropes and mechanisms used to normalize *Heroes*' fantastic events are drawn from this medium. However, these were not developed as the series continued and the archetypes either became diluted (through combination with a television aesthetic) or were repeated until what once seemed fresh and original stagnated into cliché.

Multiple superhero name checks run throughout *Heroes*: D.L. Hawkins and his son Micah are "Like Batman and Robin only no tights" (1:9), Claire berates Nathan because "you were supposed to be Superman" (3:21) and in season four, this is taken to the extreme as Hiro is reduced to speaking entirely in fantasy, science fiction and comics metaphors which reference *Star Trek*, *Star Wars*, *Battlestar Galactica*, *The Matrix*, *Sherlock Holmes*, *Don Quixote* and Arthurian legend (4:12). The *Ninth Wonders* comic created by Isaac Mendez is another recurring symbol whose reuse ultimately becomes repetitive. Isaac's precognitive ability is reincarnated in Matt Parkman (season three), who paints a mural of an explosion in Washington, D.C. (3:17) on the floor in Isaac's loft, where Isaac's painting of New York exploding once was (1:1). Isaac's crucifixion with paintbrushes (at Sylar's hands: 1:19), a shockingly violent scene the first time round, is also recalled and diminished as Peter does something similar to Sylar with a nail gun (3:24).

Ninth Wonders' artwork (by Tim Sale) and the cinematic style of *Heroes* also reference the comics industry. Director/co-producer Greg Beeman says his aim was to "see the spaces, see the faces" (*Heroes Unmasked* #5), a strategy reminiscent of comics artwork, where wide-angle establishing shots are combined with emotive closeups (although Fiske (1987) notes that closeups are also characteristic of soap opera). Writer/director Tim Kring qualifies the comics connection, commenting, "We wanted a lot of shots to have a very 'graphic novel' kind of feel to them; the camera's in places that you very rarely see it" (*Heroes Unmasked* #5). Subtitles that are positioned like speech bubbles also recall a comics' aesthetic. However, paratextual material get more showy in later series (for example, 3:20, where Tracy Strauss breathes ice over the episode title "Cold Snap" which then melts away) and it is arguable that this dilutes the original impact of this creative positioning by removing the resemblance to comics. The series also uses frames and shots that represent comic book panels. Strong vertical lines (such as thick, contrasting doorframes) characterize the *mise en scène* throughout *Heroes*, and this aesthetic normalizes the fantastic events by quite literally framing them, flagging a comics' sensibility to the audience. For example, walls are often used to split scenes, visually recalling the comic book panel (see, for example, 1:1 as Noah Bennet plunders Chandra Suresh's apartment); volume four (which begins midway through season three) opens with Tracy and Nathan framed by a television screen, and shortly after Matt appears bordered by a door and window frame (3:14). Later in this season Hiro, Ando and baby Matt Parkman hide from Janice, separated again by a doorframe that acts as a comics "gutter" (3:20), and in the following season Samuel's hall of mirrors shows us the past in a series of paneled images (4:6). Michael Cohen notes the use of similar signifying techniques in his discussion of *Dick Tracy* (whose matte painted sets, cartoonish *mise en scène* and abstracted props create a "fiction effect"), commenting, "The frozen posture is the event of the panel" (28), and characters who pause in these vital framed moments recall a comics aesthetic.

Structurally, too, the series resembles the periodical format of comics publishing as individual story arcs are built into the wider arc of the overall plot and episodes are named as "chapters" within "volumes." Comics' narrative strategy of retroactive continuity ("retcon") — the process of expunging past events or adding new ones in order to create a coherent history for a character — is also present throughout the series. Hiro's self-imposed mission in season four can be read by the comics' reader in this way, as he tries to undo his past mistakes while still keeping a coherent history alive (4:6). Samuel's magic ink can rewrite history, such as in the news story photo he shows Peter (4:6). More significantly, we realize that, in true comics style, we have already been "retconned," as the real relationship between Noah Bennet and ex-partner Lauren Gilmore is revealed in "Once Upon a Time in Texas" (4:8, an episode which revisits the events of season one).

Other tropes of the comics medium are also present; most notably the exploitation of Hatfield's "art of tensions" or McCloud's "interdependent" combination (and what I name an "aesthetic of excess"), i.e., where words and pictures comment on each other for effect, such as the Petrellis' toast "to closure" over a visual demonstrating that Sylar is still alive (4:3). Switches between scenes are also linked in this way, as in comics such as *The Killing Joke* (1988), whose scene changes are frequently linked by having a visual or thematic similarity. In episode 4:4, Emma Coolidge and Peter Petrelli both have unsatisfactory conversations with their mothers, in which the parallel sentences "I think this whole filing girl act is finally getting to you"/"I think this whole focusing on work thing is getting to me" link the two scenes, both of which end with the children walking out on their parents, and which also seem characterized by a similar theme: where Emma is literally deaf, Angela is not listening. These aesthetic and structural similarities with comics sit alongside a use of archetypes that familiarizes *Heroes*' content.

The Golden Age of Comics

The golden age of comics began in 1938 with *Action Comics* #1, featuring Jerry Siegel and Joe Shuster's Superman, followed by Bill Finger and Bob Kane's Batman in 1939 (*Detective Comics* #27). These golden-age archetypes remain the most famous superheroes in the world and their popularity has scarcely diminished in the last seventy years; both have featured in a range of other media and recently enjoyed revivals in their own blockbuster movies. It is worth noting that there is a strong opposition between them: while Superman is nearly omnipotent, and an all-American good guy (despite his alien origin), Batman has no tangible powers and dark, obsessive tendencies.

Although these basic character elements have remained constant, their stories have developed to include realism in various ways. *Action Comics* #1 introduced the "Man of Steel" as an omnipotent god, but this tactic soon began to tire, as an unbeatable man made for fairly unsatisfying adventures. Superman's one weakness, kryptonite, first appeared in 1943 on the Superman radio series and first featured in the comics (albeit initially colored red!) in *Superman* #61 (1949). Introducing kryptonite via the radio and then transferring it to comics demonstrates the role of a cross-media feed of ideas (or Henry Jenkins' transmedia storytelling) in the construction of tonal — if not actual — realism. Despite being a fictional invention, kryptonite added variety and realism to the stories by creating a hero who was more accessible to his readership than an invincible man; and the notion has a literary and mythological precedent, as, for example, in legends such as Achilles, whose heel was his only weak spot. The introduction of kryptonite into the Superman mythos is mirrored by the strategies used in *Heroes*—as we are reminded time and time again, everybody has a weakness. All the heroes mysteriously lose their powers during the eclipse in season three, and even the regenerative powers enjoyed by "Indestructible Girl" Claire Bennet are quickly shown to be vulnerable to a branch or object positioned in the right place at the base of the skull (1:3), an "Achilles heel" that extends to Peter Petrelli and Sylar, too, and is emphasized at various points (1:3, 1:19, 3:13). With their ever-expanding collections of powers, Peter and Sylar most obviously fit the Superman archetype (Sylar showcases his vast array of powers at 3:14), but remain fallible in this way. In addition, Peter's abilities are later reined back still further as, after having his ability stolen (3:6), he then gains an altered version of his original ability, whereby he may only have one power at a time (3:13).

Conversely, Batman stands out in the superhero ranks: he has no apparent superpowers and instead uses extensive martial arts training, detective skills, intellect, technology, and psychological warfare to combat crime. Although the notion of a non-powered superhero who can do what Batman does is actually in many ways *more* unbelievable than the standard superhero template, Batman's methods ascribe a sense of realism to the superhero. It also adds the "everyman" motif, implying that any reader could become a hero if he or she wanted it enough. In his initial incarnation, Batman was primarily a detective, solving crimes such as society kidnappings ("Batman versus the Vampire," *Detective Comics* #31–32, 1939). Mark Fisher (2006) situates Batman's evolution within film tradition, noting that while the early comics and the Oedipal nature of Batman's origin recall 1930s horror, this is superseded by the emergence of film noir in the cinema of the 1940s, which sparks a similar trend in the comics.

Heroes pays homage to film noir and the detective genre through the character of Noah Bennet, who is introduced to us only as "HRG"—the man with the horn-rimmed glasses. These glasses are initially our sole anchor regarding his identity and in this sense operate as a clue: a visual marker of the type used in comics where "the requirement on the viewer is not so much analysis as recognition" (Eisner 38). We are at first unsure which side Noah is on; he is framed as a villain—anonymous, working for a mysterious company, threatening Mohinder Suresh, and plundering Chandra Suresh's apartment (1:1). Yet soon he is working against his employers and has become a vigilante, like Batman; and although he subsequently switches partners many times, he seems to remain on the side of good (although often outside the law) for the remainder of the show. Like Batman, he lives a double life, and later seasons emphasize the number of lies he has told until Mr. Bennet the family man is ultimately revealed to be as fabricated an identity as Bruce Wayne (4:18). Noah's "origin story" also has inverted echoes of this superhero's beginnings, as his first wife was murdered by a "special" during a home mugging that went wrong—as Claire concludes: "That's how you became Mr. Bag-n-tag" (4:18). He also shares the Batman's amoral tendencies; for example, he is willing to kill a child (Molly Walker) to ensure the safety of future generations of heroes (1:22, 1:23) and comments more than once that he's "comfortable with morally gray" (1:17, 3:17). Again, this recalls Batman, whose vigilante status and violent ethos and methods are often emphasized (see, for example, Frank Miller and Lynn Varley's *The Dark Knight Returns*, 1986).

Mohinder Suresh is another example of the unpowered hero who references Batman through his intelligence, science, and technology. Mohinder is the catalyst for the whole show, whose events stem from his inquiries into his father's death, and this is emphasized through philosophical introductions and conclusions which bookend many of the episodes of the first three series and which recall a comics-style narration in their reflective tone and indirect address to the reader, both of which imply omniscience. Although ostensibly unpowered, Mohinder is super clever and super moral, and by the end of season one it even transpires that he has "super blood," making him the one person who can heal Molly Walker. It should be noted that Mohinder's disastrous transformation when he gains the power of "activating evolution" in season three sits somewhat uneasily with his character as we know it, and later the series collapses his parameters still further (as he first becomes power-hungry, then returns to his stoic self, then simply absent and unmentioned at the start of season four) before finally being excised completely from the series' climax with the somewhat flimsy and unlikely excuse, "I broke a promise to a girl" (4:15).

This nod to unpowered heroes is expanded in season three where a second eclipse causes the heroes to experience a temporary loss of powers. Not only does this add tension (for example, as Noah Bennet attempts to kill Sylar before his regenerative powers return (3:11)) but it also marks a reiteration of the everyman motif, such as when Daphne Millbrook is revealed as reliant upon crutches without her superspeed ability (3:10). Comics lore states that the superhero and alter ego will often be radically opposed (consider weedy Clark Kent/omnipotent Superman; superficial Bruce Wayne/obsessive Batman; and timid Peter Parker/brash Spiderman), and this strategy is apparent in *Heroes* as characters are given traits that complement their alter egos, as Kring comments:

> I thought about a lot of these powers as metaphors for the characters. Take ... Nikki, who's a single mother stretched about as thin as you can be, so I started

thinking of a single mother stretched so thin that her power is she can literally be in two places at one time. Greg Grunberg plays a cop, and I started to think what would be the ultimate power if you were a cop? ... Being able to read other people's thoughts [Douglas 2006].

In this context, Ando's "enhancing" ability (season three) reinforces his role as the sidekick rather than hero, and later episodes, in which his "crimson arc" power (a name played for laughs, as befits the comedy sidekick (3:24) is used independently and variably to open door locks and give electroshock therapy to Hiro's brain (4:14), weaken this innovation. Like Batman's sidekick Robin, Ando functions as comic relief, and he also takes on the impetuous quality associated with this example, such as when he wants to help the Vegas dancer Hope (1:15) or decides to attack Sylar by himself (1:22). Both events contribute to Ando's status as blundering sidekick; his "rescue" of Hiro prevents him from destroying the formula (3:2), and later he causes the destruction of the catalyst (3:13). His attempts to be a real superhero are played for laughs, with Hiro (stealing tropes from Batman) using hi-tech resources to give him the "Andocycle," whose name and function recalls the Batmobile — for example, as Ando comments, "The Andocycle is a chick magnet" (3:14), recalling Chris O'Donnell's character in *Batman and Robin* (1997): "I want a car. Chicks dig the car." As Ando concludes, "I guess I am the sidekick" (4:12).

The child or teen sidekick was originally introduced to comics to attract a young readership and give these readers someone to identify with, proving extremely successful in this regard. Robin the Boy Wonder first appeared with Batman in 1940, in *Detective Comics* #38, an appearance that doubled the sales of Batman-related comic books (Daniels 36). *Heroes* also features child characters such as Micah Sanders and Claire Bennet, and, although they are heroes in their own right, their positioning still conforms to the comics model, as Robin went on to multiple solo features and was later reinvented as the superhero Nightwing (Micah's own recreation as Rebel may be a nod to this). In *Heroes* both Micah and Claire are presented as children. Although Claire is often shown wearing her cheerleader uniform and referred to as "the cheerleader," the sexy contemporary stereotype is deliberately avoided; and "Claire Bear" is consciously presented as a "special" little girl through various methods. She "always" drinks chocolate milk rather than plain (1:3, 4:4), and a variety of scenes show her surrounded by soft toys (1:9, 4:1), making cupcakes with her mother (1:6), coloring in (1:8), and playing games such as *Guitar Hero* (4:1). The adoption storyline of the first season also establishes her as a child and later episodes which feature her interacting with not one but two fathers reinforce this (as she claims: "I just wanna be Claire Bennet, daughter of Noah Bennet" [4:1]). Throughout the series, her school and college life feature prominently (particularly in seasons one, two and four), which emphasizes this point, particularly when she is bullied as the "new girl" at school (season two). Even her college experimentation/lesbian storyline is non-sexualized and phrased in childish terms: Gretchen describes her feelings as a crush (4:4), a single kiss is shown (4:6), and the climax of Claire "owning up" to her feelings is when they hold hands in public (4:15).

It therefore seems unconvincing when Claire is also shown as a "badass" action heroine in later series; on a rebel mission to save "specials" from the government, or in flirty scenes with Alex (West, as a high school boy, seemed more convincing). Tight black leather may work to signify a new, serious Claire, agent of the Pinehearst Company, in a potential future (3:1, 3:4) — just as similar clothing delineates a stern and melancholy "Future Hiro" who has lost Ando (1:20) — but seems a little incongruous on the everyday "Claire Bear" that the main storyline follows. This shift to a *Matrix*-style aesthetic and a violent plane-jacking (3:15) is another example of the dilution of comics archetypes that occurs in later episodes of *Heroes*.

The Silver Age of Comics

The silver age of comics saw a reinvention of many elements of the golden age as characters were rewritten or combined in new ways. In this way the superhero team-up was born, most famously in Stan Lee's *Fantastic Four* (first published 1961), the titular family who became the direct inspiration for *The Incredibles* (2004). Although Kring has famously stated he is not a comics reader, he does cite "the premise of *The Incredibles*, people trying to live ordinary lives while having these superpowers," as one of the inspirations for his series (Douglas 2006). *The Fantastic Four* (Reed Richards/Mr. Fantastic, who can stretch his body; Sue Storm/Invisible Girl; Jonny Storm/The Human Torch; and Ben Gunn/The Thing) contrast strongly with the majority of golden-age goody-goody heroes. They are a literal family (Sue and Jonny are siblings, and she is engaged to Mr. Fantastic) with distinct personalities, who bicker and argue, such as when the Human Torch quits the group (#3) and the others blame each other (#4).

There are obvious parallels here with the super-powered Petrellis, whose first screen appearance together is tense, as Nathan greets Peter with "I don't have time for this" (1:1), and who are frequently on opposing sides. However, themes of the family become even more obvious in later episodes of *Heroes*. Season four offers us three organizations with strong familial links: Samuel's carnival, Claire's sorority and the new company set up by the Petrellis. Samuel tells both Sylar and Tracy that his carnival is "home" (4:4, 4:5), and two further episodes also close with his rousing speeches, concluding: "We will finally be home" (4:11) and "our new home" (4:12) — although admittedly the sound bite has become a little tired by this point. Doyle also describes the carnival folk as "a family" (4:12) and, most tellingly, Samuel explains the carnival to Claire in similar terms, saying, "You will *inherit* this new world, it's your *legacy*" (4:17, emphasis mine). The sorority that Claire is invited to join is, of course, also a sisterhood, as is emphasized ("we're sisters"; 4:4), and Angela Petrelli also redefines her proposed new company as a family (3:23). A restaurant scene between Angela and Millie Houston also underlines this point, as the two matriarchs battle wits (4:3).

The struggle with normality is another theme that runs throughout *Heroes* and has its basis in silver-age titles such as *The Fantastic Four*, where Sue Storm just wants to get married or *Spiderman*, where Peter Parker's "great responsibility" prevents him from being with Mary Jane. Stan Lee's great invention was these reluctant heroes, for whom the responsibility of being a protector is a struggle in itself. This reaction is expressed most obviously by Claire many times throughout *Heroes*, and volume four opens with Claire, Matt and Daphne struggling with normality: the latter couple trying not to use their powers in an attempt to experience normal life. Matt is even enrolled in an AA-style group designed to help him stop "using" (4:2).

These sort of everyday touches add realism to the series and echo another trope that developed in comics' silver age: the introduction of pseudo-science. The pseudo-scientific origin has its basis in silver-age characters such as the Fantastic Four (who gained their powers from exposure to "cosmic rays" while on a space mission) and Spiderman (whose abilities come from being bitten by a radioactive laboratory spider). In *Heroes* we discover that genetic makeup is linked to the possession of abilities, and that these can be synthetically created. The previous generation of heroes include Arthur and Angela Petrelli, Kaito Nakamura (Hiro's father) and Charles Deveaux (father of Isaac Mendez's girlfriend Simone), among others, although it should be noted that the construction of this genetic theory seems somewhat random, as neither Simone or Hiro's sister Kimiko seem to possess powers. Yet despite these inconsistencies, the theory that super abilities are genetically encoded still sounds convincing. The Human Geonome Project involved in Chandra Suresh's research is real: it was a global study coordinated by the U.S. Department of Energy and the National Institutes of Health that ran 1990–2003 and aimed to identify all of the 25,000 genes in human DNA and improve analysis techniques. This gives a greater sense of realism to *Heroes*' pseudo-scientific model through familiarity with convention and everyday terminology.

The Dark Age of Comics (1980s–Present)

Modern comics have continued to explore troubled heroes, for example, by offering aging characters (Mark Waid/Alex Ross' *Kingdom Come*, 1996) or incorporating dystopian, realistic environments, drawing on the depressing politics of the 1980s. *The Dark Knight Returns* (1986) is one of the best examples of this: set in a futuristic Gotham ruled by gangs after Batman's retirement. While the silver age was an era noted for focusing on the personal issues associated with being a superhero, the dark age takes this theme further towards the psychological, offering us "dark knights" whose methods and motivations are often twisted and troubled. While these tendencies were of course present in many earlier comics, they frequently dominated superhero titles towards the end of the twentieth century.

Modern comics explore the negative side of being a superhero: exploitation, persecution, madness and more. In *The Dark Knight Returns*, the brutality of Miller's backdrop adds realism but more telling is the inclusion of Superman in this text as a government-sanctioned weapon. This notion of a company or government branch dedicated to controlling, categorizing or experimenting on superhumans also appears in concurrent titles such as Alan Moore/Dave Gibbons' *Watchmen* (1986). In this way the application of contemporary politics to the superhero model resulted in more realistic settings that incorporated dystopian surroundings and governmental interest. We can see this represented from the very start of *Heroes* by the Primatech Paper Company (whose business is concerned with tracking and tagging people with abilities) and the introduction of the Pinehearst Company in season three extends this trope further by performing experiments on U.S. marines (3:12) and receiving presidential sanction for their continued activities (3:13).

All these realistic elements feature in contemporary superhero comics. Warren Ellis/John Cassaday's *Planetary* (1998–2009) uses alternate worlds to redefine the good versus evil perspective, and characters who bear more than a passing resemblance to the industry's archetypes, such as Sue Storm's invisibility or Ben Gunn's indestructibility. This title also explores the notion of government experimentation and references actual political concerns in this regard; for example, one of the test subjects is introduced as "The screenwriter. Pacifist. Communist"—a description which implies he has been selected for experimentation for these reasons. As the narrator of this chapter explains: "We were the big joke; dirty reds being used as guinea pigs for the special anti-red super-army to come," although she continues, "There was no real 'red threat.' [The] angle just got them the initial funding and the secrecy they needed" (Ellis). A similar treatment is also found in titles such as Neil

Gaiman/John Romita Jr.'s *Eternals* (2006), such as when the regenerative powers of the Eternal Icarus are tested to their limits by a mysterious agency.

Pseudo-science is also at play in *Eternals*—Makkari, a character with super speed, needs armor to protect his body when moving at ultra-high speeds. Again, this finds a parallel in *Planetary*, where Ms. Süskind (the homage to Sue Storm) must wear special goggles while invisible in order to see so that light does not simply pass through her eyes (2004). Although *Heroes* evokes pseudo-science (Daphne finds her super-speed ability enhanced to the stage where she can actually travel back in time and the explanation is offered that "you must be going faster than the speed of light" [3:13]), it stops short of exploring the physical contradictions of abilities in this way.

Contemporary comics offer a reconstruction and exploration of heroic identity as fragmented and fractured. Although many of the *Heroes* characters struggle to accept their new identity, figures such as Niki/Jessica Sanders most obviously represent the kind of psychological torment and fragmented identity associated with the superhero condition. As mentioned, the alter ego is often directly opposed to the superhero identity, and in this sense the two halves define each other. The superhero is a postmodern symbol of fragmented identity (Round 2005), and supports a view of personalities as not only multiple but constructed, where neither "Clark Kent" nor "Superman" accurately reflects the whole, complete person. Within *Heroes* Niki's ability (to transform herself into the super-strong mercenary Jessica) is originally presented to us as a psychological disorder. For example, one of the first times we encounter her ability is in retrospect, when she awakes to find the corpses of some men who threatened her literally torn apart around her (1:1). A video camera is conspicuously present in this scene but its contents (which would presumably show Niki herself killing them) are never revealed to us. This attempt to muddle the issue of superhuman ability with dissociative identity disorder continues in the first series, as Niki alone encounters Jessica in mirrors. The reuse of this very effective visual trope to represent Matt Parkman's struggle with the consciousness of Sylar, who is imprisoned in his head, removes all such subtlety from it (4:6). Matt and Sylar are so physically different and their characters so well established that fear of one's reflection can no longer be an explanation, and Sylar's threats towards Janice seem clumsy and clichéd.

Niki's initial presentation is intentionally designed to imply that she may not have superpowers at all. However, her fragmented identity also serves another purpose — to illustrate the antithesis between alter ego and superheroic identity. The construction of Niki's psyche—and therefore her character's realism—is drawn from this source, and it is also used in other characters; the ambitious Nathan Petrelli (as Peter comments: "Even in your generosity,

Nathan, you are selfish" [3:23]) ultimately sacrifices himself—not once, but twice. Sylar's search for an identity in the final season is also expressed in these terms by Lydia, who comments, "It's like there are two sides at war in him" (4:5). Of all the heroes, only Sylar is introduced as having a constructed "supervillain" identity that conforms to the standard superhero model. He keeps his "real" name of Gabriel Gray a secret, taking on the name Sylar for his villainous activities. These characters in particular invoke this superheroic stereotype of hero and alter ego that owes a direct allegiance to comics. However, the other characters keep their abilities secret and separate from their everyday lives, thereby using the same divided identity construction.

A common linguistic construction is also apparent in these titles. Rather than superpowers, the characters of *Heroes* have "abilities," and are later referred to as "specials." Gaiman's Eternals have "skills." *Planetary* refers to "talents." This linguistic shift is one of the more obvious attempts to redefine the notion in everyday terms. There are, therefore, both visual and textual parallels to be drawn between contemporary comics and *Heroes* that include the presence of a mysterious agency and governmental involvement: the use of pseudo-science and a linguistic reformulation of the much-maligned and clichéd term "superpowers."

The analogy between hero and villain is also explored in modern comics, such as *The Dark Knight Returns*, which questions the sanity of its hero, or Alan Moore/Brian Bolland's *The Killing Joke*, which states this duality from its very opening ("There were these two guys in a lunatic asylum" [Moore 3]) and has the Joker make a similar point, asking Batman:

> I mean, what is it with you? What made you what you are?
> Girlfriend killed by the mob, maybe? Brother carved up by some mugger?
> Something like that, I bet. Something like that...
> Something like that happened to me, you know [39].

This parallel between hero and villain has also been noted by writer Frank Miller, who comments, "The Batman folklore is full of Doppelgängers for Batman.... Two-Face is identical to Batman in that he's controlled by savage urges, which he keeps in check, in his case, with a flip of a coin. He's very much like Batman" (Pearson and Uricchio 36). This doubling has been explored many times in comics history; for example, Dr. Doom was introduced to the *Fantastic Four* comics in a story voiced by Reed Richards as a rival scientist whose genius resembles his own (*Fantastic Four* #5, 1962).

In *Heroes* this alignment is most apparent in the Peter Petrelli/Sylar relationship. Firstly, they are paralleled in their abilities: Peter's power of empathic mimicry echoes Sylar's more violent form. The show's structure also aligns them since, as the first series progresses, it becomes obvious Peter is the metaphorical hero (alongside the more literally named Hiro Nakamura), with Sylar positioned as his nemesis. Peter not only embraces but actively seeks out his ability, despite discouragement from all around him. He is the one given the now-infamous mission to "save the cheerleader, save the world" by Hiro Nakamura (1:5). The exploding man plot from season one also contributes to this issue, as at various times throughout this season both Peter and Sylar think they (or the other) might be it (1:11). Even the characters themselves are aware of the parallel, as Sylar gloats: "Turns out you're the villain, Peter" (1:23). The point is also emphasized visually, as both begin this climactic fight dressed nearly identically (in black mid-length jackets and jeans), until Peter removes his jacket, replacing the similarity between them with a black-versus-white contrast.

These tensions are continued in subsequent seasons, as hero and villain roles swap throughout *Heroes* and, as a whole, the series intentionally blurs the lines between heroes and villains. The Primatech Paper Company and the Pinehearst Company are both little more than unreliable touchstones for right and wrong as their employees and motivations change constantly. Individual characters at best seem "morally gray" (indulging in murder, revenge, and similar activities), and their roles too morph between the heroic and the villainous as characters continually switch sides and allies. In this way *Heroes* demonstrates exactly how meaningless these terms are.

It therefore seems that intertextual references and following both cultural and universal convention give *Heroes* a sense of familiarity and therefore a "tone" of realism. This is also achieved by the use of pseudo-science and vulnerability — tropes that give an air of respectability, although their inconsistent treatment or presence in fact undermines a strict notion of realism. There is a development of characterization similar to that seen in silver-age comics, that shows relationships to be familial and people flawed, and this again privileges the believable elements over the unbelievable. Contemporary comics are also referenced via the use of convincing backdrops and engagement with world politics, and a denial of Manichean morality that is achieved by offering multiple viewpoints and drawing parallels between hero and villain, exploring the psychological impact of the superhero condition. So, although the subject and treatment of *Heroes* might seem new to television, it can be argued that many of the conventions that its creators originally relied upon to construct this realism have evolved in comics over the past seventy years.

However, later series of *Heroes* seem to dilute these ideas by bringing in tropes and genres drawn from cinema and television. Unconvincing romances, police procedurals and soap opera melodrama became the genres of choice, clumsily melded with comic book tropes that, although originally innovative, are repeated to the point of tedium. The series is also weakened by a plethora of continuity errors, loose ends, and unfinished storylines. Such questions might include if the body or the mind holds the abilities. How is Ando able to sustain adventuring with Hiro in the reality where he is married to Kimiko? Why does Peter's Haitain ability not prevent Sylar from shapeshifting? Do Sylar's clothes transform along with him? Why would a drugged Japanese man speak in English? What happened to Micah? Who/where is Barbara Strauss? In this way, *Heroes*' transmedial nature works against the series, as many loose ends are resolved in the comics and webisodes, but to the casual viewer there seems instead a loss of control over what was once an elegantly plotted series.

A significant example of this is the "exploding man" trope used at the climax of season one and returned to midway through season three. The season-one finale resembles a tag-team wrestling match somewhat, as characters take their turn at rushing in and delivering a blow or two, before being injured or otherwise distracted to make way for the next. Although this structure has been criticized from a dramatic point of view (Stafford and Lavery 2007), it seems typical of a comics showdown and sets up the pairing of Peter and Sylar (as hero and nemesis), even though it is Hiro who finishes the fight. Yet when the exploding man trope is revisited in season three, it is with a quite different emphasis, as Matt Parkman is framed as a terrorist, drugged, and released in central Washington with bombs strapped to him (3:18). Here, terrorism has replaced the supernatural and television tropes have replaced comics' heroism, as we are shown the tension of the bomb control room (3:19) rather than the physical fight that was the climax of season one. Positioned mid-series, this reinterpretation echoes the impact of the initial fight, but weakly. Later, when the heroes converge on the carnival at the climax of season four (all will play a part, just like the first series) the impact is again diminished as this seems a pale imitation of the first season, with Peter again in a duel (or dual) with his opposite, having stolen Samuel's "terrakinesis" power (4:18).

Television genres and aesthetics are used increasingly in later seasons, such as the melodramatic reaction shot (for example, focusing on Noah Bennet as Nathan is accused of being "one of us" [3:19]), which John Fiske notes is a defining characteristic of soap opera (184). Fans noted this shift; as one commented, "Think of it as a soap opra [sic] with super powers" (empath2380). Plot devices that would not succeed in comics, such as shapeshifting, are brought to the fore. Numerous romances (another Hollywood trope and one that was ill-received in silver-age *Batman* comics) appear, meeting with mixed reactions; as Tim Kring later admitted, "I've seen more convincing romances on TV. In retrospect, I don't think romance is a natural fit for us" (Jensen 2007).

Nods to various movies and series start appearing: parallels between Claire and Joss Whedon's *Buffy* are commented upon (4:6) and Claire and Gretchen's friendship has further similarities with Buffy and Willow, such as when super-smart (and gay) Gretchen explains a "physics thing" to Claire (4:6). Mood music eerily similar to the *Halloween* (1978) theme tune is played as the pair undergo what they think is a sorority initiation in an abandoned abattoir (4:6). Claire and Alex share an underwater kiss that recalls Baz Luhrmann's *Romeo + Juliet* (1996) (4:7). Nathan's demand, "What's in the box?" (3:21) echoes Brad Pitt at the conclusion of David Fincher's *Se7en* (1995). Hiro pays homage to *Quantum Leap* (1989–93) by gulping, "Oh boy," when Sylar shows up. Matt's self-inflicted injuries (as a result of Sylar controlling his consciousness) again contain echoes of Pitt and Fincher, this time referencing the denouement of *Fight Club* (1999), which revealed Edward Norton fighting himself (4:7).

Even the aesthetic changes place more emphasis on cinematic genres and visual effects. Claire becomes a plane-jacking action heroine in a tight black leather jacket (3:15), and the glamorous staff present when Daphne is rushed to hospital recall an *ER* drama more than a real-life emergency ward (3:20). Black-and-white flashbacks dominate some episodes (3:17), as well as slow motion (3:20). Lighting effects are also used to emphasize the carnival's unreality: it is frequently filmed in a blur, showing trails from spotlights as the camera lens gently lists from side to side (4:14). Introductory sequences that rely on televisual codes to create tension (such as the extended shot of Agent Denko shaving that opens 3:20) emerge and, although a comics aesthetic still appears at times (wide closeups of Nathan in 3:19, and occasional framed shots evoking panel borders), it is arguable that the effect has become predominantly cinematic by this point.

That said, season four's attempts to return to the series' beginnings run against this trend, by (to my mind at least) invoking the reliance on origin that characterizes comics lore. Comics are often all about the origin story: Pearson and Uricchio note that Batman's origin is frequently revisited by Batman writers in "compulsive recountings and variations" and argue that, while irrelevant details may change, this "reiteration of the basic origin events holds together otherwise divergent expressions of the Batman" (194). In these comics, "constant repetition of the basic origin events has turned them into the central touchstone of the character" (196). Season four of *Heroes* reveals that Chandra Suresh's original investigation was actually the source of the latest threat (by alerting Samuel to his power; 4:9) and the repetition noted above, although sometimes redundant, also retains the focus on comics tropes by recalling earlier episodes. We find Sylar again hunting Claire, returning us to the overused tagline of "save the cheerleader, save the world" as he labels her similarly: "Hello, cheerleader" (4:13). Although diluted by televisual and cinematic convention, the comics flavor of *Heroes* remains — but it seems that for the majority of the audience the joke has become tired through reuse and knowing irony is now glib cliché, as the same tropes are repeated or transferred to new characters. Perhaps it is appropriate, then, that the series ends through a television lens as Claire reveals her abilities to the world with the now-familiar phrase, "My name is Claire Bennet and this is attempt number ... I guess I've kinda lost count" (4:18).

WORKS CITED

Daniels, L. *DC Comics: A Celebration of the World's Favorite Comic Book Heroes*. New York: Billboard Books/Watson-Guptill Publications, 2003.
DeNardo, J. "*Heroes* Season 2 Officially Sucks." *SFSignal*. 1 Nov 2007. http://www.sfsignal.com/archives/2007/11/heroes-season-2-officially-sucks/ (accessed 22 Sep 2010).
Douglas, E. "Exclusive: Heroes Creator Tim Kring!" *Superherohype*. 29 Aug 2006, http://www.superherohype.com/features/articles/91801-exclusive-heroes-creator-tim-kring (accessed 15 Sep 2010).
Doux, B. "Heroes." *Reviews by Billie Doux*. 2010, http://www.billiedoux.com/heroes.html (accessed 25 Sep 2010).
Eisner, W. *Comics and Sequential Art*. Expanded ed. Tamarac, FL: Poorhouse Press, 1990.
Ellis, W., and John Cassaday. *Planetary: Leaving the 20th Century*. La Jolla, CA: Wildstorm Productions, 2004.
_____. *Planetary: The Fourth Man*. La Jolla, CA: Wildstorm Productions, 2001.
Empath2380. "Sylar and Peter are Brothers? Unacceptable." *9th Wonders*. 28 Aug 2008, http://boards.9thwonders.com/index.php?showtopic=64427 (accessed 20 Oct 2010).
Fisher, M. "Gothic Oedipus: Subjectivity and Capitalism in Christopher Nolan's Batman Begins." *ImageTeXT* 2.2 (20 Oct 2010), http://www.english.ufl.edu/imagetext/archives/v2_2/fisher/.
Fiske, J. *Television Culture*. London: Routledge, 1987.
Gaiman, N., and John Romita Jr. *Eternals*. Tunbridge Wells, Kent: Panini Publishing, 2006.
Heroes Unmasked, 1–33. BBC, 2007–2008.
Jenkins, H. *Convergence Culture*. New York: New York University Press, 2006.
Jensen, J. "'Heroes' Creator Apologizes to Fans." *Entertainment Weekly*. 7 Nov 2007, http://www.ew.com/ew/article/0,,20158840,00.html (accessed 1 Sep 2010).
Lang, A. "'The Status Is Not Quo!': Pursuing Resolution in Web-Disseminated Serial Narrative," *Narrative* 18.3 (2010): 367–381.
Moore, A., and Brian Bolland. *Batman: The Killing Joke*. London: Titan Books, 1988.
Stafford, N., and David Lavery. "Finale Face-Off." In *Saving the World: A Guide to Heroes*, edited by Lynette Porter, David Lavery, and Hillary Robson. 165–179. Toronto, Ont.: ECW Press, 2007.
Pearson, R., and William Uricchio, eds. *The Many Lives of the Batman*. London: BFI Publishing, 1991.

Superpowers and Super-Insight: How Back Story and Motivation Emerge Through the *Heroes* Graphic Novels

Kristin M. Barton

It is common in today's media landscape for television shows to incorporate some type of supplemental content to enhance the experience for fans of a given series. For followers of the various *Star Trek* incarnations, there exist hundreds of published novels that continue the stories of the numerous starship crews that have populated the franchise. Many sitcoms such as *The Office* (2005–present) and *30 Rock* (2006–present) now produce online "webisodes," short, truncated stories that exist independently of the series' larger storylines. Some series, such as *Lost* (2004–2010) and *Psych* (2006–present), produce online games that allow viewers to use their knowledge of the show to compete for prizes. However, what happens in the extra content usually has no direct impact on the main show, and issues or events depicted in the show rarely work their way into the supplemental content. These supplemental elements largely serve as short vignettes or stand-alone pieces to provide viewers with some extra content between new episodes.

Heroes is one major exception to this rule. In launching its line of online graphic novels (a term used synonymously with "comic books" in this context), *Heroes* managed not only to appease fans with additional content and stories, but also to use that content to create more fully formed characters and provide the necessary back stories of principle characters on the show. The content provided through the *Heroes 360 Experience* (more recently renamed *Heroes Evolution*) on the website www.nbc.com/heroes/evolutions) serves to enhance and illuminate the storylines that were running concurrently on *Heroes*. Specifically, online graphic novels were one element of the online experience that provided valuable insight and produced some of the most relevant details for fans to better understand and appreciate the show.

Released weekly, the graphic novels were intended to capture the look of Isaac Mendez's artwork (created in real life by artist Tim Sale), which became part of the iconic look of the show. Many issues of the online *Heroes* comics are also reminiscent of Mendez's *9th Wonders!* comic (both in terms of the aesthetic and content) which played a prominent role in the series. But most importantly, the online comics served to give fans of the show a deeper level of understanding when it came to the characters and why they regularly behaved in ways that seemed counterproductive to their own self-preservation.

The Nature of Television

In one of the seminal works of media criticism, *Four Arguments for the Elimination of Television* (1978), Jerry Mander outlines the abilities and limits of television. Mander argues that as a medium for conveying information, television was designed and is predisposed to depict certain types of content. Developed around the concept of projecting moving images in conjunction with an accompanying soundtrack, the nature of television is that the viewer is dependent on seeing certain things happen on screen. As Mander states, "The medium is far better suited technically to expressing hate, fear, jealousy, winning, wanting and violence" (269). These attributes and characteristics can all be expressed through broad action, whether physical violence towards another, displays of fear (such as screaming), or facial expressions, such as scowling and snarling. With reference to *Heroes*, Mander might very well see the show as the embodiment of what television was designed to do.

The depictions of characters flying, freezing time, and generally defying the laws of nature make for a visual spectacle that television is perfectly suited to show. However, the drawback, as Mander sees it, is that television does not allow for the expression or development of deeper emotions that allow viewers to more fully understand why these characters are flying, freezing time, or performing other feats of supernatural ability. This task, he might suggest, is something better suited to print, where lengthy descriptions and character insight are more customary and fitting of the medium. Media scholar Neil Postman supports Mander's view on the limitations of television, suggesting that using the medium to convey complex messages isn't practical, which he claims is comparable to trying to use smoke signals to discuss complex philosophical issues. Postman goes on to parallel Mander's critique of television by saying that "on television, discourse is conducted largely through visual imagery, which is to say that television gives us a conversation in images, not words" (7). This again supports the supposition that a show like *Heroes*, which uses numerous visual effects to create the characters' abilities, is a show that on the surface seems ideally suited for the medium. But both Mander and Postman would argue that no deeper messages (e.g., character development or evolution) can be imparted through the "smoke signals" of television. Those underlying elements, missing in the television medium, are what audience members need in order to appreciate more fully the narrative.

To illustrate the point Mander makes, try to remember the first time you had a crush on someone or fell in love. Had a television camera been following you when you first experienced those feelings, would it have been able to capture what was happening? As you slowly came to the realization that you had undeniable feelings for this person, viewers at home would merely see you standing and staring at someone across a room, an action we associate on television with stalking, not romance. The camera would not have picked up your elevated heartbeat or the fact that you suddenly started feeling much warmer. The audience may have recognized your nervousness because you might have awkwardly mumbled as you began speaking or acted jittery, but they probably would not have been able to discern the true level of anxiety you felt while asking that person out. Or maybe the viewers would have seen you acting nonchalantly while trying to "play it cool," but they would have no idea of the excitement you felt speaking to that person for the first time. What you experienced and how the TV audience would have perceived it are vastly different because TV doesn't have the ability to depict your feelings in that particular moment.

As Mander and Postman would argue, television has largely deprived us of this level of character development for so long that we no longer question the motives of television characters. One point of view expressed by Prof. Larry Johannessen is that a character's values must be articulated and explored in order for them to become fully developed (147). If Peter Petrelli and Hiro Nakamura continually put themselves in danger for others, one of the questions we should be asking is why. In the pilot episode of *Heroes* ("Genesis" 1:1), we see that Peter is a hospice nurse and that he obviously has some inherent desire to help others. But in reading the *Heroes* story as a piece of fiction, many critics would argue that viewers need to understand more fully what drives Peter at his core to do these things if he is going to be featured as one of the protagonists. It is at this junction, where characters with special abilities intersect with moral and ethical questions of right and wrong, that the graphic novel/comic book emerges as an ideal narrative vehicle. Christopher Robichaud sees this as one of the strengths of the graphic novel, when he states in an essay dealing with superheroes and responsibility, "Comic books have given rise to a universe chock-full of people with amazing abilities, and all of them face the same fundamental moral concerns. What should they do?" (178).

In issue twelve of the *Heroes* online graphic novels titled "Super-Heroics," the question of Peter's motivations is addressed (at least to some degree) by showing us how Peter perceives himself and why he is so adamant about doing good (Wilcox). The seven-page comic highlights Peter's insecurities and provides us with a glimpse into his psyche that television couldn't (or wouldn't) have provided. The comics serve to take the story started on television and elaborate on the details. As playwright Lajos Egri states, "Regardless of the medium in which you are working, you must know your characters thoroughly" (60). If television is a medium that is unwilling or unable to delve into exploring characters and their motivations, then another medium is required.

Why Online Comics?

The continuation of the *Heroes* storylines in web-comic form works primarily for three reasons. First, given the content and theme of the show, it is apropos that a story centered on people with extraordinary abilities should find a second home in the panels of comic books. The nature of the characters' abilities lend themselves perfectly to a medium that makes no distinction, in terms of cost or production time, between a character idly walking down the street and the complete destruction of a planet. Second, given the demographic of 18- to 34-year-old males who were the show's target audience, the incorporation of a digital medium reflects the awareness of the viewers' tendencies to be engaged with online content. Research indicates that sales and readership for printed comic books have been in decline over the last decade as digital comic books grow in prevalence (Kiyota 43). This fact suggests that, had NBC attempted to use traditional comic books as an extension of the *Heroes* storylines, they almost certainly would have under-performed compared to their digital equivalent. In fact, NBC did attempt to publish printed collections of the *Heroes* graphic novels, but those publications ultimately proved to be less successful than the network had hoped. After publishing volumes through the DC Comics publishing subsidiary Wildstorm in 2007 and 2008, a third advertised volume was quietly dropped from publication, presumably due to low sales and consumers' predilection for accessing the material online free of charge. The third reason the *Heroes* graphic novels have been successful is that they allow for the expansion of the story without any of the limitations or hindrances Mander prescribes to television. Here, Postman once again agrees with Mander. On this issue Postman observes, "Each medium, like language itself, makes possible a unique mode of discourse by providing a new orientation for thought, for expression, for sensibility" (10). Since their inception, comic books have been recognized for their inclusion of dialogue boxes that explicitly communicate story exposition or characters' inner monologues. In these boxes, motivation, explanation, and justification can all be provided for a character's actions and behavior. On television, the function of this type of omniscient narration is primarily to recap events or explicate plot details for the audience at the beginning or end of acts within the story. And in many cases the use of this type of narration to convey plot information results in adding to the humorous elements of the show (whether intentionally or not) rather than clarifying anything of substance (some notable examples include the Balladeer from *The Dukes of Hazzard* (1979—1985) and the deceased Mary Alice Young on *Desperate Housewives* (2004—present). *Heroes* employed voice-over narration as well, but the narration primarily featured Mohinder's philosophical and ideological considerations that did not serve any significant expository function and were eventually phased out of the show.

Looking at this technique in a more literary context brings to mind examples from classic playwrights such as Euripides and Sophocles who used the chorus as a means of speaking directly to the audience and informing them of exposition and character motivations. Even Shakespeare held to the belief that character development was paramount for any dramatic opus. Though limited in use, Shakespeare also incorporated a chorus to explicate plot points, as in *Henry V* (1599), in which the chorus serves to keep the audience aware of developments occurring off stage. When the chorus declares, "Now all the youth of England are on fire" (act 2, prologue 30), this is a means for Shakespeare to convey the deliberations of his characters and their collective decision to follow their king (i.e., their commitment to war). Allowing his audience to fully understand what was happening to his characters helped those watching to become more engaged and invested in the story. Contemporary scholars see this as one of Shakespeare's strengths as a writer and a storyteller. As the late literary critic John Gardner noted, "The center of every Shakespearean play, as of all great literature, is character" (6). The use of a chorus by these early playwrights is equivalent (in a manner of thinking) to the modern-day comic book text box.

However, unlike the plays that required a chorus to provide the audience with information, graphic novels allow for a character's inner thoughts to be on display and understood at any moment of the story. Readers rely on text boxes to gain insight into a given character's psyche and to understand the situation as it evolves and how the protagonist is responding. In fact, it would most likely seem atypical (not to mention boring) if we were to see Spider-Man swinging across the New York City skyline without text boxes providing us with his inner thoughts and turmoil. Or imagine the confusion of seeing panel after panel of Batman perched atop one of Gotham City's skyscrapers looking down into the night, without the aid of the writer providing some explanation of his thoughts or feelings. We expect exposition in comic books, which makes the online *Heroes* graphic novels an ideal vehicle for creating more fully formed characters than could otherwise be achieved through television alone.

Filling in the Gaps

In looking at the 173 total issues of the *Heroes* graphic novels that were released on the NBC website, it appears that the original intent was for them to serve as vehicles to supplement story details that were never explored on the show. The early stories presented in the graphic novels predominantly focused on the primary characters on the show and explored events that were alluded to but never explicitly detailed. Certainly one reason why these story elements may not have been included in the show could be the limited amount of time a weekly primetime network show has to tell a story, made even more difficult for *Heroes* due to the multiple storylines taking place simultaneously, featuring the numerous leading characters. But another, more plausible explanation may be that these stories, while having visually stunning components to them that would make good TV, conveyed too much exposition and character back story for them to be properly shot for television. Mander and Postman would again argue that understanding the thoughts and feelings that motivate people is not something that can be easily displayed on TV or visually imparted to the audience. Mander explains the nature of television is one where "the medium, in effect, chooses its own content from a very narrow field of possibilities" (47).

One example of this use of the graphic novels to supplement back story can be seen in issue five of the graphic novels, "Snapshots" (Pokaski). Here the audience is shown the back story of D.L. Hawkins that is alluded to on the show. The issue begins with D.L. being interrogated by the police in connection with the murders of his former criminal associates (murders committed by his wife Niki Sanders and explained in issue six, "Stolen Time," also by Pokaski). The story continues by showing D.L.'s early, inadvertent use of his powers, his time in jail, and his eventual escape. Throughout the short, six-page story, the reader is provided with insight into what D.L. is thinking and his rationale for breaking out of jail. His primary motivation, which is never articulated on the show, is concern for his family. Despite his innocence, his reasons for escaping stem from a need to protect his family more than the frustration of being wrongly convicted. D.L.'s inner monologue expresses this sentiment within a panel on the third page: "The trial was a joke. I never stood a chance. But that's not what's been bugging me" (Pokaski, "Snapshots").

Similarly, issue two of the *Heroes* graphic novels, titled "The Crane," provides readers with more insight into the character Hiro Nakamura and his compulsion to be a superhero. On the show, Hiro is shown to be a mid-level employee at a large company in Japan, and viewers are led to believe that Hiro's desire to do great things stems from his longing to escape the doldrums of the cubicle farm to which he's been relegated. But within the five pages of story contained within "The Crane," the audience is provided with new insight that better explains Hiro's motivations (Coleite). The issue, which features a soliloquy from Hiro, serves to reveal why he feels the need to be more than he is and what motivates him to feel that way. In this issue (primarily on page four), a flood of information is provided about Hiro that never made its way on to the TV show. The graphic novel reveals that Hiro's deceased grandfather is the motivating factor in his desire to live an extraordinary life, as his grandfather was a survivor of the bombing of Hiroshima and heroically fought the cancer that ultimately took his life. In fact, it is here that we learn that Hiro was named in honor of Hiroshima. During his monologue in front of a memorial, he affirms, "My mother named me Hiro, so that we would never forget" (Coleite, "The Crane").

By the end of the issue, he concedes that living his life the way he has is not worthy of the legacy his grandfather left him. The final two panels of the issue depict Hiro placing a paper crane in front of a Hiroshima Peace Memorial and proclaiming, "I believe I have done a disservice to your memory, grandfather. I will not let this happen again" (Coleite, "The Crane"). In these five pages, we are provided with a completely new understanding of Hiro and why he feels the need to try to be like the superheroes he's idolized in comic books. Once again, Mander might note here that Hiro's five-page soliloquy works well in comic book format, since it's a longstanding convention of the medium that's widely accepted by its audience. If this were to be translated on to television, it would most likely appear strange and off-putting, as most characters on television don't wander morosely through on-screen environments talking to themselves. The print medium, and particularly comic books, are uniquely suited to provide a graphic representation of Hiro's journey through the story as well as an insight into his thoughts and feelings in a way that doesn't seem forced or out of place.

Populating the World

Another function that the *Heroes* graphic novels provide is an outlet to explore the lives and stories of secondary characters from the TV show. With so many main characters, it can be hard to work in significant or meaningful stories that incorporate supporting characters. Writers and producers were quick to observe that viewers were intrigued by these characters and wanted to learn more about them. Chuck Kim, writer of the episodes ".07%" (1:19) and "Dying of the Light" (3:6) as well as numerous issues of the graphic novels, observed this trend and stated in an interview, "I think maybe Angela and maybe Claude from Season One are the fans' most beloved characters" (Stewart). This observation translated into a shift within the online graphic novels away from supplemental stories of the primary characters and toward stories featuring other characters populating the *Heroes* universe. Beginning around the start of the second season, the weekly comic began featuring auxiliary characters in prolonged storylines (up to eight issues), including Ted Sprague, the Haitian, Bob and Elle Bishop, Adam Monroe, Claude Rains (Bennet's invisible partner), various members of the Sullivan Bros. Carnival, and the founding members of the Company.

A popular character on the show who found his way into numerous graphic novel storylines was the Haitian. Powerful and mysterious, the Haitian (whose real name is René) was initially utilized on the show to provide an impetus for the heroes and as an insurance policy for the Company in dealing with information leaks. But as he appeared more frequently, the Haitian was revealed to be a character with feelings and moral judgments that sometimes ran counter to those of the Company. Perhaps with that growth in mind, the graphic novels allocated a four-issue series devoted to The Haitian's background titled "It Takes a Village," Parts 1–4 (issues 35–38). In the series, the Haitian is presented as a young boy whose father, Guillame, is a village leader who possesses the ability to influence the dispositions of those around him, ranging from inspiring trust to inciting rage. During the course of the series, we see the Haitain's abilities manifest for the first time and negate his father's abilities at a crucial moment when Guillame is attempting to protect his village. Ultimately, Guillame kills himself and the Haitian is left with feelings of guilt and responsibility for what has happened. The series ends with Agent Thompson arriving in the village looking for Guillame, but instead he leaves with the Haitian to begin his association with the Company.

The series serves a number of purposes, including showing the Haitian's origins and giving readers some insight into how he perceives his powers. But perhaps most importantly, the series explains his involvement with the Company despite what he ultimately reveals is a disagreement with the philosophical approach they have towards people with abilities. Some may have questioned why the Haitian would work for the Company and hurt people the way he does by erasing their memories, but the graphic novels suggest a reason: his respect for authority figures and his loyalty to those whom he sees as surrogate parental figures (Agent Thompson, Noah Bennet, Angela Petrelli).

Adam Monroe, the would-be immortal formerly known as Takezo Kensei, is another character who populates numerous issues of the *Heroes* graphic novels. Having lived for over four hundred years, Monroe is a character ripe with opportunity for expanding his story. One such example comes from issue 66 of the online comics titled, "The Ten Brides of Takezo Kensei" (Kim). Here we are given a glimpse of how Adam Monroe has lived his life through the women he has loved as he recounts his relationship with each of them during his time buried alive (Hiro buried him alive in the season-two finale, "Powerless," 2:11). Through his recollections, Monroe walks the reader through his marital experiences, ranging from true love to mere flings, from a relationship that lasted 62 years to an adulterous wife whom he killed as she slept. As a tool for understanding character, this story suggests that Monroe was a multifaceted individual who was more than just the selfish villain depicted on the show. The fond manner in which he remembers several of his former wives indicates that he is a man capable of love and trust, characteristics that were absent from his personality on television. Once again, using the graphic novels to provide more back story for Monroe functions as a way to create a more complete character that seems more realistic than the two-dimensional miscreants who populate many television programs.

Previews and Introductions

In a move that serves as both a promotional tool and vehicle for storytelling, the third function the graphic novels fulfill is to introduce the *Heroes* audience to new characters prior to their incorporation into the show itself. Numerous characters who have appeared on screen made their initial debut through introductory stories designed to establish these characters as part of the *Heroes* universe. Once again, the relatively limited amount of time available to tell story on the television show necessitates the omission of certain story elements in order to keep the action moving and progress the overall narrative. But the graphic novels, with their weekly release schedule and varying lengths, provide an outlet to deliver information to the audience prior to the characters appearing on the show, in effect priming the viewers for what is to come

(Bryant and Thompson 88). Whether intentionally testing the waters or merely providing a sneak peek of things yet to take place, the graphic novels function as prologues for many of the stories carried out on the show.

Two of the most maligned characters ever to appear on *Heroes*, Maya and Alejandro, made their initial debut in the graphic novel "Maya y Alejandro" (issue 51, Warshaw). This issue (which was released the week before the duo made their first television appearance in the episode "Four Months Later," 2:1) highlights the events that trigger Maya and Alejandro's journey to New York to find Chandra Suresh. When we are introduced to them on the show, the two are already on the run and evading authorities who are pursuing them. While the origin of their flight may not be critical for a television audience to know, the graphic novel examines the death and mayhem the two have left in their wake and reveals the moment when the police identify them as being responsible for numerous gruesome deaths.

Hana Gitelman is another character who made her debut in one of the graphic novels, but unlike Maya and Alejandro (who appear in only one issue of the graphic novel but fifteen and seven episodes of the show, respectively) Gitelman is a character whose story is told primarily through the online comics. First appearing in the issue "Wireless, Part 1" (Coleite), Gitelman makes her first televised appearance almost two months later in the episode "Unexpected" (1:16). Played on the show by Stana Katic, Gitelman appears in only two episodes but is featured in several storylines within the graphic novels, including "Wireless" (four-part series), "How Do You Stop an Exploding Man?" (two-part series), "War Buddies" (six-part series), and "The Death of Hana Gitelman" (two-part series). During her run in the graphic novels, Gitelman encounters several primary *Heroes* characters, including Noah Bennet, Micah Sanders, and Matt Parkman, and her fate ultimately is to sacrifice herself in order to protect others who possess abilities as well. This storyline, though never directly referenced on the show, underscores the capacity that the online graphic novels provide as a supplementary storytelling vehicle.

As Gitelman makes her decision to sacrifice herself to protect the identities of others like her, the audience is given some insight into her character through an inner monologue that, as stated before, may have been perceived as "awkward" or "clunky" on television. In her final moments, she reflects, "I didn't want to be a martyr. And I wasn't doing it for revenge, or because I had a death wish. I did it because it was the right thing to do" (Coleite, "The Death of Hana Gitelman, Part 2"). Whereas on the television screen her determination and grim façade may have caused her to come across as someone seeking retribution, readers are given insight into the person she was and how she viewed her role in helping others.

In exploring the achievements and benefits derived from the *Heroes* graphic novels, this chapter was not intended to slight or disparage the medium of television. Television serves as a vital tool in almost every aspect of our lives, but like any medium it has its limitations. Recognizing those limits, the producers and writers of *Heroes* (many of whom contributed to the graphic novels) have created a more complete, complex, and vivid experience for fans of the show. While many television series have had comic books adapted from or produced in concert with an ongoing series — (*Chuck* (2007–present), *Fringe* (2008–present), and *True Blood* (2008–present), among others)— there cannot be many that have the longevity of a four-year run while at the same time serve as canon for the overarching story.

It could be argued, in fact, that no other medium could convey the pertinent information for the *Heroes* narrative as well as the graphic novels do. Combining television's visual elements with the print media's ability to relate exposition results in a vehicle seemingly designed to tell these stories. Rocco Versaci mirrored this sentiment when he compared the literary value of comic books to the literatures delivered through other media such as film and traditional print. He notes that when compared to other media outlets, graphic novels "can achieve artistic and political feats that are unique to the medium and thus unavailable to authors of these more respected forms" (183). The amalgamation of media used to tell the *Heroes* story is fitting, considering the hybridized nature of the show as an action/drama/comedy/science fiction series. Using multiple media outlets serves to create a more expansive and cohesive narrative that a complex and multifaceted show like *Heroes* deserves.

WORKS CITED

Bryant, Jennings, and Susan Thompson. *Fundamentals of Media Effects*. Boston: McGraw-Hill, 2002.

Coleite, Aron Eli. "The Crane." *Heroes Graphic Novels*. NBC.com. 2 Oct 2006, http://www.nbc.com/heroes/novels/downloads/Heroes_novel_013.pdf (accessed 20 Feb 2011).

_____. "The Death of Hana Gitelman, Part 2." *Heroes Graphic Novels*. NBC.com. 22 May 2007, http://www.nbc.com/heroes/novels/downloads/Heroes_novel_013.pdf (accessed 24 Feb 2011).

_____. "Wireless, Part 1." *Heroes Graphic Novels*. NBC.com. 25 Dec 2006, http://www.nbc.com/heroes/novels/downloads/Heroes_novel_013.pdf (accessed 24 Feb 2011).

Egri, Lajos. *The Art of Dramatic Writing*. New York: Simon and Schuster, 1972.

Gardner, John. *The Art of Fiction*. New York: Knopf, 1984.

Johannessen, Larry R. "Enhancing Response to Literature through Character Analysis." *The Clearing House* 74.3 (2001): 145–150.

Kelly, Joe. "It Takes a Village, Parts 1–4." *Heroes Graphic Novels*. NBC.com. 29 May–19 June 2007, http://www.nbc.com/heroes/novels/downloads/Heroes_novel_035.pdf (accessed 22 Feb 2011).

Kim, Chuck. "The Ten Brides of Takezo Kensei." *Heroes Graphic Novels*. NBC.com. 31

Dec 2007, http://www.nbc.com/heroes/novels/downloads/Heroes_novel_066.pdf (accessed 22 Feb 2011).
Kiyota, Yoshiaki. "Japan's Publishing Distribution in the Internet Age." *Publishing Research Quarterly* 17.2 (2001): 43–47.
Mander, Jerry. *Four Arguments for the Elimination of Television*. New York: William Morrow and Company, 1978.
Pokaski, Joe. "Snapshots." *Heroes Graphic Novels*. NBC.com. 23 Oct 2006, http://www.nbc.com/heroes/novels/downloads/Heroes_novel_005.pdf (accessed 20 Feb 2011).
_____. "Stolen Time." *Heroes Graphic Novels*. NBC.com. 30 Oct 2006, http://www.nbc.com/heroes/novels/downloads/Heroes_novel_005.pdf (accessed 20 Feb 2011).
Postman, Neil. *Amusing Ourselves to Death*. New York: Penguin, 1985.
Robichaud, Christopher. "With Great Power Comes Great Responsibility: On the Moral Duties of the Super-Powerful and Super-Heroic." In *Superheroes and Philosophy: Truth, Justice, and the Socratic Way*, edited by Tom Morris and Matt Morris. 177–193. Chicago: Open Court, 2005.
Shakespeare, William. *Henry V*. New York: Grosset & Dunlap, 1909.
Stewart, Ryan. *Interview: Chuck Kim*. Heroeswiki.com. 4 Jan 2008, http://heroeswiki.com/Interview:Chuck_Kim (accessed 1 Mar 2011).
Versaci, Rocco. *This Book Contains Graphic Language: Comics as Literature*. London: Continuum, 2007.
Warshaw, Mark. "Maya y Alejandro." *Heroes Graphic Novels*. NBC.com. 18 Sep 2007, http://www.nbc.com/heroes/novels/downloads/Heroes_novel_051.pdf (accessed 24 Feb 2011).
Wilcox, Harrison. "Super-Heroics." *Heroes Graphic Novels*. NBC.com. 11 Dec 2006, http://www.nbc.com/heroes/novels/downloads/Heroes_novel_012.pdf (accessed 15 Feb 2011).

"Niki's Not Here Right Now": Fragmented Identity in NBC's *Heroes*

Laura Hilton

"Sometimes I look in the mirror, and I'm not sure it's me that I'm seeing"—Niki Sanders

In fulfilling the demands of both genre and mainstream audiences, NBC's *Heroes* has resituated elements of the comic book tradition within the context of contemporary television. On a stylistic level, the subtitles of Hiro and Ando imitate speech balloons while camera shots frequently evoke well-known examples of comics' art, such as the famous cinematographic opening page of *Watchmen* (1987) by Alan Moore and Dave Gibbons. On a thematic level, comic books themselves are often central to plot development: Isaac Mendez's comic book *9th Wonders* is a regular feature of early episodes; Isaac's individual paintings, many of which create a comic strip when arranged sequentially, are central to the storyline of the first season; and references are often made to existing successful comic books, such as *X-Men* and *The Fantastic Four*. Furthermore, the celebrated comics writer Stan Lee makes a cameo appearance as a bus driver in season one and the apocalyptic events at the end of this season take place in Kirby Plaza in homage to the famous comics artist Jack Kirby. The plot and execution of *Heroes*, thus, are both clearly intertwined with the comic book tradition.

The connections between *Heroes* and the comic book tradition can be highlighted by focusing specifically on the theme of dual and fragmented identity. This theme is a recurring trope in the comic book industry as a whole and the superhero genre in particular, where the vast majority of traditional superhero characters present us with two identities within one body (for example, Bruce Wayne/Batman) and sometimes even three identities (for example, Kal-El/Clark Kent/Superman), and where doubles are also created through the oppositional relationships between certain heroes and villains, such as that of Batman and the Joker (*Batman: The Killing Joke* [1988], by Alan Moore and Brian Bolland, explicitly explores this particular kind of doubling). The figure of the double and the notion of a dual or fragmented identity is also a prominent feature of Gothic literature, where the double threatens "the integrity of the self" and where "tales of doubling are, more often than not, tales about paradigms of good and evil" (Dryden 38). A classic example of this would be Robert Louis Stevenson's *The Strange Case of Dr. Jekyll and Mr. Hyde* (1886), where notions of good and evil are discussed through the allegorical representation of a dual personality, and several critics have noted how this particular representation of duality has influenced and inspired contemporary superheroes such as Bruce Banner/the Hulk (Fingeroth 123; Packer 124; Wright 209). A contextual awareness of the double in Gothic fiction thus offers a useful theoretical framework from which to approach the double in superhero texts in general and *Heroes* in particular, especially with reference to the work of writers such as Otto Rank, one of the first psychoanalysts to write about the double (1914), and Sigmund Freud, who discussed the theory of the uncanny double in his seminal psychoanalytical essay "The Uncanny" (1919).

Heroes explores the concept of duality in a number of different ways: the characters Peter and Sylar portray similar abilities and opposing moral views by the end of the first season; Candice can create the illusion of identically resembling (or "doubling") another person in seasons one and two; Alejandro neutralizes the destructive ability of his twin sister, Maya, in season two; a version of Peter returns from the future and experiences conflict with his present self in season three; Eli can create identical replications, or clones, of himself in season four; and Sylar comes to embody the internal conflict between good and evil as the narrative of the whole series develops. Duality is thus a central element of *Heroes* and this chapter is predominantly concerned with the duality inherent to the relationship between the characters Niki and Jessica Sanders, who are both portrayed by Ali Larter. The traditional superhero often represents a characterization where one "identity" contains traits that contrast with the other "identity," such as Bruce Banner's reserved demeanor in relation to the Hulk's uncontrollable emotions. In reflection of this, a single actor portrays the often conflicting identities of both Niki and Jessica in what we might describe as a contemporary, female-centered narrative with clear connotations to Stevenson's *Jekyll and Hyde*. Indeed, in addition to portraying loose versions of both Jekyll (Niki) and Hyde (Jessica) as female, many central characteristics of both Niki and Jessica are related to the acceptance or rejection of the traditional female roles which are notoriously marginalized in Stevenson's novel (Dryden 101; Hurley 199). For example, these roles include protective mother of Micah; dedicated wife of Micah's father, D.L., once his innocence is proven; and female member of the sex industry as both an internet stripper and occasional prostitute, such as when Niki is asked to seduce Nathan Petrelli ("Collision," 1:4). The way in which *Heroes* presents the notion of dual identity and its significance in relation to these female contexts, roles and preoccupations is central to understanding Niki.

The divide between Niki and Jessica is primarily portrayed in season one, with the final episode implying an apparent unification of the fragmented "Niki" and "Jessica" identities. Firstly, the initial presentation of duality occurs in episode one ("Genesis," 1:1) and the Jessica personality can be best understood in relation to Freud's discussion of the uncanny double. Beyond season one, Niki's personality split gets increasingly complicated in the other three seasons of the series, especially when dealing with the significance of Niki and Jessica in relation to the other characters played by Ali Larter: Gina, Tracy and Barbara.

Exploring the Double: Niki's Reflection

Despite the fact that the identity of Niki's second personality is not revealed until episode seven ("Nothing to Hide" 1:7) and its origin is not explained until episode nine ("Homecoming" 1:9), the unusual characteristics of Niki's reflection are portrayed from the very first episode of the series ("Genesis") through a variety of special effects involving cameras, mirrors and other reflective surfaces and frames. A close reading of "Genesis" can establish what themes are introduced here and how issues relating to traditional female roles are presented.

The character of Niki is first introduced to the viewer while she is working as an internet stripper in front of a web camera and, as Porter et al. note, we can see "the position of the laptop in the foreground not only creating a frame for her but also showing the character in digital form in a frame on its screen" (80). This subtle use of frames connects *Heroes* with the stylistic qualities of the comic book (Porter et al. 80), but it also raises the notion of doubles since Niki appears both in person and via the digital screen. This initial suggestion of doubling is further explored later in this scene, where Niki quickly walks past a mirror and her reflection faces the viewer rather than reflecting her face in the expected profile angle. It would appear that Niki notices the incongruity of her reflection since she returns to gaze questioningly in the mirror, confirming to the viewer that something out of the ordinary was presented, but there is nothing unusual in this second glance. Nonetheless, moments later Niki passes another mirror in her son's room and here her reflection's movement mirrors her own in terms of angle but it is momentarily delayed. This reinforces the initial incongruous reflection's presence to the reader, but it remains unclear if Niki herself believes what she has seen.

The mirror and its unusual reflection becomes a recurring theme throughout the season and it functions as a symbol of Niki's insecurity about her identity. Its presence from such an early scene in the first episode of the first season serves to introduce this theme while also creating suggestive connotations with the role of the mirror in traditional Gothic literature. As Rank explains, one type of double is the "independent and visible cleavage of the ego" which is often depicted through a shadow or reflection. Rank discusses how this type of double can be interpreted as a representation of an internal division of one person into two parts (12) and this reading can be usefully applied to the relationship between Niki and her second identity. The unusual nature of Niki's reflection in this initial scene, therefore, presents a strong connection to the Gothic theme of dual and fragmented identities from an early stage in the narrative of *Heroes*.

These initial examples of Niki's unusual reflection are developed later in the episode while also providing some further information relating to Niki's personality and her financial situation. For example, Niki visits Micah's principal in order to discuss some unpaid tuition fees, showing that Niki is currently experiencing financial difficulties despite a $25,000 donation she made in order to secure Micah's place at the school. The way in which Niki attempts to resolve this problem is revealing: at first she tries to flirt with the principal, suggestively offering to "work harder" and drawing connections with her flirtatious behavior on her internet site at the start of the episode. Her behavior here suggests that she is familiar with using her beauty and femininity both to earn money and to manipulate people into accommodating her wishes. However, her attempt at manipulation is unsuccessful and after pleading and then arguing, her final resort is to verbally threaten the principal and to physically attack him by pulling him across his desk by his tie. While no superhuman powers are displayed here, this minor act of violence foreshadows the increasingly violent actions that the second personality undertakes with her superhuman strength later in the series. Realizing that this aggressive approach is no more successful than her flirtation, Niki leaves the office without reaching a resolution for her problem and at this point she notices her reflection in a fish tank in the lobby. Here, Niki's expression of frustrated desperation contrasts with her reflection's appearance of confrontational determination and Niki definitely notices her unusual reflection at this point since she directly addresses it with an angry plea to "leave me alone." This scene, therefore, reveals that Niki is pursuing a private education for her son despite the financial difficulties she is experiencing, suggesting an explanation as to why she strips online and showing the quality of Micah's education to be a clear priority in her life. Furthermore, Niki notices her unusual reflection and addresses it for the first time immediately following her conflict with the principal. As a result, this scene suggests that Niki's emotional response to her financial problems and her inability to provide for her son are directly related to the emergence of her dual identity.

Later in the episode, Niki confides both her financial instability and her concerns about her reflection to a close friend, Tina, explaining: "I think I'm kinda losing it a little bit. I'm seeing things. Like I keep feeling someone's watching me. It's someone that I can't see." This dialogue confirms that Niki is aware of her unusual reflection while also suggesting that at this point, she has no idea who the reflection is or what its aims and objectives might be. The final two scenes involving Niki in this episode, however, suggest that whereas Niki's priority is Micah, Niki's reflection is intent on protecting Niki. Indeed, following a visit from two men working for Mr. Linderman, a man involved in the mafia from whom Niki borrowed $30,000, Niki is captured and forced to strip while her reflection watches. One of the men strikes Niki and knocks her unconscious, and when she awakens later in the episode the room is covered with blood and both of the men are dead. Niki's shocked reaction at what has happened implies that she was not consciously involved in the attack and when she looks into the broken mirror she sees a blood-covered reflection who raises a finger to her lips in an order for silence and then smiles. The difference between Niki's appearance in comparison with her bloody reflection proposes a clear divide between the two and implies that the reflection was involved in the deaths of the men whereas Niki was not. These differences in both appearance and consciousness between Niki and her reflection thus develops the initial connection to Rank's theory of the double as an internal division resulting in two separate parts, as is evident in the use of mirrors at the start of the episode.

As such, this final appearance of Niki in the first episode develops the earlier suggestions of an unusual reflection and begins to imply a consciously separate character who is able to take control of Niki's body when Niki is unconscious and act without either her awareness or her consent. The following episodes build on this introduction, featuring blackouts and occasions where Niki loses awareness for hours at a time (e.g., "Don't Look Back" 1:2 and "Collision"), her admission to Tina that she is having "violent dreams" where she is "tearing people apart" ("Collision"), and finally a conversation between Niki and her reflection soon after the return of her husband, where the reflection reveals that she framed D.L. and caused his arrest and imprisonment while effectively forcing Niki to become a single mother. This final point is particularly interesting and while Niki's initial response to this revelation is to feel remorse for her husband's unjustified incarceration, drawing attention to her role as dedicated wife, the reflection is able to convince Niki that she needs to follow the reflection's instructions in order to protect Micah, who is once again portrayed as Niki's main priority. Directly following this conversation, Niki's reflection appears to take control of her body and attacks D.L. with a briefcase, demonstrating the ability of superhuman strength on screen for the first time and showing that the dual identity may not be the only unusual ability that Niki (and/or her second identity) possess. Niki's fragmented identity thus takes control of Niki's body by convincing Niki that she is acting in the best interests of Micah, again demonstrating the differences between the two identities and indicating that Niki's approach to the role of wife contrasts sharply with that of the Jessica identity.

The opening episode of season one thus introduces a number of themes which are developed throughout the following episodes, including the significance of the mirror, the separate identity of the reflection, and the approach to roles such as wife and mother. The remainder of season one takes an interesting approach to developing this notion of fragmented identity in relation to the identification of Niki's second identity in episode seven.

Jessica and Freud's Uncanny: The Return of the Repressed

The seventh episode of season one marks the first occasion where the Jessica identity is mentioned by name. Niki explains to Tina that she sometimes thinks the reflection in the mirror is "another me" called Jessica and that "when someone tries to hurt me, it's like she comes out" ("Nothing to Hide," 1:7). The significance of this name is finally revealed in episode ten, where details of several characters' histories are explored and where we learn that Niki was adopted into a family with another child named Jessica who died aged eleven ("Six Months Ago," 1:10). Analyzing the earliest chronological appearance of Jessica through a close reading of the episode "Six Months Ago," followed by an application of Freud's theory of the uncanny, helps us to explore the psychological relationship between Niki and Jessica.

When visiting Jessica's grave, Niki is portrayed as clearly still mourning the loss of her sister despite the years that have passed since her death (1:10). The close bond between the two characters is emphasized by Niki's insistence that "it's important not to forget," but the value Niki places on remembering her sister is ironically undermined later in the episode, when she meets with her estranged adopted father, Hal. When Hal visits Niki, D.L., and Micah at their home, the following conversation takes place:

>   HAL: I feel lucky that you'd even let me through the door after all the things I've done.
>   NIKI: Stop saying that. You didn't do anything.
>   HAL: Why do you keep doing that?
>   NIKI: Doing what?
>   HAL: You're only as sick as your secrets, Nicole.
>   NIKI: I know the mantras, Hal. I've been reciting them for over a year. ["Six Months Ago"].

This conversation implies that a significant event in the past has caused the estrangement between Niki and Hal, but that Niki has either forgiven Hal or has forgotten the event. After an argument involving the gift Hal brought for Micah, Niki asks: "What did you do that was so bad that I can't have my father back?" and Hal responds with shock: "You really don't remember, do you?" before immediately leaving. After this Niki looks in the mirror with an expression of distress on her face, but the expression soon hardens, suggesting that an emotional change has occurred and her reflection, the Jessica identity, has taken control. Chronologically, this is the first occasion where the Jessica identity appears since this episode takes place six months prior to the one before and Jessica's appearance significantly emerges immediately following the return of Niki's estranged father. Since there is no indication that the Jessica identity was active before Hal's return due to Niki's apparently stable and content life with D.L. and Micah, it would appear that Hal's return triggers the dual identity that initially occurs here and continues to recur throughout the season.

A later scene from this episode depicts Niki visiting Hal in his hotel room. The use of camera angle, which begins the scene by depicting events as shown through a mirror before revealing that this is a mere reflection, suggests that the dual identity is relevant here and that the Jessica identity is in control. This suggestion is soon confirmed by the words: "Not Niki. It's me, Daddy. Jessica." The Jessica identity has spoken before, telling Niki's friend Tina that "[Niki] doesn't need your help anymore, understand?" ("Nothing to Hide") and telling Niki, who was trapped in a reflection, "We're going hunting" after buying a powerful gun ("Homecoming"), but this is the first occasion where the Jessica identity categorizes itself as differentiated from Niki in such an unequivocal manner. The fact that the Jessica identity is so explicitly identified at this point in the narrative is significant since the scene goes on to explain that when Hal abused and killed his biological daughter, Jessica,

Niki was left as his "punching bag" and that the Jessica identity was there to "protect her.... I took every punch, so that she wouldn't have to." This suggests that the Jessica identity was initially constructed in Niki's childhood as a coping mechanism to help the young Niki survive both the abuse she experienced at the hands of her adopted father and the knowledge that her adopted father killed Jessica. It would also appear that following this time of intense emotional and physical trauma, the Jessica identity was no longer required and thus temporarily suppressed while Niki enjoys a relatively calm and happy period in her life with D.L. and Micah. As the Jessica identity says, "I thought she had learned to protect herself, but no such luck" and this suggests that the Jessica identity had been dormant for some time and that Niki had been solely in control until this crucial turning point.

The fact that the Jessica identity reappears when a figure from the original time of trauma returns to Niki's life suggests a close connection between the dual fragmentation of Niki's identity and Freud's theory of the uncanny double. In "The Uncanny," Freud argues that the double often results from the return of something that was once repressed and that "is actually nothing new or strange, but something that was long familiar to the psyche" before the act of repression (147–148). In this case, we might argue that the memories of Niki's abuse at the hands of her father and the fact that her father abused and killed her adopted sister is the knowledge that is both "long familiar" and repressed, and that the reappearance of her estranged father triggers the return of these repressed memories and it results in the uncanny doubling of her psyche. As such, a division is made between one identity who is aware of exactly what has happened in the past (Jessica) and another who can only access certain memories (Niki).

Another connection can be drawn to Freud's essay through his later argument that one particular type of double is represented through the person who "may identify himself with another and so become unsure of his true self" or "may substitute the other's self for his own" (142). These ideas apply interestingly to how the relationship between Niki and Jessica has developed up to this point. Firstly, Niki becomes "unsure of [her] true self" when she looks in the mirror, as discussed above. Secondly, the Jessica identity is substituted for Niki's identity on an apparently unconscious level at the start of the series, with Niki experiencing confusing blackouts (e.g. "Genesis") and often finding herself in new locations or clothes without being aware of how these changes have occurred (e.g., "Don't Look Back"). Even when provided with evidence of events that occurred when the Jessica identity was in control, such as the video of her seduction of Nathan Petrelli ("Collision"), Niki is unable to access the actual memories.

However, these apparently unconscious substitutions are eventually replaced with a conscious, consenting substitution that significantly occurs when Niki considers herself to be unable to rescue Micah from D.L. without help. Here, Niki looks into the mirror and begs, "Help me" but nothing happens. It is only later, after telling Tina that, "I tried to protect my son, but I couldn't. I failed him" and that "the part of me that needs Micah back wants to let [Jessica] [take control]" and finally smashing a mirror, that Jessica becomes the controlling identity ("Nothing to Hide"). This situation is significantly different: Niki does not simply experience a blackout while Jessica is in control and instead she appears to be aware of Jessica's actions as she watches from Jessica's previous position behind the glass of the mirror ("Homecoming"). We might read this as a direct result of her invitation for Jessica to take control and this conscious substitution of the Jessica identity for Niki's own marks the beginning of the battle between Niki and Jessica for control of Niki's body. The fact that Niki is consciously trapped behind the mirror while Jessica is in control seems to invoke an increased awareness of Jessica's actions and a consequentially increased conflict with them. Indeed, Niki's unwillingness to kill D.L. and Niki's dismay at Jessica's accidental harming of Micah ("Fallout," 1:11) mark the first conscious disagreement between Niki and Jessica, highlighting the difference between Niki's priorities here (Micah and, to a lesser extent, D.L.) and those of Jessica (Niki alone). Niki's realization that both Micah and D.L. are at risk from Jessica results in her decision to surrender herself to the police in order to protect her family from Jessica's unpredictable actions. As such, Freud's theme of the substitution of the double for the self is represented as both an unconscious and a conscious action in *Heroes*, and the struggle for control is triggered only when Niki learns more about Jessica's intentions and actions, and subsequently begins to fear for the safety of her husband and their son.

Consideration of Freud's writing on the uncanny thus offers additional insight into Niki's emotional instability and the resultant relationship that emerges between Niki and the Jessica identity. In the final two episodes of season one, an apparent unification between Niki and Jessica occurs. This unification would appear to be the only possible resolution for Niki since, as several critics have noted, an attempt to destroy a double invariably results in the destruction of either the "original" or both the "original" and the double (Rank 79; Royle 190). The unification takes place as a result of a series of events in which the power struggle between Niki and the Jessica identity begins to change and they begin to fight together towards the same goal. For example, in the penultimate episode, Mr. Linderman offers the Jessica identity, who is currently in control, $20,000,000 if she will kill D.L. ("Landslide,"

1:22). Jessica is sorely tempted, but she admits that she knows Niki would be devastated and instead relinquishes control over Niki's body and allows her to reunite with D.L. This marks a rare occasion where Jessica places Niki's desires over her own notion of what is best for Niki, suggesting that Jessica is beginning to realize that she cannot protect Niki from danger at the cost of everyone she loves. As such, here Jessica is no Hyde to Niki's Jekyll and here she instead demonstrates concern for Niki's emotional, rather than physical, well-being.

The Jessica identity's unusual behavior is further developed in the final episode of the season, where Niki has to abandon an injured D.L. in order to search for their abducted son ("How to Stop an Exploding Man," 1:23). Niki eventually finds a room containing a woman who is identical to her in appearance and who is eventually revealed to be the shape-shifter Candice. Niki initially believes Candice to be a physical embodiment of Jessica and struggles to overcome her shock when Candice attacks her. It is only after Niki glimpses the real Jessica identity in a shard of broken mirror and, hears her reassurance that Niki can defeat Candice, that Niki is able to finally embrace characteristics of her second identity and subsequently tap into the confidence, independence, and superhuman strength that she has had the potential to access all along. Niki finds Micah soon after defeating Candice and when he asks if she is really Niki, she looks into the mirror and sees only her own reflection. This suggests that the Jessica identity has now become redundant since Niki is now able to protect herself, her son, and her husband.

For the remainder of the episode, Niki is both confident and powerful. She is able to access her superhuman strength in order to destroy a door handle to aid her escape and to briefly join the fight against Sylar before returning to her family in reflection of her desires throughout the entire series. However, the resolution of fragmented identity is predominantly temporary in superhero comics: for example, unification may be established (e.g., the resolution between Bruce Wayne and Batman at the end of *Batman: The Dark Knight Returns*) but fragmentation almost always returns (e.g., *The Dark Knight Strikes Again*) due to its role as a central theme of the superhero narrative. In reflection of this tradition, the resolution between Niki and her fragmented identity is also temporary and the fragmentation in Niki's identity returns in season two.

Conclusion: (Re)Fragmented Identities Beyond Season One

Despite playing a less central role in the second season, Niki remains of interest due to her attempt to permanently remove her fragmented identity with the help of Bob Bishop, the current chairperson of the Company, an organization involved in hiding the existence of those with evolved abilities from the general public ("Kindred," 2:3). Niki's initial attempt to use medication ends disastrously due to her inability to consistently take the tablets, which results in the emergence of a third identity called Gina ("Four Months Ago," 2:8). Gina is based on an alias Niki first created when she used to live in Los Angeles ("Four Months Ago") and her first appearance takes place in a flashback episode, just like Jessica's first appearance in "Six Months Ago." This reinforces the suggestion that Niki's fragmented identity is due to her inability to process and cope with events that have happened in her past.

In a striking contrast with Niki's family-oriented priorities throughout season one, Gina is presented as the epitome of selfish hedonism and is taking drugs and dancing with several men in a club when she is eventually located by D.L. Niki is only able to regain control of her body after D.L. shows Gina a photograph of Niki, D.L., and Micah together, emphasizing once again both the importance Niki places on her family and how this provides Niki with the strength to fight her internal fragmentation. However, D.L. is shot and killed outside the club, leaving Niki as a single mother in an echo of her position at the very beginning of season one. Niki's response to this situation is to entrust Micah with family in New Orleans and initiate her own incarceration with the Company in a final attempt to battle her fragmented identity.

While staying with the Company, Niki is shown as initially attacking her allies in a violent reaction against her treatment ("Fight or Flight," 2:5) then making swift progress in her attempt to achieve a stable identity ("The Line," 2:6) before being manipulated by the telepath Maury, who uses her fear of her fragmented identity to convince her to murder Bob. In an attempt to escape future manipulation and the potential harming of others, Niki injects herself with a virus that negates her abilities and threatens her life ("Out of Time," 2:7). Powerless and unwell, Niki returns to Micah just before he places himself and his cousin, Monica, in grave danger ("Truth & Consequences," 2:10) and Niki chooses to save Monica's life at the cost of her own in the season finale ("Powerless," 2:11). However, the fragmented identities portrayed by Ali Larter continue to play a central role in *Heroes* even after Niki's death, with the introduction of a new character, Tracy, at the beginning of season three ("The Second Coming," 3:1). Tracy is revealed as one of a set of identical triplets, including Niki and another woman called Barbara ("I Am Become Death," 3:4), and similarities between Niki and Tracy can be identified through examination of their comparable struggles when dealing with their abilities and the morality of their actions. For example, in a direct parallel of Niki's actions in seasons one and two, Tracy tries to confess when she accidentally kills someone ("I Am Become Death"), she sleeps with Nathan

("Angels and Monsters," 3:5), and she is prepared to sacrifice her life for Micah ("Cold Snap," 3:20). As such, Niki's death at the close of season two does not prevent the significance of fragmented identity, or the relevance of female roles in relation to this, from continuing to feature as a recurring element of *Heroes* throughout the remainder of the series. Instead, the lack of closure in relation to Niki's death and the way that her past is echoed in the portrayal of Tracy draw further connections with the Gothic double through the tropes of hauntings, resonances and repetitions: Niki may be dead, but she is constantly evoked through the continued presence of her literal mirror-image, Tracy.

As Catherine Spooner observes, the female double plays a relatively minor role in eighteenth- and nineteenth-century Gothic literature in comparison with the male double, but "as the notion of woman as a unified speaking subject has become more stable within the twentieth-century, female doubles have become more prevalent" (128–129). If Gothic and superhero narratives continue to interact in the literature and television of the twenty-first-century, series such as *Heroes* may force the male double to finally share the spotlight with its female counterpart.

WORKS CITED

Dryden, Linda. *The Modern Gothic and Literary Doubles: Stevenson, Wilde and Wells.* Hampshire: Palgrave MacMillan, 2003.
Fingeroth, Danny. *Superman on the Couch: What Superheroes Really Tell Us About Ourselves and Our Society.* New York and London: Continuum, 2004.
Freud, Sigmund. *The Uncanny.* 1919. Trans. David McLintock; introd. Hugh Haughton. London: Penguin, 2003.
Hurley, Kelly. "British Gothic Fiction, 1885–1930." *The Cambridge Companion to Gothic Fiction*, edited by Jerrold E. Hogle. 189–207. Cambridge: Cambridge University Press, 2002.
Miller, Frank. *The Dark Knight Returns.* 1986. New York: DC Comics, 2002.
_____. *The Dark Knight Strikes Again.* 2001. Santa Monica, Titan, 2002.
Moore, Alan, and Brian Bolland. *Batman: The Killing Joke.* New York: DC Comics, 1988.
_____, and Dave Gibbons. *Watchmen.* New York: DC Comics, 1987.
Packer, Sharon. *Superheroes and Superegos: Analysing the Minds behind the Masks.* Santa Barbara: Praeger, 2010.
Porter, Lynnette, David Lavery, and Hillary Robson. *Saving the World: A Guide to* Heroes. Toronto, Ont.: ECW Press, 2007.
Rank, Otto. *The Double: A Psychoanalytic Study.* 1914. Trans. and ed. with introd. Harry Tucker Jr. Chapel Hill: University of North Carolina Press, 1971.
Royle, Nicholas. *The Uncanny.* Manchester: Manchester University Press, 2003.
Spooner, Catherine. *Fashioning Gothic Bodies.* Manchester: Manchester University Press, 2004.
Stevenson, Robert Louis. *The Strange Case of Dr. Jekyll and Mr. Hyde.* 1886. Ed. Martin A. Danahay. London: Broadview, 2005.
Wright, Bradford W. *Comic Book Nation: The Transformation of Youth Culture in America.* Baltimore and London: John Hopkins University Press, 2001.

Science Fiction and the Uncanny Realism of *Heroes*

David Hipple

Heroes displays affinity with multiple popular genres. In depicting evolutionary, global, dynastic struggle, it has the scope of the epic. Episodes are punctuated by tumultuous beats as characters oppose either each other or threatening circumstances, appealing to fans of pure action. This supports season-spanning character arcs involving diverse individual quests, lending *Heroes* the flavor of the adventure genre, and as these personal journeys collide or intertwine, it also fosters the shifting interrelationships of a soap opera.

This chapter concentrates on *Heroes* as a science fiction show, and on its makers' strategies to establish its first season as such. Science fiction (henceforth SF) is popularly associated with the uncanny, the unreal and (particularly in its visual form) the exultantly spectacular. M. Keith Booker (2–5) traces these insistently visual conventions in television SF back to Georges Méliès' early cinematic tricks, through the *Flash Gordon* serials (1936–1940) and *Star Wars* (1977). *Heroes*, however, demonstrably rejects this conventionally populist attitude, in its policy of *refusing* to emphasize the spectacular and the marvelous. This discussion suggests considering *Heroes* using a more productive general conception of SF's narrative strategy that I elaborated in "*Stargate SG-1*: Self-possessed Science Fiction" (2006): SF has no central thematic preoccupation, and is not primarily reliant on spectacle; it takes stories of experiences and relationships that could essentially be told "realistically," but tells those stories in plausibly unreal contexts that emphasize their impact.

Heroes usefully exemplifies a critical distinction between SF and fantasy, also discussed below, exhibiting SF's ideal (not always emphasized in traditional visual SF) of quasi-realistic "explicability." This emerges partly from the writing and partly, perhaps counter-intuitively, from its downplaying of remarkable visual techniques that in SF we might conventionally expect to be accentuated and celebrated. Indications of this are found in landmark sequences and in some that go relatively unremarked. We therefore find *Heroes* asserting itself from the outset as mature SF, challenging audiences' conventional visual expectations.

The "making-of" series *Heroes Unmasked* (2007–2008) constitutes a kind of "official" commentary from the show's makers. In "Mohinder's Journey" (1:11), Anthony Head's ironic and skeptical narration considers denouncing *Heroes* as mere SF, inherently lacking credibility. *Heroes* creator Tim Kring provides an answer:

> When it comes to *Heroes*, are we talking science fact, or is it a right load of old science fiction? It is somewhat the stuff of science fiction, but at the same time ... it's grounded first of all in the idea of the human genome project.

Both of these components indicate SF's problematic position within popular film and television: the question playfully dismisses the entire genre on the level of narrative seriousness; and the answer rather defensively admits that there is something of SF in the series but that it is seriously grounded as well. This invokes an issue that has occupied criticism of visual SF for decades. Many serious SF critics reserve the frostily diminutive term "sci-fi" for trivial, unchallenging SF, typically including all mass-market material on the big and small screens. Isaac Asimov even proposes the term "eye-sci-fi" as a further means of distancing visual SF *en masse* from more demandingly thoughtful manifestations of SF in print (132). *Heroes* deploys complex narrative material throughout — and thus directly confronts this awkward status of visual SF.

The characteristics that make SF a *genre* in the first place are subject to a great deal of discussion. Many attempts to define SF concentrate on the idea that it is essentially *about* science, "the future," "the other," or some similar theme, which seems to be a basic mistake. The fundamental operations of SF (like the detective story) occur not in content but in narrative method. This discussion will focus on SF not as being *about* any particular theme — but rather as a strategy for storytelling, where a comprehensible and logically explored alteration (or simply an exaggeration) in an otherwise conventional human environment provides a means of accentuating the human story at hand. Here, postulated superpowers brighten the colors in which human conflicts and other familiar relationships can be sketched, making those relationships all the more vivid.

This might invoke shadows of Darko Suvin's *novum*, the "new thing" that he proposes as SF's essential feature (4, 7–8), but my approach here connects to different and older ideas. Suvin's conception of SF depends upon intrinsic, formal mechanisms. Patrick Parrinder observes that the Brechtian policy of "estrangement" that Suvin attempts to co-opt was "a strategy for provoking audience-response and a means towards the reader's political education," but that in Suvin's hands it becomes "a matter of choosing a plot that is non-realistic in the sense that it is determined by the *novum*" (39). For Suvin, the consequences of each *novum* force SF characters to enact a Marxist critique of contemporary society. He expresses negligible concern for narrative strategies, but SF's appeal is precisely that of intriguingly dressed-up yet still accessible stories of individual experience. Suvin casually implies equivalence of his *novum* with HG Wells' "fantastic elements" (208), without fully accommodating Wells' description of their true function:

> The fantastic element, the strange property or the strange world, is used only to throw up and intensify our natural reactions of wonder, fear or perplexity. The invention is nothing in itself and when this kind of thing is attempted by clumsy writers who do not understand this elementary principle nothing could be conceived more silly and extravagant [241].

Later, we will see a Wellsian emphasis on human stories emerge from the evolution of "space opera" narratives, paralleling the rejection in *Heroes* of spectacle for its own sake and its privileging of sympathetic individual experience. Its narrative strategy emphasizes not fantastic new things but their consequences in accentuated human experience, reflecting JRR Tolkien's analysis of authentic fairy stories: "Stories that are actually concerned primarily with 'fairies' ... are relatively rare and as a rule not very interesting. Most good 'fairy-stories' are about the *adventures* of men in the Perilous Realm or upon its shadowy marches" (17).

Assessment of the standing and effectiveness of *Heroes* purely as drama is complicated by ongoing evolutions in the wider TV industry during the show's creation and transmission. This "TV show" was quickly represented in other formats, such as graphic novels intended to flesh out some characters' background stories, and the privileged "backstage access" documentary conceit of *Heroes Unmasked*. *Heroes* mounted a multimedia promotional assault on the marketplace, including an interactive internet vector. For example, websites were set up for Daniel Linderman's Corinthian Hotel and for Primatech Paper, the latter purporting to seek employees in the real world and coyly announcing the evidently problematic departure of Noah Bennet. A disguised link led viewers to an "Assignment Tracker," Primatech's profiles of assorted superpowered characters. (These sites remain, with limited content — for example, a brief video of the fictional hotel's demolition, as if to explain its absence from the real world should anyone seek it out. Original content from "Assignment Tracker 2.0" is archived at the Heroeswiki site.)

The show's host network NBC released a range of video material online in the form of ancillary "webisodes" and extensive documentaries. In one such segment Tim Kring discusses newer projects embodying lessons learned from

Heroes. His multimedia *Conspiracy for Good* endeavor is centered on a website providing a wealth of textual and video narrative, serving as a focus for participation via various communication media and real activities in a live-action roleplay with positive social outputs. Its "Who We Are" page describes the project as "a first-of-its-kind interactive story that empowers its audience to take real-life action and create positive change in the world. Call it Social Benefit Storytelling." This naturally extends the efforts noted here to present the *Heroes* narrative as a credible real-world occurrence available for direct exploration.

Beyond this vivid demonstration of media convergence both in and arising from the broad *Heroes* megatext, basic philosophies of both making and consuming TV are becoming increasingly sophisticated. Outside the *Heroes* discourse, Kring has commented comprehensively on this development in contemporary television when interviewed for the Interactive Advertising Bureau's compilation of analyses by authoritative commercial media practitioners. (The IAB is an alliance of media and technology companies with commercial interests in multimedia advertising.) In a segment from the 2008 IAB MIXX conference Kring discusses the establishment of modern drama series as "brands," amidst contemporary audiences' actively selective consumption of TV entertainment:

> You no longer have a big sort of lazy, sloppy kind of audience out there that will be entertained by anything that's ... you know: "There are three networks on, and I'm watching the one show that's on one of them. So, it may not be just [perfect] for me but I'll sit here and watch it anyway." Those days are completely gone, and so it is now by appointment that someone finds you, and by a desire and passion that they find you, and so you therefore have fans who are passionate fans, and that cuts both ways — consumers who are passionate consumers, and it cuts both ways. They can either love you, or they can very quickly turn against you. And so it just becomes very important, I think, to try and stay very true to a narrative that connects with those people's heart, or connects with their passion.

Here, Kring characterizes the modern relationship between series-maker and audience not as simply identifying provider and recipient, but as a continually *re*negotiated reciprocal understanding. In *Heroes Unmasked* "The Director's Cut" (1:20) John Badham, director of two episodes, draws attention to a related escalation in visible production values, intended to signify appealing "quality" in television:

> It's really interesting that television in the last few years has gotten so ambitious that they're spending a lot more money on their shows to make them look like little movies. [That costs] almost double what normal shows cost because they're trying to have all the effects and all of that kind of magic that normally would be reserved for a big movie.

Complicating matters further, Badham then tackles aspects of visual SF's problematic public image. He knows that effective drama essentially tells compelling human stories, and that SF is concerned with doing so in intriguingly novel worlds; but also that SF is nevertheless widely condemned as the undemanding "sci-fi" that most stridently asserts its popular marketplace presence. Barry N. Malzberg observed, "Science fiction is the only [genre] whose poorer examples are almost invariably used by critics outside the form to attack all of it" (174). Like Kring, Badham argues for *Heroes* being dramatically convincing while guardedly disconnecting its fantastic elements from a naively orthodox conception of SF:

> The stories and the characters [in *Heroes*] are so complicated. It's not just like doing [a] very simple action-hero type of movie. In, say, *Spider-Man* they did some interesting character work. You know, you got really involved with Spider-Man and his girlfriend and his uncle. That really works, and is very effective, and they've been trying to do that on *Heroes*; and they're good at it, so it's not just about hands glowing and people blowing up and doing weird effects things.

This hesitation arises from the lineage that leads critics such as Booker (above) to note SF's persistent association in popular media, from *Flash Gordon* to *Star Wars* and beyond, with celebration of its own creativity through extraordinary spectacle. The calm naturalization of the fantastic in *Heroes* is unusual in visual SF. To grasp the expectations in entertainment that it resisted, we must first consider this heritage. This chapter will now examine the trends in popular SF cinema to which Badham alludes, the sometimes simplistic conception of SF narrative that was confronted by Kring, and the unhelpful confusion of SF with fantasy, its fellow genre of the unreal.

Trailers for the Flash Gordon cinema serials (1936–1940) energetically promised innovative visual flourishes. One example available online proclaims the "GREATEST SCOOP in Motion Picture History," showing the launch of a dramatic space vehicle and its visually dynamic encounters with apparently hostile saucer-shaped craft. About half of this trailer features text inviting audiences to "ROAR through space aboard the rocket ship!" "SHOOT through the stratosphere at killer speed!" and "LAND on the mystery planet Mongo!" Each exhortation proffers dramatic footage but no indication whatever of narrative context. We are promised "amazing scenes caught by the camera for the first time!" including "the death fight between shark and octopus," "the City in the Sky!," "The Hydrocycle Submarine!," "The Undersea Empire!," "Weird shark-men!" and "The beasts of Mongo!" Snippets of action and dialogue then suggest an awkward wedding, but further text simply declares, "Nothing like it ever before attempted on the screen!" The trailer promises novel spectacle and excitement, not dramatic engagement. The narrative connecting these attractions seems rather an afterthought. In just this way, Tom Gunning associates early visual SF with the "cinema of attractions" phenomenon of film-as-vaudeville:

> To approach even the plotted trick films, such as *Voyage dans la lune* (1902), simply as precursors of later narrative structures is to miss the point. The story simply provides a frame upon which to string a demonstration of the magical possibilities of the cinema [58].

Children, *Flash Gordon*'s principal audience, enjoyed this circus-level aesthetic — but visual SF remains culturally associated with spectacle. Marketing of the philosophical SF series *Total Recall 2070* (1999) emphasized its infrequent CGI sequences, implying an action series, and failed to attract significant audiences. A film as cerebral and scientifically accurate as *2001: A Space Odyssey* (1968) still structures its finale around a psychedelic ride and a newborn cosmic superbeing. Films can come to be more meaningfully *about* their own presentation than their narrative content. Examples such as *Star Wars* (and much imitative material) delightedly embrace this stereotype.

Flash Gordon figures prominently in George Lucas' comments on influences in *Star Wars'* conception, such as when interviewed by Paul Scanlon on its release:

> I was a real fan of *Flash Gordon* and that kind of stuff.... I didn't want to make a *2001*, I wanted to make a space fantasy that was more in the genre of Edgar Rice Burroughs; that whole other end of space fantasy that was there before science took it over in the Fifties.... I said, this is what I'm going to do. It's *Flash Gordon*, it's adventure, it's exciting, sort of James Bond and all this kind of stuff.

This thinking fuelled screen SF's growth towards the monolithic presence that it enjoys today, and consequently informed studios' assumptions in producing SF as profitable product: it privileges heroic adventure and exciting visual techniques. In celebrating *Flash Gordon, Star Wars* actively positioned itself — and thus the subsequent wave of SF film and TV — as a genre not of reflection but of visceral stimulation, of conventional space opera. In this emphasis, visual SF most consistently distinguishes itself from the printed form.

Or it might be fairer to say that print and visual SF have followed reasonably similar stylistic courses, with SF onscreen generally following some decades behind print. The two media have exhibited similar ambivalence over the subgenre of space opera, for example. The debate on print SF, however, has largely taken place in a relatively small community concerned with the entire genre's technical features and artistic ambitions; while the debate on visual SF emphasizes a wide public expressing views on an entertainment sector whose products are typically so expensive as to rely upon pleasing as large an audience as possible (now in the increasingly demanding marketplace described by Kring, above). *Heroes* confronts issues that have long occupied print SF commentary, but from within a relatively naive critical atmosphere.

This asymmetric situation has both divided and united SF across media. *Le voyage dans la lune* Méliès spoofed Jules Verne's serious storytelling as satirical but primarily light entertainment. In 1915 E.E. "Doc" Smith began his *Skylark* series of square-jawed, heroic space operas, which in 1928 began serialization in the issue of *Amazing Stories* magazine that introduced *Buck Rogers in the 25th Century*. Both prefigured Buster Crabbe's onscreen heroics as *Flash Gordon*'s star, before also starring in the functionally equivalent serial *Buck Rogers* (1939). Gardner Dozois and Jonathan Strahan discuss Wilson Tucker's 1941 coinage "space opera" for what he described as "the hacky, grinding, stinking, outworn space-ship yarn, or world saving," pointing out that Tucker's complaint was almost redundant even while being made: the 1940s and 1950s saw writers using space opera's general form to tackle far weightier themes than before (2–3). In the 1960s and 1970s this increasing earnestness led to space opera *per se* being virtually abandoned by "serious" writers — but on screen this was when *Star Wars* reinforced all the charges of vacuous escapism that had ever been leveled at SF, and *Star Trek* made its journey from small-screen collapse to big-screen franchise. From the 1980s writers such as Iain M. Banks reappraised space opera's possibilities as a balance of narrative muscularity positively energizing political thoughtfulness, but only recently has such a sensibility shown any sign of becoming a minor but recognizable convention in film and TV SF. *Battlestar Galactica* (2003–2010) is one such product, and *Heroes* another. Their makers have addressed difficulties of genre noted here, apparently independently but with comparable results.

One crucial principle here is the critical distinction between SF and fantasy, two genres that for some purposes are commonly conflated (bookshops frequently present undifferentiated "sf&f" sections), but which for this discussion display informatively different properties. Charlie Lippincott, Advertising Publicity Supervisor for *Star Wars,* made a knowing point to David Houston on that film's original release:

> The only people we're going to offend are the die-hard science-fiction people who are into the whole idea that science fiction is what Hugo Gernsback [see below] said it was: dealing only with plausible science of the future on a fictional level.
>
> Our hardware is so fantastic as to be really impossible.... It's a fantasy film, a space fairy tale. That's why we call ourselves space fantasy and not science fiction [21].

The term "science fiction" quickly evolved from Hugo Gernsback's editorial neologism "scientifiction" when launching *Amazing Stories* in 1926. His prescription took its cues from Jules Verne, H.G. Wells and Edgar Allan Poe: an instance of scientifiction should be "a charming romance intermingled with scientific fact and prophetic vision." That is, what Gernsback personally found in these writers was scientific fact underlying predictive speculations delivered as narrative entertainments — a very narrow and arguably wrong-headed reading of all three authors. In any case, only a tiny proportion of *Amazing*'s published output ever flirted seriously with Gernsback's formulation of romance, science and prophecy. Gernsback did, however, inspire the rather different evaluative generic measure of *explicability*.

"Science fiction" certainly need not be "about" scientific speculation (although its predisposition to rationality makes it well-suited to that if necessary): *The Day the Earth Stood Still* (1951) is unconcerned with the technical means whereby Klaatu and Gort reach our world, or with the source of the destructive power that threatens Earth unless its civilizations cease warfare; *Forbidden Planet* (1956) never elucidates the Krell machinery in terms of known science, because it is interested in ideas about human philosophical development; and *Children of Men* (2006) concerns itself not with explaining widespread female infertility, but with its social consequences. What makes these films science fiction is a narrative sense of the universe following logical, mechanistic rules. The unrealistic element present in each story (a threatening interstellar government, advanced sciences of the mind, a hazard to human reproduction) functions as a rationally comprehensible and acceptable starting point from which each story can then explore the plausible consequences for characters whose challenges and dilemmas may resonate with our own plausible experiences.

Space battles and artificially intelligent robots aside, *Star Wars* is the story of a provincial farmboy unexpectedly setting out to save a beautiful princess from an evil wizard, using a marvelous sword provided by a benign wizard as part of a noble heritage of which he was previously unaware. Lippincott's "space fairy-tale" recounts its hero's induction into what amounts to magic, with a growing sense of personal destinies careering towards a moment of truth. *Star Wars* may simultaneously be read as exploiting certain pleasures of the Western genre, and epic, and romance; and while its hardware lends a flavor also of SF, its narrative logic is most faithfully that of fantasy. A widespread perception of its success *as SF* has created considerable confusion.

Heroes specifically denies unsteady positioning between fantasy and SF, by insistently invoking rational, mechanistic and (supposedly) scientifically testable causes and effects. A superhero narrative, like all others, must define its relationship to the audience's world of experience. Certain kinds of metaphorical story are available that turn upon matters such as destiny or warring gods, fantasy forces that providentially interrupt normal expectations of causality for the especially significant individuals that we encounter as protagonists. While the radioactive bite that creates Spider-Man might be pragmatically regarded as being at least as "fantastic" as those forces, it conversely asserts a world of inescapable scientific causality.

Heroes adamantly locates itself in this kind of un-miraculous world, contributing to a minor trend in modern visual SF and helping to explain its muted presentation even of spectacular powers. Its narrative and visual styles constantly assert rational causality along lines suggested by Farah Mendlesohn and Edward James: "The most obvious construction of fantasy in literature and art is the presence of the impossible and unexplainable. This helps to cut out most SF which, while it may deal with the impossible, regards everything as [rationally] explicable" (3). So, while our everyday experience may militate against the strict possibility of personal time travel, the "laying on of hands," autonomous flight or a bodily tendency to emit hard radiation, we may still suspend such disbelief in order to accept a narrative in terms of its own augmented rationality. Such acceptance will occur in a certain manner when unprecedented abilities are arbitrary gifts from the gods in a world of destiny; and in another when they are the result of mechanistic scientific processes in a diegetic world where their secular value as commercial, criminal and political assets immediately comes to the fore as we might realistically expect. These powers may seem exceptional; but as presented they do not offend a cultural orientation towards modernism, positivism and Darwinism.

Mendlesohn and James confront a live issue in current critical discourse that *Heroes* appears to have discovered independently, judging by its internal debate over destiny. In "Run!" (1:15) we see many objects that have been "melted" by Zane Taylor and Sylar. By now viewers are trained to accept these sights not as uniquely fascinating phenomena to be examined and marveled at but as explicable parts of the diegetic reality, representing or contributing to characters' emotional and ideological motivations. Here, we glimpse liquefied objects that prompt Mohinder's natural and diplomatic inquiry about "control" of this ability. Sylar replies, "It's like riding a bike for the first time. It's a little wobbly, and then I discovered something: a kind of peace, a sense of purpose that can only be described as destiny." The accompanying Daliesque image of a telephone half-melted into a tabletop underscores what may be recognized as Sylar's perversely triumphant allusion to his aberrant appropriation and single-minded refinement of others' talents. Equally aberrant, in thematic context, is his self-absolution on grounds of "destiny."

These stories maintain an instinct for SF's grounding in firm rules, as opposed to fantasy's appeal to neatly idealistic forces. Linderman's personal construction of destiny ("I believe destiny to be intrinsic," in "Landslide," 1:22) as a sovereign principle controlling individuals from within is revealed as false, and can be thwarted by principled impulse: he dies bearing an expression of considerable surprise. Hiro's competing construction of "destiny," as something to be *aspired to* and *created* through faithful adherence to a code, can rationally influence this world. In ".07%" (1:19) Peter reminds Nathan of future–Hiro's instruction on the train: "Don't you get it? Claire's the girl that I saved in Texas. 'Save the cheerleader, [save the world,]' and she turns out to be your daughter—*your* daughter.... Maybe if Claire's here, I don't blow up [and destroy New York]. Maybe she's going to save us. Talk to her, Nathan: we need her." Hiro's message, although from the future, is not a prediction but advice: Claire's cooperation must still be obtained. At the end of this episode Hiro encounters the three-dimensional model of past events that his future self (explained in "Five Years Gone," 1:20) has laboriously constructed to determine how New York's destruction could, in an alternate "history," be avoided. Future–Hiro retains his romanticism, while also becoming rationally influential. He does not assume that "history" will necessarily regress to an unpleasantly familiar mean and converge upon a doomed path: his message encourages people to strive to achieve a future divergent from his experience. Events are neither predetermined nor arbitrarily imposed by external forces. Reality and possible futures are contingent upon human agency and relationships, amidst familiar causal rules.

The iconographic element of *Heroes* that initially most evokes a flavor of fantasy is Isaac Mendez's precognition, especially since it is enacted in a mystical trance that supplants his conscious will. Its immediate impression is of something akin to divine revelation, striking an odd note in a diegetic world that otherwise insists on superficially fantastic events ultimately being scientifically explicable. In fact, the more Isaac's paintings come to seem *unreliable* (their depicted events need not, we find, inevitably occur), the more comfortably they sit in this rational world. They function not as infallible predictions, but probabilistic projections from current circumstances. Isaac's sensitivity to those circumstances (usually well beyond his direct personal experience) is perhaps uncanny, but no more so than Matt Parkman's sensitivity to thoughts or Hana Gitelman's to wireless signals; and his projection of probable futures is no more uncanny than a complex statistical forecast — just as Isaac Asimov's classic *Foundation* series of SF novels (1951–1953) postulates a "science" of psychohistory, a mathematically predictive discipline that anticipates future trends and events. Peter was always *likely* to fly, even if he finally does so in a fashion varying from Isaac's initial, beatific depiction. New York was *likely* to be destroyed, given the forces initially in play. Isaac's very forecast of this likelihood, however, impels intervention (however mystified) to avert it. Far from providing discordantly magical access to future "truth," Isaac's ability highlights the genuine role of uncertainty, extrapolation and testable conjecture in the formation of real knowledge. The stylized, graphic-novel *mise-en-scène* of *Heroes* in general, and of Isaac's paintings within it, constantly draws us to focus not upon spectacular, drawn-out sequences, but upon *moments* where many interrelated lives and purposes hinge this way or that in obscurely and stubbornly logical ways.

In upholding their narratives' explicability and rationality, neither Kring nor Badham ungraciously cites contrasting examples. Many viewers, however, would probably compare *Heroes* with the closely preceding superhero television series *Mutant X* (2001–2004). Joe Nazzaro asked Howard Chaykin (its writer and "executive consultant") whether the thoughtful *X-Men* sequel *X-2* (2003) posed difficulties for *Mutant X* (45). Chaykin's reply seems to confirm the continuing presence of resolutely conservative narrative models in popular TV SF:

> Not especially. My model for this show is much more to do with *Mission: Impossible* and *The A-Team* than anything else. I'm more interested in reaching an audience that doesn't care about comic books. I want to reach the guy or gal out there who, if they have read a comic book, it was years ago, and is looking for a way to spend an hour with some fun people, doing some fun stuff.... It's an action-adventure show.

In contrast, I would suggest that the makers of *Heroes* have negotiated several existing critical perceptions of SF, while also adopting a newly synergistic attitude towards (and imposing greater demands upon) their own audience. This is indicated by the complexity of the episodes themselves and by Kring's stated commitment (interviewed in *Heroes Unmasked* 1:13, "Telling Tales") to engaging rather than patronizing a knowledgeable audience:

> The writer's room is populated by a lot of comic book geeky guys that love comic books and grew up with comic books; and a huge part of our fanbase are people who grew up reading comic books and know this stuff really well. And while the show is trying to present a very ordinary world, there is still this tremendous desire that we have to reach out to those viewers.

In taking this approach, *Heroes*' makers have perhaps unwittingly refreshed debates that have previously exercised critics of print SF, such as that concerning space opera. They have independently reinvented another critically unregarded SF subgenre to cultivate thoughtful SF audiences, in the process helping us to understand the genre's nature and reception in general.

Any TV drama is both an artistic endeavor and a commercial product. In the conventional U.S. television market, studios and networks constantly seek successful, profitable models to adapt or even replicate, and constantly monitor viewing figures because the sale of advertising slots (or, in the HBO model, subscriptions) is crucial to the industry's funding. This is why an artistically promising series under a proven creator might still be summarily cancelled, sometimes only halfway through its first season (one famous example in recent years was Joss Whedon's *Firefly*, 2002) and occasionally even more quickly (such as Chris Carter's *Harsh Realm*, 1999–2000).

Each product is assessed in terms of its potential to attract an audience, and thus lucrative input from advertisers interested in gaining that audience's attention. Although Henry Jenkins' recent work suggests that any viewer engaged by and loyal to a series is statistically more likely than those seeking casual entertainment to remember and potentially act upon advertising (74–79), "genre" products are traditionally positioned to attract distinctive social types of audience, defined by demographic characteristics perceived as inherently implying receptiveness to particular kinds of advertising. The central appeal of "fantastic" TV and film is frequently perceived as the increasingly persuasive and exciting portrayal of marvelously unreal locations and events. Chaykin's remarks above demonstrate that SF can still therefore be actively promoted as undemanding material with relatively juvenile concerns. Any given SF film or series might therefore strive simply to be that much more visually impressive than the last, regardless of quality (or its lack) in other areas.

SF's contemporary popularity derives from the explosive impact (beginning in 1977) of the still-burgeoning *Star Wars* franchise and the consequent resurgence of *Star Trek* in films and spinoff TV series, long imagined by Paramount Studios but finally triggered specifically by *Star Wars*. (Documentation for this and for *Star Trek*'s similarly misleading presentation as exemplary SF is extensive, as I have indicated in "The Accidental Apotheosis of Gene Roddenberry," *The Influence of* Star Trek *on Television, Film and Culture*, ed. Lincoln Geraghty, 2008.) The marketing assumptions behind *Star Trek: The Motion Picture* (1979) led to considerable running time being devoted to opportunities to admire the proffered spectacle. This was intended as a celebration of *Star Trek*'s return, a decade after its initial TV run collapsed. Even at the time, however, the film was widely perceived as privileging lumbering spectacle over worthwhile story content. These days, even William Shatner concurs:

> Nothing happened, and it took more than two hours not to happen. The studio had spent all that money on special effects and they wanted the audience to see them. And see them. And see them. Warp speed never went so slowly.... So the film was replete with tedious shots of the *Enterprise* flying through space. There goes the *Enterprise*. Here comes the *Enterprise*. Whoops, there it goes again [201].

Such practices reflect a simplistic perception of SF while also recalling the inception of visual SF, and of cinema itself as reflected in Booker's and Gunning's remarks, above. Pioneer Georges Méliès used "in-camera" trickery (any process, however manipulated, whereby an image is captured directly at the moment of filming) to present impossible but nevertheless comprehensible and engaging illusions of space travel and other fantastic events, a lighthearted but visually appealing approach that has persisted. This is not to say that screen SF is *necessarily* so insubstantial. As early as 1927, Fritz Lang's *Metropolis* showed that it could be scathingly political; but popular visual SF has tended to follow Méliès' sensibilities far more often than Lang's. For every *Solaris*-style meditation, we receive many *Star Wars*– or *Star Trek–style* space operas.

Heroes, similarly, uses in-camera and other approaches to portray phenomena such as Hiro freezing time — but here the overall effect is intriguingly to diminish any fixation upon something astonishing occurring. The most potentially gaudy sequence in early episodes of *Heroes* occurs in "One Giant Leap" (1:3), when Hiro and Ando falteringly realize Isaac's illustration of them saving a schoolgirl from a careering truck. As it smashes towards her, Hiro halts time and moves her. Cyclists and toys flung from a crushed stall are among elements "frozen" by a mixture of special and visual effects (*special* effects are created physically on set and photographed directly, while *visual* effects are achieved through further processes such as CGI in post-production). This extraordinary scene might have been unique in TV drama, but its narrative effect is curiously muted. The event's eerie, unmusical soundtrack anticlimactically counterpoints the truck's noisy threat moments earlier; and the scene's emotional focus is not the stasis itself but Hiro's astonishment at having accomplished it. Arresting spectacle is certainly achieved by inverting chaos into stasis; but while Ando presumably sees Hiro vanish from one location and sensationally reappear elsewhere with the rescued child, the scene that we witness is unexcitingly filled with static, mundane components until Hiro restarts time and the insistently engaging bedlam of market and traffic sounds crashes back into operation. The sequence's narrative emphasis shifts quickly from the friends' exasperation over their seemingly baffling task to their exuberance at having achieved it, barely registering the extraordinary feat in between. This singular accomplishment swiftly recedes from consideration, overshadowed by its consequences for the characters.

With films often dominated by expensively elaborate multi-camera techniques that subvert expectations of speed and timing (pioneered in advertising and exploited by *The Matrix*, 1999), it is somehow refreshing that in *Heroes* this effect is founded upon surrounding actors simply (if with assistance) standing very still indeed. Subsequent CGI in post-production does not glorify the resulting technical achievement. Instead it reinforces an everyday sense of texture and detail, unobtrusively bucking the dominant trend of SF TV and cinema. Mark Kolpack (visual effects supervisor) discusses exactly this feature of the series. In "The Dreamer" (*Heroes Unmasked* 1:3) Kolpack discusses the first appearance of "Future Hiro"("Collision," 1:4, and "Hiros," 1:5), who arrives in a train carriage and stops time for the other occupants in order to talk to Peter:

> Usually we'd set up 120 cameras, *but* there's no time to set up that kind of intricate camera array on a television schedule. So the only other way to do it is to have a lot of people stand really still, in sort of awkward positions, meaning they're in the middle of an action, they're in the middle of a step.
>
> [In the scene, the camera providing the audience point of view now threads its way between the "frozen" passengers.]
>
> Now, what makes this work really well.... Everything's frozen but yet you're moving around it so you're getting a perspective change. If you just had things in the background, people can see, "Oh, that's just a visual effect back there."

Sendhil Ramamurthy (playing Mohinder Suresh) then reports a grueling two-day shoot for around a minute's screen time (in fact the total is fractionally over three minutes); yet impact is quickly transferred from the amazing fact of time stopping to surprise over the visitor's identity and perplexity over the import of his message. Casual incorporation of these fantastic events into the action contributes to their easy acceptance as part of the story, not their elevation as objects of wonder in themselves.

In the following episode of *Heroes Unmasked*, "Hiro Worship" (1:4), Kolpack expands on this approach in the schoolgirl's rescue. This was realized in two main phases. On set, various methods kept objects (e.g., a jump rope) and actors motionless, seemingly arrested during normal movement. A camera moves with Masi Oka (playing Hiro) through the scene as he raptly examines the immobile objects around him. Items thrown up by the truck's impact are suspended in midair, created by the visual effects team in post-production:

> I said to Masi, "Here's what's going to happen: ... there's going to be these toys in the air — so duck, look, and wherever you do this, I will put objects." So he went "Oooh," and ducked, and his shoulder bumped into a robot in the air, and all that kind of stuff, so in the end what you get is this really interesting, cool shot that looks like the world has stopped but yet we are moving through the space of it.

The emphasis in the writing and in the visual techniques deployed here is upon traveling through the scene with Hiro, rather than asking the audience to acknowledge the bravura accomplishment of getting this tableau onscreen in the first place.

In an online documentary, Kolpack stresses this philosophy of smuggling astounding representations onto the screen, before whipping them away in order to concentrate on the core story of human relationships:

> If we do our visual effects job well, the fans don't really pick up on anything that we've done. And I think what's really cool is that ... [when viewers discuss *Heroes*] they always just *talk about the show*. The visual effects [are] rarely ever even mentioned — which means we're doing our job correctly, because it just fits within the character, the story structure, the emotion of what's going on in a particular scene, so it's not distracting, which is what you never want to be.... You want to help suspend that disbelief, and if we do our jobs well enough, then of course the shots play really well and they become invisible.

That this is an overt policy in the making of *Heroes* seems evident from remarks by James Kyson Lee (playing Ando) in "Hiro Worship":

> Our special [*sic*] effects team is amazing — *awesome*.... Really, people don't realize, and the great part is that they do it in a way that it doesn't take away from the show. It's just like little sprinkles, and icing on the cake. But it's so spectacular and yet it makes you live in this reality even more. That's the amazing part.

This highlights an emphatic understatement, a sense almost of mundanity, informing these ostensibly fantastic depictions. The visual techniques employed are used to *naturalize* those events, to make them believable parts of the diegetic experience. The audience is invited not to gasp in awe at miraculous sights, but to share with the characters a world in which those sights are simply present, consistent with the story's emergent circumstances. In a series already dominated by a consciously contrived visual strategy (*Heroes Unmasked* 1:5, "Painting the Future," observes, "The comic book style is maintained throughout the series, and even defines how *Heroes* is shot"), it is all the more remarkable that its approach to unprecedented events can still encourage its audience to "live in this reality," as Lee puts it.

In DVD commentary for *X-Men* (2000), Bryan Singer describes a tension between an unavoidable necessity to present fantastic *spectacle* and maintain a tone that he would consider appropriate for the *character* drama that he primarily wanted to create. Singer suggests that audiences are no longer impressed by an ever-mounting onslaught of affordable CGI. He believes that the proliferation of such visual flourishes runs a considerable risk of cheapening any drama that actively flaunts them: they can be perceived as being present simply to distract audiences from basic weaknesses in the material (this became a common criticism of *Hulk* (2003), for example). Consequently Singer faced the problem of presenting powers and events that must indeed be marvelous, but doing so in a style that the audience could accept as relatively matter-of-fact. Singer's strategy was to dwell no longer than necessary upon any given fantastic event, and to move quickly to its physical or personal consequences:

it becomes a naturalized part of the diegetic reality that we are temporarily asked simply to accept. The same tension is addressed by the visual design of *Heroes*, with conscious efforts made to downplay or undermine what might otherwise be seen as celebratory flourishes of technical brilliance. A perhaps surprising, potentially risky, but in fact successful component of this strategy is the series' use of humor. Light character moments are frequently provided throughout, for example, by Hiro's amiable attempts to control his power. An isolated event from early in the first season, however, demonstrates this more pointedly.

In *Heroes Unmasked* 1:8, "The H. R. G. File," Adrian Pasdar (playing Nathan Petrelli) discusses the scene of Nathan's arrival at the *Fly By Night Diner* in "Hiros," when he hops around in discomfort after landing: "I remember skidding and saying, 'My feet kinda hurt,' and the director looked at me and said, 'What are you doing? It looks kinda foolish,' and I said, 'Well, I don't have super-*feet*.'"

As scripted, ensuing scenes would have allowed Nathan to appear ridiculous in any case. When he enters this remote diner wearing only pajama trousers, naturally the patrons stare and he responds dryly: "All right, I get it: a guy in his pajamas. Ha ha. Now we can all stare and have a good laugh, or one of you can lend me your cell-phone." In the episode's final form, however, Nathan's discomfiture begins as soon as he lands.

Although Pasdar's hopping was an *ad lib*, it was ultimately retained within a series so self-conscious and controlled in its narrative tone. This is significant for two reasons. First, it indicates not only a character but also a production team finding its feet in volatile circumstances: the script was already set to bring Nathan down to Earth in the diner; but the actor's improvised discovery of hubristic irony in his character's circumstances is preserved within evolving styles of editing and *mise-en-scène* that are intent upon subordinating visual marvels to human consequences with which audiences can directly identify. Second, this visual gesture actively undercuts any celebratory awe over a journey begun as a dramatic escape from sinister characters attempting capture. In a spectacular moment we finally see (from the perspective of his thwarted pursuers) a fully explicit instance of Nathan flying, rocketing high into the air before departing the area at what appears to be supersonic speed. If the series were waiting to display a moment of wonder worthy of dwelling upon, this would surely be it; and if nothing else we surely expect Nathan's literal flight to end with a suitable air of triumph. A potentially magnificent escape ends, however, in anticlimactic and inglorious embarrassment with the character's arrival at the back end of nowhere, with no resources and in inadvertently self-inflicted pain. We might have been shown the desperate but defiant flowering of a remarkable power, but while this power achieves the intended and impressive escape, it also immediately produces comically mundane discomfiture. As with sequences previously discussed, this one quickly discourages any temptation to celebrate its fantastic subject. Before that could have time to occur, we are presented instead with the shakily unpromising but warmly character-driven first steps towards Hiro's later friendship with "Flying Man."

Heroes constantly maintains this resolve that dazzling events and personal feats should remain subsidiary to emotional experience. Many viewers will have sensed this first season building towards a probable and pivotal confrontation between Peter and Sylar. When this occurs (in "Five Years Gone"), some undoubtedly anticipated a spectacular clash of good and evil, but again any such expectation is undercut. We see the two squaring off and readying their superpowers, but the battle itself takes place off screen as Mohinder struggles to hold a door closed so that Hiro and Ando may escape. The centrality of believable personal experience upheld here has been proclaimed from the outset.

Despite its cosily inclusive behind-the-scenes demeanor, *Heroes Unmasked* clearly represents sanctioned comment promoting the series, part of the elaborately orchestrated multimedia campaign to establish a franchise and a commercial brand. Unsurprisingly, therefore, its first edition ("A New Dawn") includes various cast and crew positively characterizing *Heroes* overall. Their perspectives contrast, but in their variety must also be understood as approved propaganda for the show. They therefore convey a promotionally useful "something for everyone" sense of *Heroes*, while firmly reinforcing certain common threads. The most significant here is that of *Heroes*, however fantastic its iconography, consistently delivering accessible emotional dramas, relevant to the TV audience's everyday encounters and challenges. Masi Oka suggests, "It's about the *characters*, not necessarily about their powers. It's about the story. The powers are *part* of it, but it's *always* about the characters."

I have discussed SF as a genre that examines *conventional* human experience, through a lens of extraordinary novelty. Santiago Cabrera (playing Isaac Mendez) offers an informal assessment of *Heroes* that supports this theoretical position: "It's people with problems. It's people that make mistakes. It's everyday people that aren't perfect. They have their own problems to deal with. And suddenly they have [superpowers to deal with] on top."

As is contended by H.G. Wells, this "fantastic [SF] element" has no dramatic significance *in itself*, except the extent to which it plausibly (explicably) emphasizes character-centered narratives. The show does not try to persuade us that these powers might be real (even though part of its marketing conceit is to allow us to play an interactive, intellectual game in which we may pretend that they might be). Its objective is to have us invest interest in a web of believable human relationships that are at stake or otherwise affected when surprising, often inherently threatening and sometimes sinister circumstances exert pressure upon them. Milo Ventimiglia (playing Peter Petrelli) merges the cast views already quoted: "Extraordinary abilities, but set in the real world. People have to pick up their kids, work, deal with any kind of personal issues. So I think it's that combination of the unreal with the real."

We are dealing here (as in all SF) with stories whose human significance (matters of conflict, loyalty, etc.) could always be played out in some entirely realistic context. This strategy for storytelling that we term SF, however, operates precisely by introducing and logically justifying a narrative element that we recognize as unreal but accept, since it logically accentuates its chosen story. The makers of *Heroes* display no active awareness of this as a fulcrum of generic critical debate. Indeed, the sheer vagueness with which Jack Coleman (playing Noah Bennet) in "A New Dawn" unashamedly but imprecisely invokes SF as a genre suggests complete unfamiliarity with the genre's historical criticism: "Epic storytelling, sci-fi in its scope and nature, but with much more *realistic* human consequences."

Those involved with *Heroes* (alongside others such as Bryan Singer) appear to have struggled from first principles with contemporary attitudes to their genre. They have reached a conception of it that contributes to an ongoing rehabilitation of visual SF consistent with that of its print form, and congruent with primal ideas of fantastic narrative upheld by Wells and Tolkien. Their fruitful arrival at much the same point, independently of existing debate, suggests that a truly fundamental part of SF's nature is indeed its strategy for storytelling, and that its habit of novelty or spectacle functions most powerfully in support of narrative credibility, not as a whimsical end in itself. By actively understating its own spectacular presentation, *Heroes* contributes to a modern visual style whose articulate *realism* in its deployment of the fantastic enhances SF's ability to tell compelling human stories.

Works Cited

About the IAB. 9 Jan 2011, http://www.iab.net/about_the_iab.
All Heroes Videos. 9 Jan 2011, www.nbc.com/heroes/video.
Asimov, Isaac. "The Boom in Science Fiction." *Asimov's Science Fiction Magazine* (Fall 1979): 132–135. Reprinted in *Asimov on Science Fiction*. London: Granada, 1983.
_____. *Foundation.* New York: Gnome Press, 1951.
_____. *Foundation and Empire.* New York: Gnome Press, 1952.
_____. *Second Foundation.* New York: Gnome Press, 1953.
Assignment Tracker 2.0. 9 Jan 2011, heroeswiki.com/Assignment_Tracker_2.0.

Banks, Iain M., *Consider Phlebas*. London: Macmillan, 1987.
Booker, M Keith. *Science Fiction Television*. Westport, CT: Praeger, 2004.
The Corinthian Hotel and Casino. 9 Jan 2011, www.corinthianlasvegas.com.
Dozois, Gardner, and Jonathan Strahan. "Introduction." *The New Space Opera*, edited by Gardner Dozois and Jonathan Strahan. 1–5. New York: Eos, 2007.
Gernsback, Hugo. "A New Sort of Magazine." *Amazing Stories: The Magazine of Scientifiction* 1.1 (April 1926): 3. Reprinted in *Forrest J Ackerman's World of Science Fiction*, edited by Forrest J Ackerman. 31. Los Angeles: General Publishing Group, 1997.
Gunning, Tom. "The Cinema of Attractions: Early Film, Its Spectator and the Avant-Garde." In *Early Cinema: Space, Frame, Narrative*, edited by Thomas Elsaesser with Adam Barker. 56–62. London: British Film Institute, 1990.
Hipple, Dave. "The Accidental Apotheosis of Gene Roddenberry, or, 'I Had to Get Some Money from *Somewhere*.'" *The Influence of* Star Trek *on Television, Film and Culture*, edited by Lincoln Geraghty. 22–40. Jefferson, NC: McFarland & Company, 2008.
_____. "*Stargate SG-1*: Self-Possessed Science Fiction." *Reading* Stargate SG-1, edited by Stan Beeler and Lisa Dickson. 27–47. London: I. B. Tauris, 2006.
Houston, David. "Creating the Space-Fantasy Universe of *Star Wars*." *Starlog* 7 (Aug 1977): 18–28.
IAB MIXX Conference & Expo 2.8 —Tim Kring. 9 Jan 2011, www.youtube.com/watch?v=bFa7VKJJ8g0.
Jenkins, Henry. *Convergence Culture*. New York: New York University Press, 2006.
Malzberg, Barry N. "The Engines of the Night." In *The Engines of the Night*, edited by Barry N. Malzberg. 174–176. New York: Bluejay Books, 1982.
Mendlesohn, Farah, and Edward James. *A Short History of Fantasy*. London: Middlesex University Press, 2009.
Nazzaro, Joe. "Howard Chaykin." *Writing Science Fiction and Fantasy Television*. 36–45. London: Titan: 2002.
1930s Flash Gordon Serial Movie Trailer Ad. 9 Jan 2011, www.youtube.com/watch?v=NVNBBLt00ZY.
Parrinder, Patrick. "Introduction." In *Learning From Other Worlds: Estrangement, Cognition, and the Politics of Science Fiction and Utopia*, edited by Patrick Parrinder. 1–16. Durham, NC: Duke University Press, 2001.
Primatech Paper Company. 9 Jan 2011. www.primatechpaper.com.
Scanlon, Paul. "The Force Behind *Star Wars*." *Rolling Stone*. 25 May 1977, www.rollingstone.com/news/story/7330268/the_force_behind_star_wars (accessed 3 May 2009).
Shatner, William, with David Fisher. *Up Till Now: The Autobiography*. London: Sidgwick & Jackson, 2008.
Smith, Edward Elmer. *The Skylark of Space*. Buffalo: Buffalo Book Company, 1946.
Suvin, Darko. *Metamorphoses of Science Fiction: On the Poetics and History of a Literary Genre*. New Haven, CT: Yale University Press, 1979.
Tim Kring's New Projects. 9 Jan 2011, www.nbc.com/heroes/video/timkrings-new-projects/1250848.
Tolkien, J. R. R. "On Fairy-Stories." *Tree and Leaf; Smith of Wootton Major; The Homecoming of Beorhtnoth*. (Lecture given 1938; enlarged for publication 1947; reprinted "with only a few minor alterations.") 11–79. London: Unwin, 1975.
Visual Effects. 3 May 2009, www.nbc.com/Heroes/video/clips/visual-effects/137166/.
Wells, Herbert George. "Preface to *The Scientific Romances*." In *H. G. Wells's Literary Criticism*, edited by Patrick Parrinder and Robert M Philmus. 240–245. Brighton: Harvester, 1980.
Who We Are. 9 Jan 2011, http://www.conspiracyforgood.com/about.php.

Super Style:
Notes for a Stylistic Analysis

Sérgio Dias Branco

In "Superheros for Sale," David Bordwell looks briefly at the exaggerated visual style of some films based on superhero comic books such as *Watchmen* (2009) or clearly influenced by this type of comic like *The Matrix* (1999). *Watchmen* was released six months after the publication of Bordwell's text (and postscript) and therefore he does not mention it as an example, but it fits in well with his arguments. In these films, motion is altered, perspective is distorted, some shots are extremely low- or high-angled. Bordwell focuses on recent examples and argues against zeitgeist readings of the increasing amount of superhero films after the 9/11 attacks (17–22). Instead, he favors a palimpsestic understanding of their style, disclosing visible traces of other art forms and contending that the images contained in these movies are evocative of "[c]omic book panels, those graphically dynamic compositions that keep us turning the pages. In fact, we call such effects 'cartoonish'" (Bordwell 50).

Taking *Heroes* (2006–2010), the popular drama series about a group of ordinary human beings with superhuman abilities, as a case study allows us to expand on these ideas. This chapter aims at contributing to a stylistic analysis of the series without attempting to examine every major stylistic feature of the series in detail. Instead, the scope of this essay is limited to the scrutiny of the links between the imagery of the show and that of films and comic books. Scrutinizing these links is also a way to exemplify the kind of work on television fiction that can issue from the analysis of the style of particular series. Such an approach is not so much interested in the communicational facet of television as in the representational, expressive, formal, and experiential aspects of televisual art works (Carroll 1999). At the same time, this chapter, which will concentrate on salient visual elements of the show, demonstrates the faults of an essentialist view of television aesthetics, contributing instead to a historically contingent understanding of the nature of television.

That is to say, television is seen as a form which is not ontologically different from cinema, but which has a particular history of technical and aesthetic development — a history that is not determined by an essence, but that is rather the product of multiple factors (like technological advancements such as non-linear, digital editing systems) and numerous influences (from cinema and comics, for example). The visual style of *Heroes* is exemplary from this point of view because it can be considered as "impure," amassing elements from various art forms and rejecting a purist approach to television as a creative practice. It is this "impurity" that makes the series an illustrative example of how television fiction series, as televisual works, integrate diverse references (cf. Bazin, "In Defense of Mixed Cinema," 53–75).

The first section of this chapter defines the contemporary technological and stylistic context of *Heroes*. The series epitomizes aspects of this context in a limpid and explicit manner, namely in the connections it establishes between television and cinema. The second section concentrates on how the aesthetics of comics have influenced the visual style of the show. The result of this influence is at times an overt disregard for prevalent filmmaking practices.

1. The Abilities of Television

John Ellis claims that the use of new digital technology to manipulate and create images sets cinema and television apart. He sketches the opposition this way: "Cinema uses the new potential to make ever more realistic, yet impossible, images. Television uses it to make constantly changing collages of images. In doing so, television has discovered a means of enhancing its particular social aesthetic" (Ellis 107). This is a deterministic way of thinking about media, which sees every new instance as a confirmation of the intrinsic features of a medium. Ellis is right when he highlights the use of digital technology in segments of television news programs such as weather forecast simulations and contrasts it with the use of special visual effects to create lifelike dinosaurs in *Jurassic Park* (1993). Yet his conclusions lack nuance, when he asserts that "[d]igital image manipulation allows television to combine images; it allows cinema to continue to present a spectacle of reality" (Ellis 107). To counter this sweeping generalization, we need only to recall that some series employ digital visual effects in ways that are similar to their use in *Jurassic Park*. *Heroes* is one of these series.

The show is a product of the technological changes in the production of television fiction over the past thirty years. John Thornton Caldwell points out six devices that have been paramount to this change: one, the *video-assist*, a video camera mounted alongside the camera that allows technicians and artists to adjust the shot based on the information gathered from a monitor; two, *motion control* equipment like mountings and robotic or motorized contrivances that produce smooth, controlled camera movements; three, *electronic nonlinear editing*, which allows random access to the footage; four, *digital effects* that broaden the range of imaging possibilities; five, *Tabular* or *T-grain film stocks*, with flatter crystals in the emulsion that make them expose more easily to dim light, increasing resolution and decreasing granularity; and six, the *Rank–Cintel equipments* for transcribing film into video tapes and data formats in high-definition (*Televisuality* 78). It is worth enumerating and detailing these technologies to make clear how they can be seen at work in *Heroes*, a series shot with care and precision, containing dynamic and fluent camera movements, crosscutting between multiple story lines, abounding with digital imagery, displaying high photographic resolution, and released on high-definition. The machinery and equipment that Caldwell lists has been developed and used both in cinema and television production, a fact that by itself goes against any arguments that the two are essentially different because they are technologically different. For Caldwell, these innovations are the historical roots of the stylistic exhibitionism that governed the television of the 1980s and '90s and that he has termed *televisuality*. According to him, televisuality oscillates between two modes: the videographic and the cinematic. The former involves electronic images, captured or created, simply processed or complexly manipulated, and it has been more associated with television.

> The cinematic refers, obviously, to a film look in television. Exhibitionist television in the 1980s meant more than shooting on film, however, since many nondescript shows have been shot on film since the early 1950s. Rather, cinematic values brought to television spectacle, high-production values, and feature-style cinematography [Caldwell, *Televisuality* 12].

The cinematic therefore seems to be less technical and more stylistic than the videographic — and therefore more vague, since cinema allows many looks and styles that do not fit in with Caldwell's definition. There is a more rigorous way to approach the connection between television and other media. If we brush presuppositions aside and look closely at works like *Heroes*, it becomes clear that the relationship between television and cinema is often one of mutual contamination. This becomes clear when we realize how television has used the aforementioned technologies to produce programs that forgo live broadcast. An essentialist approach would lead us to declare that by opting for this path television loses its essential, defining feature: the possibility of transmitting images of events at their time of occurrence. Indeed, theorists such as Umberto Eco have identified the live broadcast as the most characteristic and unique aspect of television (107). Eco also connects live transmissions with improvization (109) and therefore with the openness of life—live television can be said to organize the chance of life into "a cluster of possibilities" (116). His words take for granted that live television is somehow planned, but never scripted. Yet live episodes from scripted series demonstrate that this assumption is false—"Ambush" (4:1), from the medical drama *ER* (1994–2009), and the entire second season of the sitcom *Roc* (1991–1994) are just two examples. To sum up, considering the totality of the televisual output, it is more accurate to acknowledge that televisual works have changed and diversified, within a specific system of production and means of distribution. High-definition television broadcasts have been steadily increasing since the mid-nineties— exactly when Caldwell published his book on televisuality. Today, television series are released on high-resolution formats like DVD and Blu-ray. The sharpness of their images and sounds and those of their cinema counterparts are basically indistinguishable. Even so, we must avoid seeing this change and diversification as a radical, unexpected alteration. In later writings, Caldwell calls attention to the fact that media mixing is not determined by the technological shift to the digital, but is symptomatic of more fundamental logics present throughout television history. The use of digital technologies confirms the importance of the aesthetic influences of other art forms and media in the creative process of television. These technologies "merely served to accelerate and legitimate these well-practiced industrial strategies" (Caldwell, "Convergence Television," 68).

Heroes exemplifies the technical sophistication and aesthetic intricacy of present-day television fiction series. The post-production visual effects give an arresting visual form to the dazzling abilities of the characters—when Nathan Petrelli (Adrian Pasdar) self-propels himself in order to fly away at high speed or when Hiro Nakamura (Masi Oka) freezes his surroundings, suspending the march of time. Technological sophistication lures the television spectator with the promise of something amazing and fresh—just like superhero movies. Promotional materials like trailers and previews displayed the choice to use visual effects to impress, especially in the first seasons. At the same time, the episode "Company Man" (1:17) is an expressive display of the stylistic elaboration of the series. It employs black and white and deep-focus cinematography in the flashbacks of Noah Bennet's (Jack Coleman) personal history within the Company, cramming the screen with objects to visualize the grimness and messiness of his personal drama. It also uses low-angle framing, for example, after Matt Parkman (Greg Grunberg) shoots Claire Bennet

(Hayden Panettiere), to emphasize the position of the other characters towering over her lying body in the foreground. Images like these rely on a consciousness about the significance of *mise en scène* and framing that appears to be inherited from the history of cinema.

2. *The Powers of Comics*

The serial nature of *Heroes* is especially relevant when discussing its relation to comics. The first film adaptations of comic books were serials like *Adventures of Captain Marvel* (1941). Yet, for reasons that range from changes in production to alterations in exhibition, films have forgone this structure for less planned, non-periodical franchise releases like *Spider-Man* (2002, 2004, 2007). In contrast, *Heroes* is divided into volumes and then subdivided into chapters, just like a graphic novel. This division is in some way independent from the usual season-episode structure of television series — the first and second seasons correspond to the first and second volumes (*Genesis* and *Generations*), but the third season comprises the third and fourth volumes (*Villains* and *Fugitives*), and the fourth season returns to the former structure with just the fifth and last volume (*Redemption*).

Moreover, the show makes the connections with comic books visually evident. Comics are key narrative elements — Issac Mendez's (Santiago Cabrera) drawings, paintings, and the comic series *9th Wonders!* that features prominently in "Don't Look Back" (1:2) provide information about future events because they record his precognitive visions. They are also an aesthetic inspiration — the typeface used in captions and credits imitates traditional hand-rendered comic book letters, as in the beginning of "Lizards" (2:2) where "Chapter Two" is roundly inscribed inside a glass and the name of the episode over the egg at the bottom of the glass. However, there are subtler stylistic influences throughout the show.

Comics were established as a mass art form in the late 19th and early 20th century, a time when film itself was just starting. Both comic strips and comic books consist of sequences of panels. In this sequential form, we are invited to read the dialogue or narration, to follow the drawings or scan the page, and we comprehend the story being told and the significance of the verbal and visual details by inference. David Carrier explains, "Comics are like realist novels: a few odd transitions are possible only because we are accustomed to reading the body of the text as straightforward narrative. What we often infer from transitions are causal connections" (51, 53). In general, each page contains multiple drawings that lack real movement and, consequently, the potential visual continuity of motion pictures. For a comic to work narratively it has to allow the reader to comprehend the "causal connections" between *discontinuous images* that Carrier mentions. The principles of image composition and linkage that comics need to follow to ensure narrative continuity are therefore loose — as long as they avoid "such large gaps as to make the action seem jumpy" (Carrier 53).

Filmmaking rules are stricter or at least, as a rule, more strictly followed. In "The Butterfly Effect" (3:2), a conversation between Angela Petrelli (Cristine Rose) and Elle Bishop (Kristen Bell) is filmed and edited using shots and reverse shots from just one side of the axis of action, the imaginary line that passes through the actresses. This basic rule of filmmaking preserves spatial continuity on screen. Nevertheless, *Heroes* often disregards the 180° system and disobeys this rule, sometimes within a scene that has previously abided by it. Later in the conversation, Angela turns to the sedated Sylar (Zachary Quinto), faces the camera, and dispenses with Elle's services, seen in profile in the background. This planimetric composition is followed by a close-up of Elle and then by another one of Angela in profile. Crossing the line of action introduces inconsistencies in the relative positions within the frame. The moment is not too disorienting only because Angela and Elle are immobile — Angela with her hands joined over the stomach and Elle with her arms crossed over the ribs. Their lack of movement enables us to make sense of their relative positions in the room more easily, even if not immediately. The perspective changes 90° and then 180° in geometrical fashion, emphasizing the contrast between Angela's and Elle's perpendicular eye-lines. The spatial discontinuity between images suggests the estrangement of the characters.

This sequencing of images as connected yet independent brings to mind the aesthetics of comics. Consider "The Crossroads," written by Joe Kelly and drawn by Michael Gaydos, the 53rd chapter of the short web comic that develops further the narrative and characters of *Heroes*. It opens with a page containing a series of five long horizontal frames. Four of these pictures depict a dialogue between the Haitian and the geneticist Mohinder Suresh whose rendering contains two jumps across the axis of action; between the first and the second images and between the second and the third. The position of the characters within the room is unclear, but despite it, links are easily established between the images based on their sequential composition and narrative content. Of course, any expectation that a comic book would comply with the 180° rule is unfounded. Readers are used to the visual discontinuity of comic books. The same cannot be said about television viewers and series. Nevertheless, unexpectedly, *Heroes* explores this possibility from time to time, as the scene from "The Butterfly Effect" demonstrates with clarity.

There may be other possible factors that explain the unusual framing and editing choices of *Heroes*. Maybe they are not really choices—that is, maybe the filmmaking is unsystematic, perhaps even careless. Therefore, when the series does not follow conventional rules like eye-line matches, which rely on the directionality of a character's look to match it with what the character is looking at in the next shot, perhaps it is not deliberate. Yet the series has provided ample evidence that this is not the case. From the very first scene, its images seem to have been created to become memorable as well as carefully composed to produce a haunting effect: Peter Petrelli (Milo Ventimiglia) dropping from a high city rooftop is shown in a bird's-eye shot that foreshortens the height of the building, flattening the perspective to visually express the absence of danger and hint at his ability to fly. The careful composition of many of the shots in the show is sustained rather than sporadic. The *mise en scène* of *Heroes* repeatedly looks to emulate the same graphic autonomy that we see in the drawings of many comics—and the creators of the show try to achieve the same astonishing effect that comic book drawings, through their concision and precision, often seek and achieve.

Nevertheless, comics and television series are not identical forms. As Robert C. Harvey points out, "Cartooning is not the same as filmmaking" (173–191). He argues that the narrative in moving pictures is measured in time, whereas in comics it is measured in space (Harvey 176). Certainly, the fact that pictures move makes the duration of this motion a key factor in the depiction of actions. Yet, as we have seen, visual framing is equally important for making an action comprehensible and an image more expressive. Harvey notes that another difference is that films are usually audio-visual whereas comics are only visual, which means that the latter have to convey the narrative information by purely visual means. In fact, television series are also audio-visual works. However, it is not to belittle the use of sound in *Heroes*—think, for instance, of the contribution that Mohinder's (Sendhil Ramamurthy) voice-over narration makes to set overarching themes and a solemn tone—to argue that its images are even more emphatic in expressing meaning. This emphasis seems tied to the aesthetic influence of comics on the series.

3. The Skills of Heroes

This brief stylistic analysis of *Heroes*, which has highlighted its manifest visual connections with cinema and comics, shows how this kind of examination can be a productive approach for the study of the aesthetic properties of series. The excessive, emphatic style of *Heroes* is a product of technical developments, media convergence, and aesthetic influences. The individuality of the show lies in the way it combines these aspects to tell a story that is reminiscent of the adventures of *The X-Men*, a group of mutants who also have to negotiate and defend their individuality in a world that is predominantly human. The series is exemplary of trends in contemporary television because, much like its characters, it defies purist and essentialist categorizations, embedding the themes of difference and miscegenation within its style.

A moment in "Shadowboxing" (4:9) exemplifies this process. Peter Petrelli uses his mimicked healing power to save a critical patient in the emergency room. He puts his open left hand on the patient's chest and the burning wounds of his left arm gradually disappear as if they are being rubbed out. The show could have presented the peeling off of layers of damaged skin to reveal healthy skin beneath them, thus preserving the whole healing process as a sheer corporeal event. Instead, the wounds are made vivid and almost tangible — the damage of the skin is severe and the white burn ointment over the raw flesh is visible — and then are turned into pure visual elements, graphic components of the image that may be erased as though they have been drawn. The skillful style of the series gives prominence to the ability of television series to develop patterns from episode to episode, like those concerning the use of visual effects, and also to the integration of powerful aesthetic influences, like those that come from comic books.

The singularity of the style of *Heroes* lies in the combination of these two aspects: the serial development and the aesthetic fusion. This *serial hybridization* relies on regular installments that may be compared to issues of a comic series. This is therefore a distinct process from the one displayed in single composite works like *Dick Tracy* (1990), with its limited and bright color palette, and *Hulk* (2003), with its insistent and conspicuous multiple frames, that make explicit their visual connection with comics. There are strings of comic book film adaptations that are consistent in their style, like the succession of *Batman* films directed by Christopher Nolan. Yet they lack the regularity of television series and the extensive creative planning that supports it. In *Heroes*, every volume and chapter title is announced in a comic book typeface, but the visual style of the series goes beyond the direct use of components that are usual in comics. The series opts for a subtler approach that results in impressive graphic compositions and elements, which transfigure the space and concreteness of the scenes.

Works Cited

Bazin, André. *What Is Cinema? Vol. 1*. Trans. Hugh Gray. Berkeley and Los Angeles: University of California Press, 2005.

Bordwell, David. "Superheros for Sale." *Observations on Film Art*. 16 August 2008, http://www.davidbordwell.net/blog/?p=2713 (accessed 3 March 2011).

Caldwell, John. "Convergence Television: Aggregating Form and Repurposing Content in the Culture of Conglomeration." *Television After TV: Essays on a Medium in Transition*, edited by Lynn Spigel and Jan Olsson. 41–74. Durham, NC: Duke University Press, 2004.

———. *Televisuality: Style, Crisis, and Authority in American Television*. Piscataway, NJ: Rutgers University Press, 1995.

Carrier, David. *The Aesthetics of Comics*. University Park, PA: Penn State University Press, 2001.

Carroll, Noël. *Philosophy of Art: A Contemporary Introduction*. London: Routledge, 1999.

Eco, Umberto. *The Open Work* [1976]. Trans. Anna Cancogni. Intr. David Robey. Cambridge, MA: Harvard University Press, 1989.

Ellis, John. "*Speed*, Film and Television: Media Moving Apart." *Big Picture, Small Screen: The Relations Between Film and Television*, edited by John Hill and Martin McLoone. 107–117. Luton: University of Luton Press, 1996.

Harvey, Robert C. *The Art of the Comic Book: An Aesthetic History*. Jackson: University Press of Mississippi, 1996.

Kelly, Joe, and Michael Gaydos. *Heroes: "The Crossroads."* NBC.com, 2 October 2007, http://www.nbc.com/heroes/novels/novels_display.shtml?novel=53 (accessed 3 March 2011).⅔

PART 3: IDEAS AND CONCEPTS

Heroes, Control, and Regulation

Lorna Jowett

Heroes is about ordinary people discovering they have extraordinary powers. Thus three main concerns arise: individual control of the ability; moral regulation that maintains some characters as heroes rather than villains; and social control of the (secret) knowledge that abilities exist. Ben Strickland notes that superheroes like Spider-Man exist in a world that imitates reality and are thus affected by external factors outside of their control (87), while *Watchmen* (comic series 1986–1987, film 2009), the *Powers* comic series (2000–present), and *The Incredibles* (2004) directly question how superheroes might function in a "real" world concerned with power and in/equality. Similarly, *Heroes* highlights the possibility of public panic about people with abilities, the probability of that knowledge being used as power, and the presence of covert agendas and actions by governments and private companies to regulate and control this part of the population. The dominant spheres of social control are political, scientific and familial. "Political" control of the heroes or, more accurately, of the knowledge that they exist, takes in corruption, secrecy, double-dealing, economic gain, internal power struggles, and media "spin" juxtaposing "superpowers" with a variety of real world powers.

The series establishes a science-fiction approach to abilities and draws on ways science has been used for social regulation. As J. P. Telotte notes, science fiction is based on "a culture that is intent on exploring, understanding and codifying our world, as well as any others we might encounter," underpinned, as he suggests, by "a rational perspective, a thoroughly modernist view of the world, and indeed the universe, as essentially knowable, reducible to cause-and-effect terms, and thus accessible to human manipulation" (17). The dominance of such representations explains why, as Mary Alice Money observes, in *Heroes* the "Company consistently sacrifices humans and humanity to gain power by tracking, controlling, and experimenting on" those with abilities (158), using methods familiar from dystopian fictions of all kinds and, as Porter, Lavery and Robson note, even the manipulative Linderman files, collects, and catalogues everything from people to artworks (132). Mysterious powers manifest in ordinary people, then, should be explainable through science. Furthermore, once science understands the powers, we can control and even benefit from them — knowledge is power. Science becomes both a disinterested means of explaining abilities and a tool of social regulation.

The spirit of scientific inquiry may be heroic but Mohinder (and his father, Chandra) Suresh discover, as Aylish Wood notes, that "the nature of contemporary research, dependent on expensive equipment and facilities, inevitably results in the incorporation of the researcher into a system they cannot fully control" (37). Both Drs. Suresh find themselves implicated in morally dubious research, and Mohinder is often forced to return to the Company (or its equivalent) when his own resources are insufficient. As in *The X-Files* (1993–2002), World War II's strategic deployment of science (including eugenics) is also invoked, not least by the Coyote Sands Relocation Center, and details of medical experimentation dating back decades are revealed in seasons three and four. Mohinder says at one point that those with abilities are "like ... a separate species" ("Five Years Gone," 1:20) and scientific language frequently objectifies them. By medicalizing, even pathologizing abilities and those who have them, a "scientific" approach supports the notion that abilities are a disease that can, perhaps must, be "cured" or eradicated.

This depiction of scientific power and control is nothing new. Telotte notes that the popular 1930s serials tended to show both good and bad science, with the former focused on protection and the latter on destruction (186). *Heroes'* representation of the battle to control knowledge of abilities constantly switches between the two. Thus Strickland describes Linderman as a "villainous humanitarian" who is "trying to create a utopia" by dubious means (99). The same could be said of season four villain Samuel Sullivan, and even the Company sees itself as working for the "greater good." The emphasis on different generations of those with abilities allows the show to align this notion of control as protection with familial care. Thus, Porter, Lavery and Robson note, even in season one the Company is largely a "global regulatory group of rich parents" (132) and Money describes how storylines focus on "conflict between blood relations and chosen families" (160).

The show thus presents science, politics and the family as social institutions designed to regulate citizens, either through benign protection or total social control — one person's utopia is another's dystopia. "We find people and make sure they don't become dangerous," Bob Bishop tells Mohinder as he tries to persuade him to work for the Company ("Four Months Later,"

2:1), though the show also offers many variations on the question, "What would people do if they knew what we were capable of?" as Nathan Petrelli rhetorically asks Matt Parkman, before replying, "They'd lock us up and throw away the key" ("Nothing to Hide," 1:7). Morality and ethics are foregrounded by this constant debate about means and ends.

Moreover, for the individual, having a "power" does not automatically mean becoming powerful. The characters of Niki/Jessica Sanders (prominent in early seasons) and Claire Bennet (a major role throughout the series) provide a complex view of power/lessness. Niki complicates the notion of regulation, since her defining feature, and the characteristic that requires control, relates primarily to her personal identity and only secondarily to her ability. Claire, a young adult with a developing ability growing restive under parental regulation, offers a further perspective on social and personal control. The depictions of both Niki and Claire as "heroes" also inevitably intersect with, and sometimes consciously play with, a range of conventions for representing female characters.

Niki: "What I Am, You Can't Fix"

All those with abilities initially have problems controlling their powers, and characters like Hiro Nakamura and Peter Petrelli maintain that the burden of a hero is to use the power for good, to regulate the self—the "with-great-power-comes-great-responsibility" angle familiar to Marvel fans. *Heroes* creator Tim Kring notes that in moral terms Niki/Jessica Sanders is more complicated even than Sylar. She is "the most complex to wrap your brain around," he states, continuing, "I've always thought that if you looked at it like Dr. Jekyll and Mr. Hyde or like the Incredible Hulk, then you really weren't too far off." Like both Jekyll and David Banner, Niki does not control transformations into her alter ego, superstrong Jessica. Moreover, Niki's life as a single mother (her husband is in prison) seems designed to show how she lacks control and power in the real world. Her socioeconomic position makes it impossible to take control of her life and she earns a living as an internet stripper. It is difficult to disagree with Strickland's comment that Niki/Jessica is a character "most consistently defined by her roles" (96): her position as mother, stripper and killer continue to identify her across several seasons.

Profit, as Porter, Lavery and Robson note, is always a motive in the show, and heroes at the lower end of the economic scale like Niki resent and suspect the wealthy behind the Company (134), offering a stand-in for the viewer (131). Viewers may also be aware that Niki's story, with husband D.L. initially in prison, reflects how real-world economic hardship tends to hit women and children hardest. She is willing to let her estranged father, Hal, back into her life because it could benefit the family, especially her gifted son, Micah, telling D.L., "He's got money. He could help with tuition. We can get Micah into that private school" ("Six Months Ago," 1:10). Indeed, when Hal visits he gives Micah a $2,000 computer — and is appalled that Micah promptly takes it apart to see how it works. When Jessica violently threatens Hal, telling him to leave them alone, she not only reveals his secret (according to her, he abused Niki and sister Jessica and killed Jessica) but rejects his money, stuffing his blank check into his mouth. Lacking control of almost every aspect of her life, including Jessica, Niki tries to be a good wife and mother; Jessica takes control and acts to change things, though in morally dubious ways.

Porter, Lavery and Robson compare Niki with Kate from *Lost*, describing them as "pragmatists who do whatever it takes to remain free" (32). Niki's work as a stripper can be categorized in this way — she is forced into it to support her son — but it remains problematic. When regular online client Ando turns up on her doorstep unannounced, she tells him, in a foreshadowing of her split personality, "You got the wrong girl. That person that you see on the Internet, that's not me. You get the difference, right?" ("Hiros," 1:5). Viewers may sympathize but Niki's control over her clients and how they perceive her is demonstrably slippery. Even after her death, Niki's roles as stripper and mother haunt her sister, Tracy Strauss (as revealed in "I Am Become Death," 3:4, they are two of triplets engineered to have different abilities). When, four years in the future, speedster Daphne Millbrook is urged by Matt Parkman to "slow down" and be responsible now that she is "a wife and a mother" ("I Am Become Death"), viewers understand that she defines herself through her ability, not her family roles. Niki, on the other hand, is defined by motherhood, not by her ability, nor even by her pathology.

She is, however, pathologized more than any other character except Sylar. When Jessica first speaks to her, Niki thinks she is hallucinating and Jessica calls her "poor little crazy girl" ("Better Halves," 1:6). Niki's friend Tina clearly thinks she is having some kind of breakdown (season one), Micah and D.L. talk about Niki being "sick" ("Mom's sick. She can't control it," Micah tells his father in "Homecoming," 1:9), and eventually Niki is incarcerated in a secure hospital after giving herself up to police, believing she is a danger to Micah (as always, he is her main concern). A history of alternate personalities is hinted at in "Four Months Ago" (2:8, when a flashback shows Niki becoming Gina, another personality) and the switch between Niki and Jessica draws on conventional representations of split personalities, as seen in her consultation with Dr. Witherson ("Distractions"). Niki's backstory of paternal abuse suggests that her split personality is caused by childhood trauma and the ability (superstrength) merely adapts to it. Given the rhetoric of control as protection that surrounds abilities in the show, the way Jessica speaks to Hal is notable: "Niki doesn't remember. But I do. Someone had to be there to protect her. I remember the stink of alcohol on your breath. I took every punch, so that she wouldn't have to." Later, Jessica tells Niki that she is taking action "because you're not strong enough" ("Fallout," 2:11). Here the character both requires protection from an abusive family relationship and offers protection to a family member out of love—a pattern replicated in other families, most notably the Petrellis, where abuse is displaced onto political maneuvering. Niki's determination to be a good mother, it is implied, derives from her contrasting experience as a child.

Niki's alcoholism (she meets Hal at an AA meeting in "Six Months Ago") is another symptom of her pathology and perhaps inspires her to believe (like some with abilities) that it would be best if she were "cured" and was able to lead a normal life. Her ability and her mental state are not always clearly distinguished, however (initially her power only manifests through her split personality), and she tells Dr. Witherson, "What I am, you can't fix. Just give me another shot and go away" ("The Fix," 1:13). When Suresh finds her at the Company facility in "Fight or Flight" (2:5), he assumes she needs help to escape: "Niki, you're a prisoner." She explains, "I'm not. I came here on my own. I gave up my son to be here. I'm sick." The connection between Niki's mental health and her ability highlights the medicalization or pathologization of abilities—achieved through the scientific investigation of both Drs. Suresh—and the subsequent step of reducing those with abilities to objects of scientific scrutiny. In Niki's case, the pathology is "real" but Molly Walker is just one other example of a pathologized female "special"—to the Company she is simply "the tracking system" and another opportunity to study the Shanti virus. Niki is also eventually infected with the virus (season two) via Maury Parkman's mind control and since the virus is designed to suppress powers, Niki becomes what she claims she wanted, a normal person. However, she is soon killed trying to rescue Monica Dawson from a burning building in "Powerless" (2:11).

Viewers recognize Jessica not just by reading cues to discern her different personality: she is also physically distinguished from Niki by the tattoo on her shoulder and by her physical skill and superstrength—this is her real power. (Since they are technically the same person, Niki should be able to access this strength, too, and eventually does, in "How To Stop an Exploding Man," 1:23). Niki is introduced by one kind of bodily spectacle (stripping), Jessica is defined by action scenes and physicality (strength and enhanced sexuality). While Niki is most frequently shown in the domestic sphere, even working from home, Jessica is the ultimate professional, displaying physical competence and icy control, whether seducing Nathan Petrelli or disposing of Linderman's debt collectors. She is competent enough to have stolen $2 million from Linderman in the first place, framing D.L. (as she explains in "Better Halves"). Yet if Niki's stripping objectifies and commodifies her body in one fashion, Jessica's skill as a killer does so in another; her body is still at the service of others. Moreover, Linderman theorizes that Jessica's profit motive arises from her past insecurity: "Like most women whose lives have been ruined by men, all Jessica really wants is security, and money buys that. Money's all she's ever really cared about" ("Landslide," 1:22). Her rejection of Hal's financial assistance in "Six Months Ago" may give the lie to this but both incidents gender her behavior and reduce Jessica, as well as Niki, to a product of family abuse. Tracy, despite her complete professionalism, is also vulnerable to gendered typing, her position in the political world threatened by accusations of a spicy past (as internet stripper Niki Sanders) even though she claims she "can spin anything" ("Dual," 3:13). Tracy's polished exterior and high-flying job simply mean that she has more to lose — her apparent control breaks down immediately with the onset of her ability, also denoted as highly physical.

The show explores some aspects of gender and power through Niki, then, but ultimately it regulates both amoral Tracy and immoral Jessica by subordinating them to Niki, the good wife and mother (Porter, Lavery and Robson seem to approve of this, 134). (Niki is also contrasted with several "bad" mothers; see, in particular, "The Hard Part," 1:21, which focuses on Niki/Jessica, Angela Petrelli, and Sylar/Gabriel Gray's mother). Jessica's actions are often condoned because they help Niki and Micah and when Tracy finds her double-dealing has put Micah in danger, she lets him escape. "My mom, who *was* the everyday American, was a hero. You're just a — politician," he tells her, forcing Tracy to live up to his ideal of Niki ("Cold Snap" 3:20). At the beginning of season four she hunts down and murders the Building 26 employees who "killed" her but eventually repents and is redeemed by saving Claire and Noah Bennet after Samuel buries them in a carnival trailer ("Brave New World" 4:19), once again doing family work and living up to Niki's memory.

Claire: "Just a Girl Who Happens to Have Powers"

If Niki's selfless maternal devotion is valorized by the show, Claire Bennet is caught in a more ambiguous web of parental protection and control. "As long as you live under my roof, you will do as I say," Noah Bennet tells her in "Homecoming" (1:9) and Claire's story is as much about her trying to break free of that control as it is about her ability (bodily regeneration). She is raised by the Company (given to Noah Bennet as a baby, on condition that any ability will be studied), though it continually fails to control her. Moreover, for Claire, family and social control are conflated time and again, whether she is the adopted daughter of Noah, long-time Company employee and specialist in "morally gray" (a phrase used for the first time in "Company Man," 1:17) or the illegitimate daughter of Nathan Petrelli, aspiring senator and granddaughter of Angela Petrelli, Company co-founder, and Noah's sometime employer. For Niki, social powerlessness is juxtaposed with warm parental care; for Claire, parental protection sparks off teenage attitude, playing with her presentation as spoiled daughter. Like Niki, Claire is consistently defined by family and framed in the domestic sphere. Yet her character arc demonstrates the frequency with which family and Company regulation collapse and require restructuring.

The famous season-one catchphrase, "Save the cheerleader, save the world," presents Claire as a nameless type. She is a kind of "cartoon character," as Strickland points out, and the show "cleverly maintains the initial impression that she is a stereotype" (90). However, the show soon begins to play off the cheerleader and spoiled daughter models and her character develops. First, Claire tries to come to terms with the fact that despite being blonde, popular, and a cheerleader, her newfound ability makes her a "freak." On the face of it, this sounds like a typical teen superhero story, reworking Peter Parker via Buffy Summers. In common with other contemporary superhero protagonists, Claire says she wants to be normal. Even in season four she admits, "I like to think of myself as just a girl who happens to have powers. And it's just one thing in a list of attributes — loyal, friendly, regenerative, good skin, you know" ("Pass/Fail," 4:16).

Family relationships and especially parental control develop Claire's character while reminding us that, just as the heroes are mostly ordinary people, she is in many ways just a girl. Noah's involvement with the Company is a secret he hides from his family, just as Claire initially hides her ability. Claire's biological father Nathan is also drawn in moral shades of gray, but his investment in Claire never matches Noah's: despite initially being married with two sons, Nathan's weakness is his brother, Peter. In fact, Kring explains, "The relationships between the two brothers, Peter and Nathan, and Claire and her father were much more profound than I had envisioned in my head originally, especially Claire and her father." He goes on to elaborate, "In a strange way, it was almost a classic love story between two people who are star crossed and can't quite get together." This description demonstrates the intensity of their bond and explains why potential romances for Claire quickly fizzle out—she already has a deep emotional bond with a partner, another is redundant. Family, even chosen family, is always more important than romance in *Heroes*. Claire and Noah's relationship involves frequent betrayals and breakdowns and the "star-crossed" aspect Kring describes echoes in Claire's anguished "you're my dad, for better or worse," as their air runs out after being buried underground by Samuel ("Brave New World," 4:19).

Noah's love for and fierce desire to protect his adopted daughter, and Claire's ability to forgive his moral waverings and stand by him as her "real" father, contrasts Elle and Bob Bishop's more obviously destructive blood relationship. Another blonde beauty with a Company dad, Elle is an insecure, homicidal sociopath. Noah reveals to her how Bob authorized testing of her power from a tender age, though she has no memory of this ("Cautionary Tales," 2:9). Bob is certainly abusive towards Elle, as in "Powerless" (2:11) when he castigates her for provoking Claire's threat to go public and, as with Niki, this paternal abuse scars Elle for life. Eventually Elle asks for Claire's help when her ability is out of control ("Eris Quod Sum," 3:7) and the two function as foils all along. Elle meets the tragic demise of an unloved and abused daughter, while Claire's stable childhood results in a strong young woman who wants to change the world.

While Claire's introduction, documenting her latest "attempt" to test her powers by throwing herself off an 80-foot drop ("Genesis," 1:1), alludes to teen suicide, the show deflects the grim nature of the subject matter through its approach to her ability. As Steven Peacock notes, the show "revels in the violence inflicted on the body before it inevitably heals" to the point that any scene featuring Claire being injured "has a Looney Tunes quality to it" (145). For instance, her "death" during jock Brody Mitchum's attack is shocking but when she wakes up on the autopsy table her gruesome injuries are played for laughs as she literally has to pull herself together before she can leave ("Collision," 1:4). She absent-mindedly puts her hand in the waste disposal to retrieve a ring, losing a finger ("Genesis"); takes cupcakes from the oven barehanded ("smells like something's burning," Sandra comments, "Better Halves"); cuts off a toe to see if it will grow back ("Lizards," 2:2); has her hand crack off her body after she is frozen by Tracy ("Brother's Keeper," 4:10); and demonstrates her ability to others by cutting or burning herself. Yvonne Tasker has noted that action heroes are often characterized by both restraint (in using strength) and excess (of strength), and observes that the tension between these may be mediated through "both horror and comedy" (9). Claire's ability is treated in a somewhat different fashion, though its representation relies on horror and comedy. She is not a superstrong action hero (like Niki/Jessica), more a passive hero with the ability to withstand and recover from severe physical punishment, a kind of hyper-vulnerability presented as excessive spectacle. (Both Claire and Niki are associated with specularization, being watched, as well as spectacle.) "I have busted, like, every bone in my body, stabbed myself in the chest, I've shoved a two-foot steel rod through my neck," she says, "and I don't have a scratch on me!" ("Genesis"), a comment that also mocks the way television heroes recover unrealistically quickly from wounds.

Adam, a villain with the same ability, is first presented to us as famous warrior Takezo Kensei but Claire is the ultimate victim. She appears, in keeping with "save the cheerleader," to be little more than a damsel in distress who, for our viewing pleasure, is threatened, attacked, mutilated and even killed. She is the beautiful woman horror-movie directors often talk about as the focus of torture and pain (see Hitchcock's famous "torture the women!" or Dario Argento's comment, "I like women, especially beautiful ones. If they have a good face and figure, I would much prefer to watch them being murdered than an ugly girl or man," in Clover 42). Yet because Claire can never be killed, we enjoy excessive horror and bodily violation in the knowledge that it is not "serious" and the character's own perverse comments on her ability add to its subversive nature. In addition, she quickly learns to use her power aggressively when she crashes Brody Mitchum's car after he attempted to rape her and left her for dead. One of the first things Noah says when he visits her in hospital afterwards is, "Your mother told me you lost control of the car," while Claire confesses, "He tried to force me" ("Hiros," 1:5). Although she can endure being "forced" to the point of death, only to recover, she finds that she was not the first young woman Brody had attacked but the others chose to keep quiet — this inspires her to act against him. Her ability allows her to take control by apparently losing it. The attempted rape scenario foregrounds gendered power as well as gendered models of active/passive behavior that continue to impact on televisual representation.

The regenerative properties of Claire's blood are capable of bringing Noah back to life ("Cautionary Tales," 2:9), as well as acting as a "catalyst" in combination with Mohinder's antibodies ("Truth and Consequences," 2:10) to cure strains of the Shanti virus but the show never shifts Claire from regenerator to healer. Retaining her identity as the indestructible girl allows her to continue a kind of passive resistance. Moreover, despite, or perhaps because of, the pain inflicted on her, she fears numbness, either when she stops feeling the pain of her injuries in season three, or when she resists Gretchen's advances because she is used to walling herself off from intimacy (season four). This emotional problem is juxtaposed with and connected to Claire's extreme physicality and eventually she takes control of the former as well as the latter, becoming an emotional subject as well as a physical body. Her tentative relationship with Gretchen also suggests a potential escape from patriarchal, heterosexual family structures that seek to regulate her.

Claire's connections (Noah and Nathan) mean that she has something of a free pass from the persecution other specials suffer, but familial regulation is multiplied. "Do you have any idea what happens if they think I can't control you anymore?" Noah asks her during season three and she simply replies, "That's the thing, Dad, you can't" ("Building 26," 3:16). During season four their arguments continue, but she now gives him advice: "Why do I suddenly feel like you're the parent and I'm the kid?" he asks her as she counsels him on the loss of his life's work and the breakdown of his marriage ("Acceptance," 4:4; see also "Once Upon a Time in Texas," 4:8). With the dissolution of the Bennet family and Claire's move away to college, parental control over her is broken. It is no surprise, then, that Claire ushers in a brave new world at the end of the series. In a bodily exhibition that reprises her introduction, she climbs a Ferris wheel under the scrutiny of news crews and TV cameras and throws herself off. Rising and rearranging her limbs, she states, "My name is Claire Bennet, and this is attempt number ... I guess I've kinda lost count" ("Brave New World"), publicly revealing her ability. Once, Claire pleaded with her brother not to tell her parents about the video recording of her ability because her parents would "think it was a mistake to ever adopt me. We wouldn't be a family anymore" ("Nothing to Hide," 1:7). Now she is willing to expose her ability to the world. When Lauren asks Noah, "What's she doing?" he replies, "Breaking my heart." For him, this moment is about being unable to protect, or control, his little girl (the political is personal); for Claire it's not about family anymore, it's about changing the world (the personal is political).

Girls Like Us?

"It's hard out there for girls like us," Tracy tells Claire as they pause for breath after Tracy's "panic attack with powers" during "Brother's Keeper." Male and female characters alike in *Heroes* are involved with family, melodrama and the domestic. However, power in *Heroes* is generational and ultimately patriarchal and representations of social control through science and politics depict a public life still dominated by men (even arch-manipulator Angela Petrelli is on the margins). *Heroes* may have its flaws in terms of characterization and storytelling yet these often make plain the various ways all fictional representations mobilize existing (gendered) models of plot and character and seek to construct new ones. Even its insistence on the importance of family bonds manages to demonstrate how the family, especially the myth of the happy nuclear family, can be as much a tool of social regulation as scientific analysis and political spin. Peter, Hiro, and Sylar (and almost every male character) kick against social and parental control, and against traditional models of masculinity. The representations of both Niki and Claire engage with a range of female stereotypes — the powerful, sexualized psycho; the self-sacrificing mother; the blonde bimbo; the damsel in distress; the surviving girl of the slasher movie. Both are simultaneously victims and heroes and while Niki/Jessica more obviously has a dual personality, literalizing the oppositions of female representation (good/bad, mother/whore, victim/agent), Claire doubly embodies the brutally assaulted female victim of horror and the final girl who survives and takes down the villain (as described by Carol Clover). Both she and Niki prove N. Katherine Hayles' point that "it is ... more unsettling to the centres of power to be a female freak (which is perhaps a redundancy) than to be either a truncated or extended male" (166). How, or indeed whether, Claire's passive resistance taking center stage in the show's finale will change models of heroism as well as models of gendered power remains to be seen.

Works Cited

Clover, Carol. *Men, Women and Chainsaws*. London: BFI, 1992.
Hayles, N. Katherine. "The Life Cycle of Cyborgs: Rewriting the Posthuman." *Cybersexualities: A Reader on Feminist Theory, Cyborgs and Cyberspace*, edited by Jenny Wolmark. 157–173. Edinburgh: Edinburgh University Press, 1999.
Kring, Tim. "Extended Interview With Tim Kring." 28 Jul 2007, http://www.comic-con.org/cci2007/cci07prog_kring.shtml (accessed 22 Sep 2010).
Money, Mary Alice. "The Heroes Kaleidoscope." *Saving the World: A Guide to Heroes*, edited by Lynette Porter, David Lavery, and Hillary Robson. 151–163. Ontario: ECW, 2007.
Peacock, Steven. "Going Dark in Heroes." *Saving the World: A Guide to Heroes*, edited by Lynette Porter, David Lavery, and Hillary Robson. 141–150. Ontario: ECW, 2007.
Porter, Lynette, David Lavery, and Hillary Robson. *Saving the World: A Guide to Heroes*. Ontario: ECW, 2007.
Strickland, Ben. "Growing Pains: Heroes and the Quest for Identity." *Saving the World: A Guide to Heroes*, edited by Lynette Porter, David Lavery, and Hillary Robson. 85–103. Ontario: ECW, 2007.
Tasker, Yvonne. *Spectacular Bodies*. London: Routledge, 1993.
Telotte, J. P. *A Distant Technology: Science Fiction Film and the Machine Age*. Hanover, NH: Wesleyan University Press, 1999.
Wood, Aylish. *Technoscience in Contemporary American Film*. Manchester: Manchester University Press, 2002.

"You're Broken. I Can Fix You": Negotiating Concepts of U.S. Ideology

Torsten Caeners

When *Heroes* premiered on NBC in 2006, the series soon proved to be immensely popular, both with critics and with an audience. However, the series was eventually cancelled after a shaky four-season run which saw a dwindling number of viewers as well as a decline in critical acclaim. Still, as a series, "*Heroes* offers something to suit every viewer: troubled teens, shady politicians, young people at odds with parents (especially fathers), idealistic do-gooders, conspirators, serial killers, students and teachers, struggling working class parents" (Porter, Lavery, and Robson 2). What is the relevance of selected U.S. ideological concepts on *Heroes*? To understand this, we must define the concept of ideology in the context of the United States of America and delineate briefly some of its central and most widely recognized manifestations, namely *manifest destiny*, the *city upon a hill*, the pursuit of happiness and the relations of those to (the even more elusive) concept of the American Dream. Obviously, these notions are all intricately linked and cannot, in practice, be easily distinguished. I will nonetheless venture to delimit some central features of each concept that can be used to trace them within the matrix of the show's complex storylines and universe. To facilitate this, the American Dream will serve as an umbrella concept.

> No matter in which respect or from which point of view, [w]hoever attempts to understand the complexities of American life ... or to come to term with American popular culture ... will time and again run up against enduring beliefs and convictions. These beliefs, which can be traced back to some American founding myths, coalesce — in ever changing patterns — in the central vision of the "American Dream" [Freese 7].

Despite his emphasis on the heterogeneous nature of the American Dream, Freese nonetheless provides a list of the "basic constituents of the Dream" (14) which can be usefully employed as a framework for the following discussion. Here are his six constituents:

1. The future-oriented belief in a steady improvement of individual, communal, and societal conditions of existence, that is, the belief in *progress*.
2. The conviction that everybody can realize his highest ambitions by means of his own endeavors, that is, the belief in the attainability of *success*.
3. The certainty that God has singled out America as his chosen country and has appointed the Americans to convert the rest of the world to true American-style democracy, that is, the belief in *manifest destiny*.
4. The assurance that, in the context of civilization's irresistible westward movement, ever new borderlines are to be crossed and obstacles to be surmounted, that is, the idea of the continual challenges of respective *frontiers*.
5. The belief in the American form of government of the people, by the people and for the people as the sole guarantor of *liberty* and *equality*.
6. The ideas that immigrants of different nationalities, different ethnic stock and different religious affiliations can be fused into a new nation, that is, the conviction expressed in such different historical mutations as the idea of the *melting pot* or the idea of *multi-ethnicity*.

I presume to add to Freese's list two further aspects which appear to me to be core features of the American Dream, namely:

7. The belief in the exceptional nature of the USA and its leading role in the world, that is, the notion of the *city upon a hill*.
8. The right and desire for self-fulfillment, that is, the *pursuit of happiness*.

These individual constituents of the American Dream are in constant flux, changing in emphasis depending on historical circumstances and the individual person(s) utilizing them. *Heroes* contains, touches upon, and directly deals with almost every example from the above list by re-fashioning, appropriating and reciprocally (inter)weaving these notions within its universe. The idea of genetically mutated human beings with special abilities, for instance, represents a new twist on the notion of the *melting pot/multi-ethnicity*, asking the question whether or not U.S. society would be able to "fuse into a new nation" that incorporates the newness represented by "specials." In this context, the idea(l)s of liberty and equality also become pertinent. Furthermore, the series refashions the frontier idea in that it presents the audience with questions about the frontier of human existence and of whether or not the series' "heroes" represent a new species, another step in human evolution, or an abomination. Another core element of the series is the characters' constant pursuit of happiness: Matt Parkman is trying to build a family, Sylar desires happiness in terms of fame and power, Peter wants to help people, Hiro seeks happiness in living his dream to be a hero. Concise as this list is, it clearly shows the central position of the multifarious facets of the American Dream in *Heroes*.

It is by means of the various manifestations of the American Dream in *Heroes* that negotiations of U.S. ideology can be traced in the series. Naturally, like the American Dream, ideology oscillates between negotiations, implications, and the effects of cultural forces and practices on the macroscopic level as well as their individual manifestations within and around small groups and individuals. Beginning with a closer inspection of ideology, my analyses of the series will be conducted between the two poles of 1) major cultural practices, institutions, and influences and 2) individual implications, i.e., the broader structure of the series on the one hand and the personal lives and identities of the characters on the other. The dialectic intricacies between personal and societal implications arising from ideology will illuminate how successfully *Heroes* manages to construct a framework of cultural diagnosis. In particular, the American Dream will be utilized in the analysis of the character of Claire Bennet. This will be followed by a treatment of Sylar emphasizing the idea of *manifest destiny*. The story arc of *Heroes*' final season will serve to exemplify the show's engagement with the notion of the *city upon a hill* and will provide a means to incorporate the previous two readings into the overall narrative arc of the show.

Heroes, Ideology, and the United States

The American Dream and its constituent parts are the palpable manifestation of the even more ephemeral structures of ideology, structures which also permeate the *Heroes* universe. Ideology as such is an extremely slippery concept, and one that is implicated in manifold connotations, both positive and negative. Very generally speaking, ideology is a conglomeration of ideas that allow groups of individuals to form a common identity. On a general level, every culture is necessarily based on, negotiates, and perpetuates a specific ideology, as it provides essential guidelines about who and what the culture in question is and how it is different from other cultures. In essence, it is a question of cultural identity: a culture's ideology is what demarcates the "us" from the "other." Sacvan Bercovitch's definition of ideology, which he puts forth in the context of U.S. literary history, is, though somewhat dated, one of the most concise definitions of the idea:

> I mean by Ideology the ground and texture of consensus. In its narrowest sense, this may be a consensus of a marginal or maverick group. In the broad sense in which I use the term here (in conjunction with the term "America"), ideology is the system of interlinked ideas, symbols, and beliefs by which a culture — any culture — seeks to justify and perpetuate itself; the web of rhetoric, ritual, and assumption through which society coerces, persuades, and coheres. So considered, ideology is basically conservative [635].

According to Bercovitch, ideology is thus at the heart of American culture, but its function is not solely beneficial. Its positive and necessary function is that it "coheres," that it binds a culture's heterogeneous elements together by means of unifying symbols, notions and beliefs. The price paid for this unity, however, is that ideology is conservative, i.e., it is averse to change and works towards maintaining the status quo. Consequently, ideology "coerces" and "persuades." The aim of these strategies of coercion and persuasion is ultimately to force or sway rogue elements into submission. These two elements of ideology work mostly unperceived, which makes it so difficult to resist them. As Bercovitch notes, with reference to Raymond Williams:

> Ideology evolves through conflict and even when a certain ideology achieves dominance it still finds itself contending to one degree or another with the ideologies of residual and emergent cultures within the society — contending, that is, with alternative and oppositional forms that reflect the course of historical development [635].

Heroes can be read as a staging of precisely this kind of conflict or dialectic, a depiction of the struggles within one ideological system, and, in the case of the U.S., an ideology which "has achieved a hegemony unequaled elsewhere in the world" (Bercovitch 636). This struggle is displayed on a variety of levels, all of which, however, always reciprocally comment upon and influence each other. The first half of season three of the series, for instance, realizes this mainly as a generational struggle. Since the Petrelli family embodies conservative American values, it constitutes a valuable source for tracing the above mentioned ideological forces. This is so despite the fact that Nathan is a dubious character as his dealings with Linderman in the first season testify. Although he certainly "embodies traits people often detest in politicians: manipulation of power for personal gain; misinformation skillfully delivered to the public; a handsome philanthropic veneer covering deeper roots in corruption ... [m]any viewers don't expect politicians to remain altruistic all the time; ... he still does nothing worse than what many viewers expect happens frequently in real-world politics" (Porter, Lavery, and Robson 130–131). Thus, Nathan's corruption is in fact the very symbol of his conservatism. Still, it is Angela Petrelli who is a master persuader, constantly manipulating people to get her way (cf., the way she tries to influence Sylar during episodes 3:1–3:6). While she often combines her suggestions with implied threats, she is in essence exercising the persuasive power of ideology. In contrast to this, Arthur Petrelli governs by means of coercion alone, ruling through power and fear. He gets what he wants by force. Thus, Angela and Arthur can be seen as representing the two primary manifestations of ideology: coercion and persuasion. There is more, however. On his return to power, Arthur Petrelli doesn't fight for the status quo, but strives to re-establish a former hegemony, one which made him powerful. This is a struggle that is clearly depicted as existing between the generations in *Heroes* with the older generation trying to either preserve what power they have achieved, or trying to regain power, and the younger generation fighting against what they perceive as being oppressive and simply wrong. Ultimately, however, this struggle is one between two rivaling ideologies.

In *Heroes* the struggle inherent in ideology is reflected in society's concern with the implications of "difference" or "otherness." People with special abilities are "other"; indeed, they are referred to as "specials" in the series, which emphasizes their difference from those people who are considered to be normal. At the same time, the "specials" are part of U.S. culture and have thus internalized its norms and values. Consequently, they challenge the hegemony of the reigning ideology while at the same time tapping into it; that is, the "specials" take recourse to fundamental notions of U.S. culture in order to re-conceptualize their own status within it. *Heroes* negotiates this dichotomy between "normal" and "special," "center" and "periphery," "us" and "them" most obviously in the second half of its third season. Here, parallels to the threat of terrorism and the pervading insecurity and suspicion that took hold of U.S. culture after the 9/11 attacks are (too) strikingly obvious. The governmentally supported hunt for people with abilities creates an atmosphere of distrust and suspicion, a phobia concerning everything "other" that is faced by means of an increasing radicalization. Hiding his own ability, Nathan Petrelli sets up a government agency designed to control people with abilities. This organization is designed to uphold the status quo and represents the coercive power of government, which itself signifies a material manifestation of the ideology in power. Other than the Company, which was not directly associated with the government and employed people with abilities in its effort to keep the world safe from villainous "specials," the organization Nathan creates works solely to preserve the current system. People with abilities are "othered" now, being continuously referred to as "them." This is clearly exemplified in the following exchange between Noah Bennet and Danko:

> NOAH BENNET: Primatech had a system — one of us, one of them.
> DANKO: Working alongside people with abilities?
> NOAH BENNET: It helps to even the odds.
> DANKO: Yes, I read your files. I think we'd be better served with one of us, and one of us.
> NOAH BENNET: I'm sorry?
> DANKO: Or ten of us — twelve of us, and none of them.

While othering via language is a relatively subtle device, the representation of the treatment given to people with abilities who have been caught is much more obviously analogous to contemporary real-world events. The treatment of "specials" is clearly modeled after the treatment of enemy combatants in Guantanamo, complete with the prisoner's orange outfits and the accompanying loss of all their civil rights (especially the episodes 3:14 and 3:15). Both levels of representation meet in the character of Danko, who symbolizes the coercive force and effect of ideology in his outright hatred of people with abilities, culminating in his proposal to wipe out "specials" completely (see 3:21). Danko's extreme reaction is determined by his deep immersion in the value system of his culture. In essence, he has been brainwashed by the ideological forces he has encountered during his life (one has to assume that this process happened predominantly through military training and education) to such an extent, that he is a) beyond questioning them and b) experiences any attack against the basis of his internalized value system as life threatening and existential. Danko is thus at the same time a victim of the broad forces of ideological conservatism and a tool of their perpetuation and constant (re-)consolidation. The French philosopher Michel Foucault has termed these forces "techniques of objectification" through which "relations are established between institutions, economic and social processes, behavioral patterns, systems of norms, techniques, types of classification, modes of characterization; and these relations are not present in the object" (*Archaeology* 45). Since these connections are not present in the object, they go unnoticed. People thus become agents of ideology without knowing it. Unconsciously internalized as these notions are, they work on the individual, by means of self-surveillance, on the level of the Freudian superego. Individuals in this state of self-surveillance and unconscious adherence to a certain reigning value-system have been described by Foucault as "docile bodies." Narrative therapists White and Epston note:

When conditions are established for persons to experience ongoing evaluation according to particular institutionalized "norms," when these conditions cannot be escaped, and when persons can be isolated in their experience of such conditions, then they will become the guardians of themselves. In these circumstances, persons will perpetually evaluate their own behavior and engage in operations on themselves to forge themselves as "docile bodies" [24].

For all his ruthless activities, Danko is a "docile body," a person who has become an unquestioning servant of a culture's ideological forces. As White and Epston rightly point out, "docile bodies" are created through "institutionalized 'norms,'" which is particularly obvious in Danko's military background and involvement with the secret government institution. In this respect, Danko's position as a "docile body" is one effect of the broader ideological forces I have discussed — persuasion and coercion first among them — and makes obvious how ideology has profound effects on the life and mental world of individual members of society as it is depicted in *Heroes*.

Ideological Individualism and Individual Ideology: Personal Negotiations With(in) Ideology in Heroes

The character of Claire Bennet epitomizes the implications and effects of ideology on individual members of a society. At the beginning of the first series, she is living in the stereotypical American middle-class family, picket fences, etc. She neither knows about Noah Bennet's true job, nor knows about her real father who is in many respects seemingly ordinary. When Claire discovers her ability, she considers her power very much a burden and desires nothing more than to be a normal teenage girl again. Her power alienates her from what she considers to be normal, which is why she has problems accepting it. For Claire, the appearance of her power is perceived as an obstacle to her pursuit of happiness. She envisions her happiness to lie precisely in a way of life that conforms to the norms and expectations of the society she has been brought up in. Claire intends to realize the American Dream in its most traditional form.

Claire can also be seen as a "docile body," albeit one that is forced to question that state through the discovery of her ability. One could argue that she has been lulled into compliance with her surrounding culture — has become a non-threatening agent — through her almost perfect childhood and adolescence: "Claire just wants to be a normal teenager, getting a spot on the cheerleading squad, being named homecoming queen, exploring friendships; she doesn't want to be labeled a freak" (Porter, Lavery, and Robson 8). She has been indoctrinated by the idea of utopian suburbia without even noticing. When it comes to Claire, the conservatizing forces of ideology become particularly obvious in her cheerleading. At the beginning of the series she is defined almost exclusively by the role, being consistently referred to as "the cheerleader." She seems to be:

> A cartoon character. *Heroes* cleverly maintains the initial impression that she is a stereotype. She is young, cute, blond, and otherwise defined by the omnipresent cheerleader outfit that she wears in episode after episode. She can think of nothing to do with her ability to heal from seemingly every injury except document it time and again, almost as if she is unsure that it really exists [Porter, Lavery, and Robson 90].

Indeed, it is almost as if Claire as a character does not really exist at this stage of the show's narrative. She lives the ordinary, conservative life of a stereotypical middle-class U.S. teenager and, because of the ideological indoctrination of which she is unaware, she is completely happy with her life. Once she discovers her ability, however, Claire is forced to question her own position in society. She now sees herself as existing outside the established conventions of not only society, but essentially humanity. This disrupts her docility and she starts searching for a new place in the world. Looking at her development throughout the course of the series, it is questionable whether or not she is really ever able to escape from her ideologically induced conservatism. Her struggle remains throughout, between her almost inbred desire to lead a normal life and her inability to do so. Roughly halfway through the series (2:11), Claire is preparing to go public with her ability, but she is persuaded to do otherwise. In effect, her desire to change the system is — successfully in this case — stopped by the conservative forces of ideology. It is mainly her adoptive mother, also at this stage an overt stereotype of the suburban housewife, who persuades her to remain "docile." At the end of the show's fourth series, Claire makes good on her plan and does indeed expose the world to the secret of people with abilities, but it has been an arduous journey for her to finally be able to break the constricting forces of her upbringing.

During the four seasons of the show, Claire's utopian environment disintegrates almost completely. It begins with the realization that she is special and continues as she learns more about both her adoptive father and her natural parents. The family moves numerous times and finally the Bennets get a divorce. Even after all these tumultuous events, Claire registers at college and continues to look for a normal, stereotypical life (4:1–4:10). This clearly shows the persuasive power of ideology which continues to hold sway over her.

This desire for "docility" is also the reason why she is so intrigued by what Samuel has to offer during the final season of the show, namely a home, family and a normal life, yet with an open acknowledgement of her ability. Staying at the Sullivan Carnival, Claire visits Lydia and when Claire's face appears on her skin with the caption "Indestructible girl," Claire says: "What, am I ... am I gonna have a circus act?" to which Lydia replies: "This isn't the future, Claire. This is your desire" (4:12). Indeed, although Claire talks about the carnival as a "freak show" (4:12), she wants to belong there, as it represents, at least on first glance, all the virtues she has been raised to cherish.

Claire's unchanging adherence to the fundamental WASP ideal of suburban America makes the ending of the fourth series so potent and fitting. By re-enacting her first-season jumps before national television, Claire becomes the herald of revolution, which is unequivocally voiced by Peter noting: "She's gonna change everything" (4:19). This change, it is particularly noteworthy, is a change that originates from within the boundaries of the conservative ideological thinking that Claire represents. In her pursuit of happiness, Claire has realized that she will not be able to find fulfillment within her culture's current makeup and takes the bold step of foregoing what little security her life still provides. In doing so, she abandons the current system for an unknown future that may well hold more peril and danger. While she jumps from the Ferris wheel to shatter the existing order of ideology, her actions remain very much within and driven by traditional notions of the American Dream. Claire's action opens up a new frontier, pushing U.S. society beyond the threshold of what the old structures can accommodate. The literal shattering of Claire's bones when she hits the ground mirror the potential destruction of the old system. Likewise, the immediate mending of her broken body foreshadows the reconstitution of society, albeit in altered form. With the jump, Claire herself leaves home irrevocably and, metaphorically, she takes on the role of the early pioneers, venturing into the unknown and hoping to create a new home and a new culture in the process. In this respect, the ideological basis of the old system therefore functions as the basis of the emerging system by reconstituting its own founding mythology.

While Claire originally lives in a suburban home and never stops in the pursuit of her happiness, a pursuit that is closely fashioned along the dominant notions of the American Dream, Sylar feels coerced by the idea of the pursuit of happiness. He perceives his own position within society as alien from the very start and, for him, the American Dream is most closely connected with such ideological notions as *manifest destiny* and the "from rags to riches" narrative. Sylar's life has always been far less idyllic than Claire's. Before the events of the first season unfold, the audience learns from flashbacks, Gabriel Gray (Sylar's real name) lived his life as a simple watchmaker. His humble existence leaves enough room for him to dream about rising from "rags to riches," but Gabriel does not become active in the pursuit of his happiness. The reason for this lies in his appropriation of the idea of *manifest destiny*. Similar to the idea of the USA as a blessed country with a population of elect people, Gabriel believes that he has a destiny, namely to be special and to become powerful and influential. Contrary to the Puritan work ethos that developed from the idea of being elect, at first Gabriel remains passive, because he literally believes that his destiny should be manifest and thus should manifest itself automatically. This indeed seems to begin happening when Chandra Suresh knocks on his door and explains his theories to Gabriel. It is only at this moment that Gabriel becomes active; spurred on by the notion that he might be special, he begins his transformation into Sylar.

Sylar's trademark phrase, "You're broken. I can fix you," epitomizes central elements of the character's origins and development. To begin with, of course, it is evocative of Sylar's character, reminding the audience of his humble (and harmless) origin as a watchmaker. At first glance, the phrase evokes positive connotations, ending as it does with "I can fix you." It is almost a physician's phrase designed to calm a patient and stimulate new hope for recovery. In the context of *Heroes* and the development of the Sylar character, the phrase contains additional surplus meaning: firstly, it is evocative of the transfer of Gabriel's skills as a watchmaker into the abilities that he applies and hones as Sylar; on a linguistic level, it humanizes the watchmaker's promise of repairing a broken watch — "It's broken, but I can fix it" — while, on the psychological level, it de-humanizes the victims in Sylar's mind. This is also evident in the name "Sylar" itself, which is taken from the brand name of a watch. In Sylar's mind, Gabriel Gray has become "a name." Unlike an anonymous watchmaker, who — despite the implications of his job title — does not really *make* watches, but in fact only repairs broken watches brought in by equally anonymous customers, Sylar takes his name and thus his identity from an origin that implies both a certain level of activity and creativity — in that the brand really does produce watches — and constitutes a brand thus signifying fame and achievement. Things are, however, somewhat more complicated. Gabriel Gray can take apart a watch, repair or replace the broken parts and then successfully reassemble the watch into a workable condition. Sylar, on the other hand, can literally take apart a human body, locate the area which makes a person "special," and integrate this into his own body. Sylar cannot, however, bring that person back to life afterwards. Sylar is thus deficient in his skill where Gabriel is not. Sylar cannot really deliver on his promise — "I can fix you"— but in order to grow in power, he necessarily has to destroy. Gabriel fashions his alter ego Sylar as a person who can be successful and attain his goals, but this is in fact not what Sylar the serial killer manages to achieve. The alter ego of Sylar is born from desire, from Gabriel desperately wanting to be special. Gabriel wants to rise "from rags to riches"; he is in desperate pursuit of his own vision of happiness. These ideas have — falsely — led Gabriel to perceive his position in society as deeply unsatisfying, as low and tarnished, whereas, in fact, Gabriel Gray is a skilled and able craftsman who, though not leading a particularly famous or grandiose life, in essence does have something to be proud of: he has found something he is good at, developed that skill, and made a living out of it. However, this is not enough for him. He states, "I wanted to be different. Special. I wanted to change. A new name, a new life. The watchmaker's son ... became a watchmaker. It is so ... futile. And I wanted to be ... important" (1:10). The discovery of being special overpowers Gabriel as it represents the fulfillment of his most intimate desires; Gabriel turns into Sylar, because the fulfillment of desire is not the end of his search for happiness, but actually inaugurates an insatiable desire that needs continuous satisfaction. Life as Sylar is eventually equally futile. Sylar is continuously caught in the pursuit of his happiness, which manifests itself in an asocial and murderous manner, which in turn leads to social isolation and thus precludes acceptance from society and, ultimately, happiness. In the end, Sylar's insatiable desire represents the tendency of ideology for constant consolidation and hegemony, something that is only ever temporarily achieved by the acquisition of additional resources and power.

The American Dream, the Puritan Legacy and Heroes' Final Season

In its fourth and final season, *Heroes* presents the audience with a clearly recognizable villain in Samuel, the leader of a gypsy-esque carnival where the magic tricks are not really tricks at all, but performed by people with abilities. However, Samuel is not a one-dimensional villain who resorts to violence and bullying to get what he wants — something that Sylar was repeatedly turned into, weakening and distorting his character over the course of the show. Rather Samuel is smart, cunning in his planning, and, perhaps most importantly, rhetorically very shrewd and charismatic. All these (for lack of a better word) "natural" abilities have allowed him to assemble a growing number of "specials" around him. Samuel pretends that he wants to establish a home for people with abilities and give them a voice in society. Ultimately, though, his desire is for power because the presence of people with abilities increases his own powers. With this setup, *Heroes* taps into the very foundational myths and values of the U.S. (and thus its ideological sub-current) in a more subtle, and at the same time, more effective manner than in its third-season arc. The Sullivan Carnival enacts the original Puritan settlement of America. Samuel is, of course, a biblical name. The biblical Samuel was a judge and prophet, which are functions Samuel Sullivan also inhabits and utilizes for his purposes. He sets himself up as the prophet of a new era, painting a picture of a world in which his family can live normally and peacefully. At the same time, he condemns, partly rightly so, U.S. culture for its treatment of "specials" and plans to eventually seek revenge upon those who have sought to oppress them.

Carnivals are at the fringes of the cultural spectrum and are often looked at with suspicion, or at least represent a form of alternative life apart from the central cultural vein. In the context of *Heroes'* final season, the Russian philosopher Mikhail Bakhtin's notion of the "carnival" comes to mind:

> "Carnival" is Bakhtin's term for a bewildering constellation of rituals, games, symbols, and various carnal excesses that constitutes an alternative "social space" of freedom, abundance, and equality, expressing a utopian promise of plenitude and redemption [Gardiner 767].

This alternative social space which cannot occupy the center and is therefore to be located at the fringes of society is exactly what the Sullivan Carnival offers. It is a position shared by the series' main characters. While this positioning allows for an easier identification of the specials' situation for the audience, it also represents the position of the Puritans in England during the 17th century. Before Cromwell's Commonwealth government, Puritans lived at the fringes of mainstream society as an outlawed group of religious dissenters. They were briefly at the center during the early days of the English civil war, but soon cast aside by other political forces. Following the restoration of the king in 1660, they were blamed for the despotic, military dictatorship of Oliver Cromwell, the so-called interregnum, and thus again cast to the margins of society. It is from these circumstances of suppression, distrust and curtailed freedoms that the Puritan fathers set out to find a new home in America.

This is the position the Sullivan Carnival epitomizes. Samuel's biblical name is thus particularly fitting, the Irish surname Sullivan emphasizing the notion of migration. Additionally, in his speeches before his congregation of specials, Samuel speaks very much like a preacher delivering a sermon, which further emphasizes the Puritan connection. The first episode of season four begins with a speech by Samuel at the grave of his brother, where he takes the place of the priest, uses Puritan rhetoric and evokes central elements of the American Dream and its underlying ideology:

> A family is something Josef and I needed.... It offers protection from the outside world, a world that never understood or appreciated what makes us different. There are others like us out there ... each grasping for meaning in a world that won't accept them for who they are. They, like us, are blessed ... haunted by their past, and those who would harm them and keep them from their destiny. Everyone of them deserves a chance to be who they really are; ... here in this place, we offer salvation, we offer hope, we offer redemption, and, one by one, they will come to our side, to our family ... and all who have gathered will stand in unison [4:1].

Clearly, Samuel sets up an "us/them" dichotomy here, "othering" the dominant culture. This is the basis on which he can construct his family as the elect ("They, like us, are blessed"). Furthermore, those outside the family are forces that "harm them" and keep them from their (manifest) "destiny." It is only among the elect community that one can experience and be granted "salvation," "hope," and "redemption." The parallels to the Puritan situation are obvious. The community Samuel envisions generating is one that will create "unison" from difference, thus setting up the family as a miniature version of the American notion of the *melting pot*. The Carnival thus, from the very beginning, embodies fundamental ideas of U.S. ideology and functions as a re-enactment of the forging of the USA. In his final speech before the carnival is transported to Central Park, Samuel employs a similar strategy, this time around the notion of the *city upon a hill*. Samuel states, "For too many years we've been shamed into believing we're second-class citizens when the truth is we're king of the hill! They should aspire to be like us, not the other way around" (4:19). This sentiment links the overall story arc with the decision Claire makes at the very end of the fourth series, namely to take the irrevocable step towards creating a new society by revealing her powers. Claire fulfills the promise that has been corrupted in Samuel. Like Samuel and the carnival, which react against the oppressive and coercive forces of the dominant ideology by reinventing its fundamental principles which are perceived to have been somehow stained, Claire also reacts from such a basis. The show's final season thus re-enacts some of the central, intricately connected dichotomies of ideology in a manner that is expressed in the myths, values, and ideals of the USA.

Works Cited

Bercovitch, Sacvan. "The Problem of Ideology in American Literary History." *Critical Inquiry* 12 (Summer 1985): 631–653.

Cullen, Jim. *The American Dream: A Short History of an Idea That Shaped a Nation*. New York: Oxford University Press, 2003.

Foucault, Michel. *The Archaeology of Knowledge & the Discourse on Language*. New York: Pantheon Books, 1972.

_____. *Discipline and Punish: The Birth of the Prison* [1975]. Trans. Alan Sheridan. New York: Pantheon Books, 1977.

Freese, Peter. "The American Dream and the American Nightmare: General Aspects and Literary Examples." *Anglistik & Englischunterricht* 25 (1985): 7–37.
Gardiner, Michael. "Ecology and Carnival: Traces of a 'Green' Social Theory in the Writings of M. M. Bakhtin." *Theory and Society* 22, no. 6 (Dec 1993): 765–812.
Porter, Lynnette, David Lavery, and Hillary Robson. *Saving the World: A Guide to Heroes*. Toronto: ECW Press, 2007.
White, Michael, and David Epston. *Narrative Means to Therapeutic Ends*. New York: Norton, 1990.
Williams. Raymond. "Literature in Society." *Contemporary Approaches to English Studies*, edited by Hilda Schiff. 24–37. London: Heinemann Educational Books, 1977.

Heroes' Internationalism: Toward a Cosmopolitical Ethics in Mainstream American Television

Kenneth Chan

> "You can never change the past. It's bad. Always. Everything is connected!" — Hiro Nakamura
>
> "We're all connected." — Samuel Sullivan

The NBC series *Heroes* is engaging television, especially in an era of globalization and transnational capitalism. While one can attribute its international success to the innovative use of unusual narrative techniques and, at times, outstanding special effects, a key reason why both American and global audiences are able to identify with the show lies in its representation of a form of cosmopolitism, where the ethics and politics of human relationships and actions are demonstrated to exert a profound effect on others across the globe. This notion that we are all connected is a central and crucial theme in the series, as the dialogue lines above from the characters Hiro Nakamura (Masi Oka) and Samuel Sullivan (Robert Knepper) illustrate. The fact that these two antagonistic characters are seemingly articulating the same philosophical position also suggests that any envisioning of an interconnected world on the basis of humanity's commonality must entangle itself in and confront the messiness of human differences and conflicts. For what constitutes the extent of our connectivity, and hence responsibility, to our fellow human beings that allows us to transcend and transgress the boundaries of our parochial loyalties to culture and nation? In addressing this difficult question that has plagued theoreticians of cosmopolitanism, Bruce Robbins reorients the concept for us in a critically productive fashion:

> Cosmopolitanism offers something other than a gallery of virtuous, eligible identities. It points instead to a domain of contested politics.... Thinking of cosmopol-

itics not as universal reason in disguise, but as one on a series of scales, as an area both within and beyond the nation (and yet falling short of "humanity") that is inhabited by a variety of cosmopolitanisms, we will not perhaps be tempted to offer the final word on the dilemmas above.... Our elaboration of the term *cosmopolitics* represents one effort to describe, from within multiculturalism, a name for the genuine striving toward common norms and mutual translatability that is also part of multiculturalism [12–13].

It is useful, therefore, to read *Heroes* as not just simply offering a representational internationalism with its gesture toward global diversity, but also to explicate from its narrative and discourses the articulation of a *cosmopolitical* ethics that one is hard pressed to find elsewhere in mainstream American television.

It is also critical to contextualize the television series within the cultural and political environment that has enabled its production. *Heroes* is possible in a post–September 11 era, where a progressive politics in the United States has been mobilized to retool liberal humanism and multiculturalism, often in the form of a critical cosmopolitanism, as a means to challenge the resurgent xenophobic racism and globalized violence, conducted in the name of patriotism and nationalism. *Heroes*, through its pop cultural mediation, enters dialectically into the conversations that many critics and theorists have started, particularly in response to the acts of military intervention in Iraq and to the grotesque imagery of torture emerging out of Abu Ghraib and Guantanamo Bay, again conducted in the name of protecting America from the terrorism that 9/11 so horrifically amplified and epitomized. Before I examine in detail some of the narrative and discursive elements within *Heroes*, emphasizing particularly the ones relating to Hiro Nakamura, I want to summarize briefly a few key arguments marshaled by a number of important theorists and philosophers in the field of cultural studies to delineate the notion of human feeling and empathy as a significant critical force field within cosmopolitanism, into which one can then hermeneutically situate *Heroes* as a pop cultural participant in this dialogue.

The Cosmopolitics of Feeling, Connection, and Accountability

Much of the recent critical work by theorists such as Jacques Derrida, Judith Butler, Kwame Anthony Appiah, Paul Gilroy, and Slavoj Žižek challenges the dangerously myopic turn to the simplistic "patriotic" call of us-versus-them, as exemplified in George W. Bush's Iraq War response to the national and global trauma of 9/11. Labeled by reactionary forces and some in the media as "a clash of civilizations" (Simpson 6), this discursive logic relies on the production of a cultural alterity, "the existence of an implacably different culture that does not march to the same beat as ours, one that is messianic, vengeful, unenlightened, premodern, other: the culture of terror" (Simpson 6). David Simpson's critique of this logic echoes Kwame Anthony Appiah's concern about the historical neatness of this "picture of a world in which conflicts arise, ultimately, from conflicts between values," which Appiah categorically judges as flat-out "wrong" (xx). What is problematic about the cultural divide that this history produces is that it truncates any possibility of discussion, empathy, and connection; or, as Appiah puts it, "the foreignness of foreigners, the strangeness of strangers: these things are real enough. It's just that we've been encouraged, not least by well-meaning intellectuals, to exaggerate their significance by an order of magnitude.... [C]onversations across boundaries ... are ... inevitable" (xxi). The ethical and material implications of global interconnection, beyond the motivations of transnational capitalism, demand a closer examination of personal and national accountability. Without these conversations to cut through this supposed cultural and historical divide, there is no progression toward a self-critical sense of accountability and responsibility.

The binary opposition of this us-versus-them historicity needs to be complemented by alternative histories of troubling interconnectivities and complicities. Renowned gender and cultural theorist Judith Butler fleshes out this mode of historicity in painfully direct terms in her book *Precarious Life* (2004) by questioning America's historical role in creating the global political climate that enabled 9/11 to occur. This historical rerouting accomplished by Butler not only ennobles national self-critique as an underrated qualification for patriotism par excellence, but also re-couples critical nationalism and cosmopolitanism as, ultimately, intersecting projects of human relations and interdependency; lessons against the isolationism and exceptionalism that America has struggled with throughout its history as a nation. What is of particular significance in Butler's critical maneuver is her appeal to the intimate realm of the emotive, an appeal to the personal sense of connection we have to our fellow human beings inhabiting this earth. She argues that when we enact violence against one another, we simply expose how "we all live with this particular vulnerability, a vulnerability to the other that is part of bodily life, a vulnerability to a sudden address from elsewhere that we cannot pre-empt" (29). This invocation of human vulnerability, while democratizing our perceptions of human life, guards us against lapses into a nominal universalism that masks Western hegemonic and imperialist conceptions of the world. To be cognizant of our own human frailty should strengthen our resolve and ability to identify and empathize with human suffering, while consistently reexamining personal responsibility and accountability that register in real political and material ways through global interconnectivity.

In this respect, I am also particularly taken by postcolonial and race studies scholar Paul Gilroy's argument that anti-racist critique is still a necessity because "this racial order or nomos cannot be undone by fiat, by charity, or by goodwill and must enter comprehensively into the terms of political culture. It is only then, in the face of a whole, complex, planetary history of suffering, that the luxury and the risk of casual talk about humanity can be sanctioned" (36). Gilroy proceeds to build this political logic into what he terms as a "'demotic' cosmopolitanism"; where, in "articulating cosmopolitan hope upward from below," it "finds civic and ethical value in the process of exposure to otherness" and "glories in the ordinary virtues and ironies — listening, looking, discretion, friendship — that can be cultivated when mundane encounters with difference become rewarding" (67). One could conceptualize this demotic cosmopolitanism as one among Bruce Robbins' "variety of cosmopolitanisms," which negotiates the "domain of contested politics." The spirit of this cosmopolitanism permeates *Heroes*, allowing it to circumvent narrative conformity to Hollywood disaster and superhero films that constitute the series' genre lineage.

Heroes: Supercharging Interconnectivity

It seems paradoxical that the notion of intimate human connections is the central theme for a television series that ostensibly belongs to an action genre reliant on spectacle. One would presume that the spectacularity inherent in the kind of superhero narratives that *Heroes* frequently references would eclipse or drown out the moments of human vulnerability and emotional sociality. One could account for *Heroes*' success in negotiating this problem through its engagement with a variety of genres — superhero action, disaster/apocalypse, horror/slasher, science fiction, satire/parody, teen flick, family melodrama, romance — which means that it intertwines special effects seldom seen on television with soap opera–style plot twists and surprise endings. Because it is television, *Heroes*' scriptwriters have the luxury of time to draw out the complex character relations and plot intricacies that help signify global human interconnectivity in ways that a two-hour superhero film format cannot. Another way of accounting for this paradoxical combination of spectacle and intimacy is to view the personal level of global human connection as not so much diminished but enabled by the spectacularity of the character's superhero abilities. Nathan Petrelli (Adrian Pasdar) zips around the world like Superman, Claire Bennet (Hayden Panettiere) acquires an acute sense of human frailty in coming to terms with her regenerative powers, Daniel Linderman (Malcolm McDowell) can heal despite his misguided role in the Company, Molly Walker (Adair Tishler) identifies locations of individuals like a global tracking device, Matt Parkman (Greg Grunberg) reads minds and controls thoughts, and, of course, Hiro Nakamura travels through space and time. All these supernatural powers materially and psychically elevate Marshall McLuhan's conception of the global village to a whole new level, hyperbolically heightening human connections (with all its attendant risks, dangers, and benefits, as illustrated by the series' narrative convolutions). One could say that *Heroes* as a series, like Hiro Nakamura, bends time and space to construct an intersection between the global vastness of humanity and a sense of our intimate identification and interdependency.

Before exploring Hiro Nakamura as a figuration of this global intimacy, it is essential to locate *Heroes* within its post–9/11 cultural milieu. While it belongs to the superhero genre, *Heroes* offers disaster and apocalyptic scenarios that Hollywood has always had a penchant for. From disaster films of the 1970s to contemporary films such as *Independence Day* (1996), *Twister* (1996), *Dante's Peak* (1997), *Godzilla* (1998), *Armageddon* (1998), and *Deep Impact* (1998), Hollywood has created a fantastical version of this imaginary that in a frighteningly uncanny manner presents us with the visual precedence in which to situate the terrifying image of the falling Twin Towers. This "strangeness looked familiar," observes David Simpson, "as an image on the television or movie screen ... like part of a pattern developing through slow time, and thus very much a part of our inherited culture." It "looked like something we had seen before in both fact and fiction" (6). In a show of respect for the 9/11 victims and their families, "Hollywood momentarily abandoned the hyperviolent spectacles that dominated mainstream late 1990s cinema"; but "soon Hollywood was back to work on a series of highly successful 'crash and burn' movies" (Dixon 3), thus returning to its old ways of commodifying the apocalypse for primarily commercial reasons: *The Day after Tomorrow* (2004), *Poseidon* (2006), *Cloverfield* (2008), *2012* (2009), *Skyline* (2010), and *Battle: Los Angeles* (2011). My goal here is not to point an accusatory finger at Hollywood, which would be too simplistic a critical gesture. Rather, what I am suggesting is that there is a cinematic range in representing terror and trauma that *Heroes*, despite being a television show, partakes of. This television and filmic overlap is significant, considering how series like ABC's hit show *Lost* (2004–2010) and Fox's more politically conservative anti-terrorism drama *24* (2001–2010) deploy similar thematic strains. But what is fascinating about

Heroes is the distinct way it attempts (at times imperfectly) to eschew essentialist conceptions of the world and politically reactionary articulations of gendered, sexual, racial, cultural, and national identities. While I admit to a progressive political bias in deriving pleasure from *Heroes*' desire to "put a message of hope and global consciousness out into the world" (Kring), it is heartening to see the series subject its own political dogma to self-reflexive critique, thus engendering complex and conflicted narrative moments that refuse reductive idealizations of its political utopian worldview. Slavoj Žižek describes this "collective of freak outcasts in the TV series *Heroes*" as "signs of an emerging emancipatory subjectivity, isolating the germs of a communist culture in all its diverse forms, including in literary and other utopias" (xii). It is in this critical spirit that I cast *Heroes* as a pop cultural work of demotic cosmopolitanism in progress — with all its failings, successes, complicities, and interventions.

Hiro Nakamura: Internationalism Personified

Acknowledging the critical and political imperfections of *Heroes* in its representation of cosmopolitanism is an important step toward appreciating the contested cultural politics of global human interdependency. The worldwide scale of the series' narrative ambitions requires an internationalism — having characters and settings that go beyond American shores — which, one could conceivably argue, relies on a multicultural tokenism, with the inclusion of both major and minor characters from Japan (Hiro and Ando), India (Mohinder Suresh), Haiti (Rene, who is mostly referred to rather mysteriously as "the Haitian"), Honduras (Maya and Alejandro), Ireland (Caitlin), and an unknown African Country (*Heroes* Wiki identifies Usutu's country of origin as Botswana, though it is unconfirmed in the show itself) to shore up the series' American characters and the otherwise geopolitical centrality of the United States. This internationalism, of course, also plays a functional role in establishing worldwide audience appeal through its multinational signification, strategically encompassing various sectors of the globe; an important reminder that the television series is, after all, a global capitalist media commodity despite its progressive political leanings.

The pleasure that East Asian and Asian American viewers derive from Hiro Nakamura, Ando Masahashi (James Kyson-Lee), and Kaito Nakamura (George Takei) is that these characters occupy such a pivotal place within a predominantly Anglo-American ensemble cast: Hiro has the all-important mission to "save the cheerleader, save the world"; Hiro's father Kaito Nakamura plays a crucial role in the Company; and both Hiro and Ando have survived all four seasons when even major characters are killed off so suddenly and surprisingly. But, on the other hand, one cannot help but feel ambivalent or frustrated when the characters are selected to carry the requisite comic relief in an otherwise consistently high-tensioned drama. Hiro's signature Japanese exclamation "Yatta!" or "I did it," while humorously charming and infectious, is also evocative of an idealism that borders on a childlike nature or, at times, even a naive political infantilism. Particularly illustrative is the sequence in season three where Arthur Petrelli (Robert Forster) attacks Hiro and scrambles his brain, thus turning our intrepid hero mentally into his 10-year-old self, a scenario that allows actor Masi Oka to play up the dorky jokester persona even more in the Japanese bowling alley sequence. The hipper Ando is similarly not immune to such reductive caricature: again in season three, as Hiro and Ando rescue Matt Parkman's son from being captured by the Department of Homeland Security agents, the dynamic duo soon realizes that "baby Matt Parkman" has the special power to drain energy from the car they are escaping in, especially when he is unhappy with his circumstances. The only way they can keep the baby entertained is for Ando to contort his face into a clownish freeze. My criticism above might be construed as a form of racial oversensitivity if not for the fact that American cinema and television have a long history of relying on Orientalist stereotypes to depict the Asian other, of which Charlie Chan is a comic instance. Eugene Franklin Wong reads the bumbling detective Chan as "symbolic of the harmless and comical cultural and racial characteristics of a people barred from American shores because of their race" (60). As characters, Ando and Hiro, in particular, comport with this racialist representational practice.

But to simply rely on these "negative" representations in order to judge the racial politics of the series would be to do a disservice to the complex cultural politics that *Heroes* embraces and negotiates. For example, in the aforementioned sequence where Hiro and Ando are on their mission to return Matt Parkman's baby son, the duo attempt to solicit roadside assistance from a passing semi-trailer truck driven by a Japanese-looking trucker (Ken Choi):

ANDO (in Japanese): You are Japanese?
TRUCKER: Whoa, don't go getting all foreign on me. Y'all from the mothership, huh? Uh, *hablo* a little *ingleso*?
HIRO: *Sí*. I am Hiro, this is Ando, and this is Baby Matt Parkman.
TRUCKER: Well, climb aboard, *amigos*. Name's Sam Douglas from Lubbock, Texas ["Turn and Face the Strange," 3:22].

The trucker's ethnicity here mattered little to the progression of the plot, so its presence is politically strategic in disrupting the "us (white America) versus them (Asia)" discursive risk that Hiro and Ando's characterizations might suggest. Sam Douglas from Lubbock, Texas, is as American as they come, despite what his ethnicized mien might suggest to the more racially homogenized parts of the United States; thereby problematizing what Rey Chow has identified as the "visual stereotype—*the-other-as-face*—that stigmatizes another culture as at once corporeally and linguistically intractable" (64–65). This contemporary mode of ethnic intervention has made its necessary presence in American media representations. It is, therefore, significant that *Heroes* contributes to this interventional mode to counteract the racial stereotypes that Asian characters suffer in American television and film.

While the critical project of unpacking ethnic representation is a worthy one, I am cognizant of the dangers of judging such imagery based on the criterion of a simplistic good/bad binary opposition. These images deserve to be further located within the intricate discourses of narrative structuring and the series' progressive cultural politics. Hence, for the rest of this chapter, I would like to reclaim Hiro as a complex character in light of his fraught and conflicted negotiations with familial relations, cultural history, and interpersonal connections, all of which present themselves as symbolic and material gestures toward a critical cosmopolitical ethics. Together with the various other character developments and narrative threads, Hiro's struggles enrich *Heroes*' public cosmopolitanism with the personalized striations of human interconnectivity and interdependence.

Abiding by stereotypical conceptions of authentic Japanese culture as being always traditional, Hiro Nakamura is obsessed with destiny as it manifests itself through Japanese history and his personal desire to be a hero: "Every hero must learn his purpose. Then he'll be tested and called to greatness," Hiro proclaims to Ando after discovering his ability to stop time at the beginning of season one ("Genesis," 1:1). This belief in a destiny greater than himself keeps pointing him to symbols of cultural history. Of specific relevance here is the ancient sword wielded by Takezo Kensei, Hiro's historical idol. In order to "save the cheerleader, save the world," Hiro needs to restore control over his time-traveling powers, which have inexplicably disappeared after he tried unsuccessfully to rescue Charlie Andrews (Jayma Mays), the love of his life, from a gruesome fate at the hands of the ultra-violent Sylar (Zachary Quinto) and, later, "from an aneurysm" ("Six Months Ago," 1:10). He believes acquiring the sword will allow him to regain those powers. The cultural fetishism of this *objet d'art* is clear: "The sword will give me ... the control over my power I need. It's my sacred object. With it my powers will return and I can fulfill my destiny" ("Godsend," 1:12). His powers do return indeed, but in a partial fashion, therefore buying him enough time to steal the sword from the museum. But as he and Ando soon discover, the purloined sword turns out to be a replica, the original of which resides safely in Linderman's control. The clichéd lesson that Hiro is supposed to learn here is that the power he seeks lies within himself and not in some iconic object, a lesson that only his father Kaito can teach him. As Hiro laments of how all is lost because Sylar has broken the sword, Kaito reminds him that "the sword is not important. Your journey is what restored your power" ("Landslide," 1:22). Hiro's humanity is where his power lies and that this potential will help him transcend the parochialism and tribalism of culture and nationality—Hiro's desire to be a hero and to save the world is an ethical cosmopolitanism that transcends the barriers of cultural and national differences in its deep emotive concern for humankind.

This lesson that Hiro only partially learns at this point is further built upon at the beginning of season two ("Four Months Later...," 2:1), where Hiro, by the sheer force of his obsession with Takezo Kensei (David Anders), unconsciously catapults himself to the year 1671, "outside Kyoto, Japan." The entire subplot concerning Hiro's time travel may feel like an unnecessary diversion to fill up episodes. However, I prefer to argue for its iterative function in deconstructing the oppressive effects of cultural mythology's disciplinary mechanisms. Because Takezo Kensei is his "hero"—"I'm your biggest fan. I know all about you, Takezo Kensei. I know all the stories about you!"—Hiro feels the need to "restore," as he sees it, the correctness of history by trying to turn the roguish thug into a champion of the masses, who "does not fight for money" but "fights for honor" ("Four Months Later..."). To further deepen the irony of this cultural mythmaking, the series' writers playfully borrow a page from Edward Zwick's *The Last Samurai* (2003), but replace Tom Cruise's predictably heroic turn with that of David Anders' anti-heroic fumbling. The fact that Takezo Kensei turns out to be British satirically corrupts and pollutes the cultural waters that purists hold dear. What is productive in this plot detail, from a cultural studies standpoint, is that it offers a popular media representation of the messy entangling lines that are cultural lineage and continuity. It reinforces the notion that culture is more hybridized and intermingled than we wish to admit. Embracing the historicity of this cultural logic may just be the antidote, however idealistic this might seem, to the boundary-drawing violence we continually witness throughout world history. The "clash of civilizations" would make less sense when one appreciates the singular cultural source that originates Islam, Judaism, and Christianity. Or how the realization of racial purity as a racist myth might have prevented the horror that is the Holocaust. Of course, as much as this is naïve liberal wishful thinking, I share this hope with *Heroes* in impressing this notion of shared human destiny and dependence, believing that any failed accountability to one another on a planetary scale could have dire political consequences for the future, as Hiro's ensuing adventures after his journey to seventeenth-century Japan soon demonstrate. Despite being blown to smithereens, Takezo Kensei returns to the present to haunt Hiro in the form of Adam Monroe, who corrals the members of the Company, kills Kaito Nakamura, and unwittingly revives Arthur Petrelli so that the latter can resume his evil plans through the Pinehearst Company to "save the world" at all costs. Hiro's actions may have reified the mythic heroism of Takezo Kensei, but they have also spawned, through the "butterfly effect," dangerous consequences outside his control.

I close my analysis by returning to the notion of vulnerability, which ultimately constitutes Hiro's redemption. In season four, Hiro learns that his time travel is taking a toll on his body and he is dying from a brain tumor. Convinced that he needs to make amends, he goes off on a mission to change bits of history for the people he loves, a mission initiated by the rhetorical trap Samuel Sullivan has laid for him:

SAMUEL: But I bet there are some butterflies that you could change. I mean, why not make this trip worthwhile?
HIRO: No. You can never change the past. It's bad. Always. Everything is connected!
SAMUEL: Not everything. Sometimes, if you wanna change one thing, that's all you do. Change one thing. You have a rare gift, Hiro, to right the wrongs of your life ["Orientation" 4:1].

Not only does Samuel contradict his own line of thinking when he tells Emma Coolidge (Deanne Bray) that "we're all connected" in order to lure her to the carnival ("Upon This Rock," 4:13), he also gives Hiro the added push, literally, to set into motion a chain of events that will affect the lives of many around the character. This chain of events accentuates the now recurring motif that our lives are all interconnected and that our actions do in fact matter. But what eventually saves Hiro is his ability to empathize, to feel, as Judith Butler points out, the "vulnerability to the other that is part of bodily life" (29). Driven by his love for Charlie, Hiro goes to great lengths to change the course of history, thus giving her a second chance to live, but not in the way that he initially intended. Samuel traps Charlie in a specific moment in time and space in order to blackmail Hiro into working for him. When Hiro finally catches up with Charlie, she is in her golden years and has lived a full life: "But, Hiro, I already had a life. I had a wonderful life. Sixty-five years is a long time.... After the war, I married a wonderful man. We had four children. I now have seven beautiful grandchildren. We had a home, friends, cherished memories. A life" ("Brave New World," 4:19). In an incredibly touching moment, Hiro witnesses from the hospital room window Charlie's family gathering around her. He finally understands that he cannot change the course of history for his own selfish reasons of wanting Charlie by his side. He knows he has to let her go. The life that Charlie has had is both vulnerable yet beautiful, and he cannot take that away from her. He learns this lesson in a dream which he has while on an operating table: in what I consider to be the most tender moment in the series for Hiro, the camera gaze offers viewers an extended close-up, capturing him in a state of utter vulnerability, as he confesses to his mother Ishi (Tamlyn Tomita) his sense of frailty and weakness in succumbing to the tumor: "I thought I could fight it, that I could beat science ... but I can't" ("Pass/Fail," 4:16). Human vulnerability has transformed him and made him conscious of the responsibility he has to others in the most selfless of ways.

In the same dream sequence when he is undergoing the operation, Hiro is put on trial and takes the witness stand to justify his own actions: "Yes, I used poor judgment, but despite the sometimes disastrous effects, it was to make the world a better place ... for family. And friendship. And love" ("Pass/Fail"). His testimony encapsulates perfectly the thematic thrust of the series: that the ethical implications of our best intentions to help and save the world around us deserve the deepest of critical reflection; for even our best hopes for humankind can sometimes lead us to the worst of actions. Hiro had the best of intentions in his desire to be a superhero to save the world, but the global grandeur of his redemptive plan blinds him to the vulnerability of life, the inextricable connectedness of humanity, and, finally, the need for accountability to one another. The flawed fictional world of *Heroes*, especially through the trial and tribulations of the character Hiro, has indeed much to teach us of how to live with feeling and hope in our real but equally flawed world, which has unfortunately been habituated to war, terror, and spiraling hopelessness for far too long now.

WORKS CITED

Appiah, Kwame Anthony. *Cosmopolitanism: Ethics in a World of Strangers*. New York: Norton, 2006.
Butler, Judith. *Precarious Life: The Powers of Mourning and Violence*. London: Verso, 2004.
Chow, Rey. *The Protestant Ethnic & the Spirit of Capitalism*. New York: Columbia University Press, 2002.
Dixon, Wheeler Winston. "Introduction: Something Lost — Film after 9/11." *Film and Television after 9/11*, edited by Wheeler Winston Dixon. 1–28. Carbondale: Southern Illinois University Press.
Dowd, Maureen. "Clash of Civilizations." *The New York Times*. 13 May 2004, http://www.nytimes.com/2004/05/13/opinion/clashofcivilizations.html?pagewanted=all (accessed 20 Dec 2010).

Gilroy, Paul. *Postcolonial Melancholia*. New York: Columbia University Press, 2005.
Huntington, Samuel P. *The Clash of Civilizations and the Remaking of World Order*. New York: Touchstone, 1996.
Kring, Tim. "Interview." *Heroes Season Four*. USA: Universal Pictures, 2010.
Robbins, Bruce. "Introduction Part I: Actually Existing Cosmopolitanism." *Cosmopolitics: Thinking and Feeling beyond the Nation*, edited by Pheng Cheah and Bruce Robbins. 1–19. Minneapolis: University of Minnesota P, 1998.
Roberts, Soraya. "NBC's 'Heroes' Cancelled After Four Seasons and 'Law & Order: Los Angeles' Is Announced." *Daily News*. 16 May 2010, http://www.nydailynews.com/entertainment/tv/2010/05/16/20100516_nbcs_heroes_cancelled_after_four_seasons_on_the_heels_of_law__order_cancellation.html (accessed 20 Dec 2010).
Said, Edward W. "The Clash of Ignorance." *The Nation*. 4 Oct 2001, http://www.thenation.com/article/clash-ignorance?page=full (accessed 20 Dec 2010).
Simpson, David. *9/11: The Culture of Commemoration*. Chicago: The University of Chicago Press, 2006.
Wong, Eugene Franklin. "The Early Years: Asians in the American Films Prior to World War II." *Screening Asian Americans*, edited by Peter X. Feng. 53–70. New Brunswick: Rutgers University Press, 2002.
Žižek, Slavoj. *Living in the End Times*. London: Verso, 2010.

"This Power, It's Bigger Than Me": Time Travel as Narrative Device and Catalyst for Character Exposition

Kevin Lee Robinson

Heroes' utilization of time travel is rather unusual in the realm of fantasy television. The concept of time travel and indeed time itself is an intrinsic part of the show's format. Past and future events underpin character motivation and development and the fluidity and fatalistic nature of time are consistently utilized throughout the show. To appreciate the specific differences in the utilization of time travel within *Heroes*, it is worth framing the show in the wider canon of fantastic fiction presentations on television.

Television narratives and time travel commonly maintain a rather comfortable status quo and the vast majority of prime time–based dramatic presentations of fantastic television tend to adopt a number of familiar formats. This repeat use of familiar narratives regarding time travel is presumably more acceptable to the sensibilities of the mainstream viewer. With some notable exceptions, such as cult favorite *Lost* (2004–2010), time travel (and its close cousin inter-dimensional travel) is often relegated to a function of the narrative construction. The idea of time traveling becomes a narrative device through which the writers frame a particular episodic plot line. As a result of this common utilization, time travel often functions as a catalyst for story construction, and the narratives which do utilize it tend to play out in highly specific, episodic ways. For example, the *Star Trek* franchise adopts the time/dimensional displacement device on several occasions, but this is usually within enclosed episodes that do not have any real impact on long-term story arcs or character development.

In many ways it could be considered that time travel is utilized in the narrative of primetime shows such as *Stargate* as an extension of the marvelous or fantastic; as a spectacle which the audience are encouraged to gaze in wonder at before moving on to focus on the episode's real story. Once the time event is established and the characters are chronologically displaced, the resulting story tends to unfold exclusively within the milieu created. To return to *Star Trek: The Next Generation* as an example, in the episodes "Times Arrow," parts 1 and 2 (5:26, 6:1), the discovery of Data's head beneath San Francisco precipitates a plot involving aliens and Mark Twain; however, the process of time travel is reduced to a narrative construct which allows the plot to develop and resolve. As is common in time-travel scenarios on television, the characters travel through time in this episode to facilitate the telling of a story set in a period that also grants the writers access to a well-known historical figure. In this case, Mark Twain is pulled through time to remind the audience of the spectacle of the Star Trek world.

A more esoteric approach often underpins the time-travel trope when screenwriters are working towards a cinematic experience. A good example of this is *La Jetée* (1962) and its remake, *12 Monkeys* (1995) where the narrative develops around the growing awareness by the central character of his own circular existence in the flow of time. This narrative strand is developed via a series of potentially confusing, disparate scenes where the chronological positioning of the protagonist is somewhat fluid. In this instance, the complexity of the plot and the presentation of the fantastic focus the narrative on the developing relationship between the main characters. In both films, the time displaced central character finds the only reliable experience to be the repeated meeting with the woman of his childhood dream. As the relationship between the two develops, the time traveling seems to take on a directed purpose, as if it is specifically being bent to the will of the two lovers, leading inevitably to the younger version of the main character being a witness to his own death. A complex narrative of this kind requires a great deal of focus on plot from the viewer and is therefore more viable in a cinema environment. The episodic nature of television does not lend itself easily to complex plots that challenge the mainstream expectation.

This is not to say that that television never ventures out of the format-based show. However, even the most superficial consideration of the narrative function of time travel on television reveals a conservative trend in its utilization and what could be considered a bookend approach in that it starts and ends episodes. As seen in the earlier example from *Star Trek*, time travel is commonly used as the catalyst that starts the events of the episode and the return to original narrative time epilogues the narrative.

Television has never shied away from using chronological displacement and there are many examples of the use of time travel as a narrative device. There is a clear preference towards two distinct narrative approaches to time displacement in terms of the protagonist: the accidental tourist and the purposeful time traveler. The accidental tourist is adrift in time. The protagonist wanders through time (or in some instances multiple dimensions) lost and searching for the route home or some other motivational objective. The accidental tourist offers the writer less opportunity of volition of purpose in the protagonist, so he often takes a supporting companion position. Once in this role, the accidental time traveler often acts as a conscience or sounding board for the traveler. The narrative role played by Ando Masahashi (James Kyson-Lee) or the companions in *Doctor Who* provide a good example of this in action. In this respect *Heroes* takes a rather tried and tested approach to the use of time travel as both Peter Petrelli (Milo Ventimiglia) and Hiro Nakamura (Masi Oka) are frequently accompanied by companions who fulfill this well-established role.

In contrast to the accidental tourist, the purposeful traveler takes an active part in their time traveling usually by utilizing a machine or similar artifact as a method of transport. Again *Doctor Who* is a good benchmark, as the writers have utilized this narrative construct for more years than any other science fiction show. While the writers of *Doctor Who* will often refer to the doctor's lack of precision when piloting the *Tardis*, this is often for comedic effect and the machine is still intentionally guided down the time corridors in a controlled manner. Clearly, then, we cannot consider any character who has control of his time traveling in the same narrative context as one who bounces around at the mercy of his journey like the last chronologically displaced peanut in the bag of time.

The guided method of time travel also usually relies on the almost magical skills of a patriarchal figure. Per Schelde discusses this idea rather well in his book *Androids, Humanoids and Other Folklore Monsters: Science and Soul in Science Fiction Films* (1993), where he compares the traditional presentation of the shaman figure within his magical cave with the filmic presentation of the scientist character. Schelde points out that the use of technological paraphernalia creates a sense of the scientist being capable of a sort of scientific magic as the presentation of the shaman and his magical accoutrements suggests supernatural abilities (Schelde 40). In terms of developing the narrative, the scientist allows the writer to insert the protagonists into a scenario with an accentuated volition of purpose unavailable to the accidental tourist.

While this rather glib traveler/accidental tourist narrative model has some merit, as evidenced by the easily observable, repeated utilization of the two character archetypes, there is a possible misnomer at work here. In truth, both these time traveler archetypes could be described more accurately as "time passengers," as the movement through time is facilitated by a time-travel device.

In the context of the story arc, the utilization of a device or time ship as a conduit for the time travel clearly has an impact on the way the characters are presented. The character leading the narrative's use of time travel will usually do so via the superior knowledge of the scientist. As the creator or operator of the time machine, the scientist is invested with a position of superiority due to the scientific knowledge they possess. While this superiority may not extend to control over the group of passengers, it certainly creates a situation where the non-scientist characters will usually adopt the role of the accidental tourist due to their lack of understanding. The device itself acts as not only a catalyst of a cause-and-effect narrative but, via an association with the higher status afforded the scientist figure, it develops a corresponding importance as an arena in which the companion characters can ask expository questions of the pilot. The time passengers utilize the narrative potential of the time-travel device by allowing it to catapult them into extreme and fantastic situations and their reliance on it is one of vehicular transport and narrative setting.

This "passenger" model, while admittedly limited in scope, would seem to offer a reasonable perspective on the use of time travel as a narrative construct. The machine and the passengers are utilized as cause for the narrative effect and the machine itself often becomes an intrinsic part of the narrative construction.

This passenger model is rather more difficult to apply to the presentation of time travel in *Heroes* and, in particular, to the characters of Peter Petrelli and Hiro Nakamura. The superpower that underpins their time traveling clearly negates the time-passenger aspect for their characters. Hiro and Peter quickly develop a control over their ability that gives them a far more intimate relationship with time. The lack of a device or machine changes both the method of time travel and the characters' relationships with the notion of time travel. For Peter and Hiro there is no process to their displacement. There are no engines to start and no waiting for a ship to materialize because the transfer is instantaneous. The lack of a device means that the time-travel process for Peter and Hiro is a matter of personal will and therefore it becomes more intimate and spontaneous in its utilization.

This personal intimacy with the concept of time travel offers the writers of the show a wealth of options when creating appropriate story lines and narrative structures for Peter Petrelli, Hiro Nakamura, and their associated companions and antagonists. The notion of time is ever present throughout the *Heroes*' story arcs. The characters are intimately linked to the passage of time and historical events are frequently used as story points. In many respects, the utilization of time as a concept within the show demonstrates a nodal structure, in that a past event is often used to explore current character exposition and motivation (see Genette for a good discussion of nodal narratives). For example, the events at Coyote Sands in the narrative past of 1961 are the motivational force behind not only the actions of Angela Petrelli (Cristine Rose) but also the creation of Primatech and the Company. Although the massacre at Coyote Sands is exposed through flashbacks (3:23) and not time travel, the final scenes depicting the present-day characters plotting the formation of a new company reflect the past events. Again, the writers use the concept of time as an underpinning narrative theme. Even in an episode that does not feature time travel, the passage of time is an intrinsic part of the narrative. As characters, Peter and Hiro are repeatedly immersed in this use of time as a narrative concept and the trope of malleable time informs much of their story arcs. In the case of both characters, a large part of their journey is an exploration of the narrative possibilities of time travel.

The "grandfather paradox" scenario is integral to Peter and Hiro's time travel. The grandfather paradox asks, "What would happen if you went back in time and killed your own grandfather?" This is of course an expression of the impossible, as killing your grandfather would mean you did not exist to kill him, in which case you would still exist and be able to travel back in time to kill him, in which case you would not exist; and so on, forming a circular argument. In the case of *Heroes*, this is a paradox which is particularly evident in season three, where Peter is trying to prevent the release of the abilities catalyst into the general populace. Despite his repeated efforts and his superior knowledge, he seems unable to affect the outcome of his own future (or past, as seen from his perspective) and the destruction of the world seems assured. To resolve this problem, the Peter from the future passes the torch of responsibility to Peter from the present, offering the reasoning that he will be better able to stop the events unfolding. This narrative construct does not bear too much inspection and crumbles quickly under the glare of the spotlight of logic. One questions how present Peter can control the flow of time better without the aid of the hindsight and research available to his future self. In the case of Peter there would seem to be some other motivation at work that overrides the more obviously appropriate character to perform this narrative function.

Heroes' other time traveler, Hiro Nakamura, interacts with time in a similar but chronologically opposite way in the second season of the show, where his ability to travel in time and space results in him becoming embroiled in the politics of ancient Japan. Rather than specifically trying to alter the future, Hiro attempts to maintain it by facilitating the creation of the legend of his childhood hero, Takezo Kensei. Hiro frequently states his admiration of the nobility of his childhood hero and when presented with the rather less admirable Adam (David Anders), Hiro attempts to fix the past and ensure the legend of Takezo Kensei. Hiro's childhood role model is of such importance to his motivation that this story line is spread over the first seven episodes of season two. Here we see the trope of the grandfather paradox emerging in the narrative and impact of the past on the present. Without the self-created myth of Takezo Kensai, Hiro would not have been driven by his strong moral code and, to all intents and purposes, would not exist as a character.

For the sake of convenience and clarity, this chapter will consider the narrative time closest to approximating the viewer's perspective of "current" time within an episode of *Heroes* as the "now" and all other chronological screen presences as being either future or past. With this fixed point of reference in place we can consider the Peter and Hiro of the "now" (the current Peter and Hiro narratively speaking) to have three character functions. In the chronology of the story arc, the writers could potentially utilize past-present Hiro and Peter, current Peter and Hiro, and future-present Hiro and Peter. If, for the sake of argument, we think of the characters' actions as intrusions into the narrative screen time, using Peter Petrelli as an example, we could describe them as the following:

- Past-present Peter: This is the Peter Petrelli who belongs to the perceived main narrative time scale as described below, and therefore probably approximating the viewer's present, when operating a historical narrative setting.
- Current Peter: This is the Peter Petrelli who operates within both his own current time and the wider perceived main timeframe within the narrative.
- Future-present Peter: This is the Peter as described above who operates in the perceived narrative chronological future.

For convenience and clarity, we will avoid a wider discussion (at this juncture) of the further available versions of historical Peter and Hiro, and future Peter and Hiro, and the multiple derivatives each of these has. These being the versions of the characters chronologically embedded into either a future or past timeframe. These potential characters are the protagonists in the narrative chronological topography of the episode but not in the chronological narrative of the now.

As an example, when Hiro travels back in time to meet himself ("Our Father," 3:12) and witness his mother's death, the two characters present are historical Hiro and past-present Hiro. The Hiro from the narrative time setting is the child who is therefore definably historical Hiro by being in the narrative past and also in his own and the specific episodic temporal narrative. Past-present Hiro is displaced from his own present and, as the actual protagonist in that particular story arc, he is therefore the focus for the "legitimate" timeline and as such is the dominant protagonist in terms of the narrative.

Having then labeled the three versions of each character, it is now a requirement to define the narrative chronology in which they can potentially operate. These can easily be defined as the narrative "future," the narrative "past," and the narrative "now" in relation to the operation of each character within the story arc. Therefore, to consider a specific perspective on this, we can look at the functions each character performs.

While in both his own and Japan's narrative past, Hiro actively shapes the future in the world he will grow up in. Hiro's actions in the past influence aspects of the version of Hiro we watch in the present. In terms of the characters' motivational cause and effect chain, Hiro and Peter work in a binary and oppositional fashion. In season two, Hiro battles to save the personality of his future self by ensuring that historical events such as the raid on Whitebeard's camp occur ("Out of Time," 2:7). In comparison in season three, future Peter desperately tries to change his past (the narrative present), erase his own future self, and with it stop the end of the world ("The Second Coming," 3:1). Should he succeed, the battle-scarred and cynical Peter of the future will change his own timeline, which, again raises the issue of the grandfather paradox.

These storylines raise interesting questions about the importance of the narrative "now" in *Heroes*. It would seem that the past is, at least partly, malleable by a present character as both future Peter and current Hiro manipulate the past to further their own ends. The narrative present gains even more relevance as the characters operating in the past and future are doing so based on motivations based in the narrative "now."

The characters' power over time in *Heroes* changes the emphasis placed on chronological manipulation as a plot device in comparison to other shows that engage with the concept of time travel. The fact that the personal motivation of the two protagonists acts as the narrative prompt for the cause-and-effect flow of the story arc means that the characters themselves are posited as more significant than the spectacle of time travel itself.

Accepting that personal motivation is paramount to the story arc, we can then couple it with the impact actions by the characters have on narrative events and measure them against the narrative importance of the result. Referring back to past-present Hiro, we can see that the dominant motivational actions take place in the narrative now and as a result past-present Hiro is embroiled in the events in ancient Japan. Hiro's desire to ensure the Takezo Kensei legend survives the machinations of Adam (David Anders) is his motivation. As a result of his time travels, there is a consistency of chronology for, presumably at least, all current and future incarnations of Hiro.

In the case of Peter, future Peter manipulates his own past and the causal flow of current Peter and therefore relatively his own past Peter. This pattern seems to create a loose hierarchy of narrative importance rooted in the chronological positioning of the event. An event happening in the character's future would seem to have less impact than an event in the narrative past and both are motivated by events in the narrative present. Past events generally appear to have narrative causal dominance over future events (which often act as a reason to visit the past only) and both these would seem to be narratively subservient in importance to current narrative events that anchor the cause-and-effect chain for the viewer. This narrative importance seems to allow the writers to use future and past with a rough hierarchy of importance. Using the previous examples from season three, it would seem that Hiro is unable and unwilling to alter the myth of his childhood hero, yet Peter from the future is able to travel back in time and alter his own past. Other examples of this hierarchy taken from another perspective can be found in the frequent use of prediction as an ability. In season one we are introduced to the paintings of Issac Mendez (Santiago Cabrera) which predict the future with remarkable accuracy until the season finale showdown in Kirby Plaza ("How to Stop an Exploding Man," 1:23) where events change the predicted holocaust. It would seem that the past and future are only "events" if the present characters allow them to exist. To put it another way, the past-present character (P) has greater narrative value than the future-present character (F) and both have less narrative value than the current character (C).

So as a general rule of thumb, a hierarchy of character's narrative dominance in *Heroes* can be expressed as

(P>F)<C

This hierarchy appears to support the suggestion that the personal nature of the protagonists' relationships with time in *Heroes* has a meaningful impact on the narrative utilization of chronological displacement in the show.

In the more common narratives the time passenger arrives in a specific location, the episode adventure plays out, and then the episode resolves. This means the motivation is often enclosed within a single episode. *Heroes*, partly due to its protagonist's more intimate relationship with time, operates differently. In the case of both Peter and Hiro, the time traveler is motivated by personal reasons in the narrative now, resulting in a conscious decision to enter a past or future period anchored to an ongoing story arc. There is a multitude of reasons for this shift in common narrative structure within *Heroes*. Not the least of these reasons is the ethos of character-driven story arcs that sets *Heroes* apart from most previous television superhero productions.

As a genre, the superhero production sits most comfortably in the wider canon of telefantasy. As discussed by Johnson (2005), there is commonly an expectation of spectacle in the narrative structure of such shows to facilitate the suspension of the viewer's socio-cultural knowledge. In effect, the use of spectacle, often via special effects, is a part of the viewer/producer contract and the creation of the fantastic, and is tied to the needs of the viewer to see the impossible in a believable, self-contained screen world. In many ways, *Heroes* is no exception to this principle and frequently fulfills its contractual obligation to the telefantasy viewer by providing visual evidence of superpowers in a spectacular way. The finale of season one and the Shanti virus–afflicted New York ("Out of Time," 2:7) both provide high spectacle as does the opening episode of season three in which we see the explosive destruction of Tokyo.

It is somewhat difficult to discuss *Heroes* in terms of genre when considering the utilization of time travel. Time travel is more commonly a trope of science fiction where the intellectual questions raised are often woven into the narrative. The superhero genre tends to lean towards powers that are visual, such as strength, flight, and teleportation. It is here that the aesthetic values and the narrative discourse underpinning *Heroes* come to the fore and this precipitates a deviation from the superhero norm.

Heroes has a focus on otherness, as do many other superhero texts. Many of the storylines in *X-Men*, possibly the clearest comparison text for *Heroes*, are analogous to the social issues faced by its teenage readers. *Heroes* consciously focuses on the affects that their "otherness" has on the ordinary lives of the central characters and explores how they react to its intrusion. There is a repeated motivational force at play throughout the production. *Heroes* frequently explores the intrusive effects the superpowers have on those that possess them and how these powers influence characters' abilities to fit in. This intrusion is usually unwanted by the protagonists and desired by their antagonists. Claire Bennet repeatedly states her wish to be normal, to dispel her otherness, but Sylar (Zachary Quinto) repeatedly seeks out otherness and dismisses the mundane as beneath him. When forced to use his shape-shifting ability to assume another character's identity after faking his own death, Sylar states that Agent Taub is "a nothing. I don't like being a nothing" ("I Am Sylar," 3:24): By the end of the opening credits of the same episode, he has brutally slaughtered and stolen the abilities of a rather ordinary-looking "special."

Heroes is, in many ways, a contradiction: it is a spectacle-based show about the mundane. The spectacular and the fantastic are often reduced to background dressing so that the show can focus on the intimate details of character development and the often familial and fraternal superhero bonding. Hiro and Ando are depicted as office drones despite Hiro's father being a powerful businessperson. Hiro does not benefit from his father's position and wealth until it is needed in later seasons as a narrative device, which allows the writers to utilize the mundane nature of his working life to highlight his character motivation and thus his use of time travel.

This application of the mundane to accentuate the otherness of the gifted characters is far from unusual in the superhero genre and it could be considered as much a part of the audience's expectation as the tropes of the secret identity and the sidekick, both of which are also utilized in *Heroes*. It is in the application of the mundane where the writers take a different approach to the presentation of characters and time travel. The presence of time travel in the story arc intrudes into the superhero expectation somewhat by borrowing a science-fiction motif. Furthermore, the use of time travel is then woven into the presentation of the mundane and takes on a role in the character development and exposition. Under the control of an individual, as is the case with Peter or Hiro, time travel moves from the mechanical and scientific and into the realm of the emotional and motivational. As a result, time travel potentially becomes the personal plaything of ordinary people, who are ill equipped to deal with the power.

The use of time travel on a personal level opens up a moral question for the writers. When considered in context of the other powers on display in *Heroes*, time travel has the most potential to elevate the user to a state of apotheosis. By season three, both Hiro and Peter have the power to make personal choices regarding the fate of millions. The power-to-responsibility ratio is a common theme of the superhero genre. The character of Spider-Man has become synonymous with the idea of great power requiring great responsibility. A hero with time-travel abilities should be able to function at a level of apotheosis, becoming almost god-like in his ability to control the fate of others. However, this does not happen within *Heroes*, partly because of the writers' desire to avoid the superhero cliché and to maintain the underlying theme of the mundane. In relation to these considerations, the ability to control time used in a god-like way could counteract the attractiveness of the characters as everymen:

> It's a show about characters dealing with extraordinary things happening to them. That is the central premise. So my sense is that if one can assume that dealing with their extraordinary abilities is something that these characters will always face, then their stories can bend and morph and evolve forever [Kring].

Where the other protagonists tend to strive for normality, Hiro is motivated by his love of a fantasy world of superheroes and Japanese mythology. With Hiro one can see the application of mythic structure to his actions. As a character, Hiro actively wishes to conform to the monomyth approach of

Campbell (2004) and mythic structure as proposed by Vogler (2007), and this dictates his response to his developing power. Inherently, then, there is a limitation to the potential for Hiro to develop a messianic story arc, as this would require a major shift in the worldview of the character and a re-shuffling of his seemingly innate sense of morality. Television is by nature episodic (see Ellis 148 and Strackzynski 23) and can be considered in terms of segments. The continuity of story over these episodes and individual segments is partially reliant on cohesion and consistency of characters. There is therefore a narrative expectation that Hiro will not change because of his acquired power.

For Hiro and Peter, time travel is literally a conscious choice, as their own will is required to perform the act of displacement. Time travel therefore becomes as much a matter of character exposition as it is a device to further the plot. *Heroes*, as we have discussed, is heavily reliant on character exposition and development to explore the characters' struggle with their powers. For Hiro therefore the act of time traveling is frequently motivated by his personality and his own history. He travels back in time to the era of his childhood hero. He returns to meet his mother. He specifically wants to see the machinations of his father and so forth. At no point is Hiro tempted to visit a moment of historical significance beyond his own personal investment as is common in other time-travel-based scenarios.

Time travel is a difficult narrative concept and additionally has the potential to act as a catchall *deux-ex-machina* resolution to any situation. Hiro or Peter need only move back through time and kill baby Sylar to prevent the deaths of many characters in the show but this would be contrary to the nature of both characters. When Peter does in fact try a similar "hand of god" resolution to the future destruction of the world he finds that the Sylar he meets is a caring father and not the devil he expected; as a result his plans unravel in a blaze of destruction. In "I Am Become Death" (3:4), Peter travels to the future and absorbs Sylar's power. As a result of his actions, albeit indirectly, Sylar's son Noah is killed. In grief, Sylar goes mad and destroys Costa Verde. This is the result of Peter stepping away from his usually morally upstanding position and seeking a god-like resolution to his problems. Hiro and Peter are both portrayed, throughout the show, as morally unambiguous and when Peter strays from the path, the result is catastrophic.

There is potentially a further science-fiction trope at work here in the portrayal of this god-like time-travel ability. There is a narrative expectation entrenched in the science fiction and horror genres that man must not trespass into the domain of the ineffable and the divine. For the super-villain, just the monster must destroy Dr. Frankenstein (as a suitable punishment for Frankenstein's act of creation); the misuse of time travel must result in the downfall of the user of these god-like powers. For Hiro and Peter living in the everyday world of *Heroes*, the misuse of time travel is not an option as heroic fantasy principles of the former and the strict moral code of the latter restricts the use of their power in this way.

Finally, it is worth considering the problems created by the god-like character. An unchallenged and unassailable hero is lacking in the conflict required for effective drama. As a result, a superman must have a limiting weakness to allow his enemies dramatic possibilities. For Peter and Hiro, their character motivation acts to limit their powers and impacts on the drama, acting like a self-imposed kryptonite chain. In effect, the character makeup of Peter and Hiro, the dramatic necessity of conflict, and the need for character cohesion over televised segments results in a reduction of the time travelers' ability to fully utilize their powers to their ultimate god-like potential. This in turn negates the option of the *deux-ex-machina* resolution and the ascendancy to the status of godhood. Peter is aware of the potential of the Shanti virus ("Out of Time," 2:7) but at no point is returning through time to kill an option. Hiro travels throughout his own timeline and accepts the death of his own mother ("Our Father," 3:12) and father ("Cautionary Tales," 2:9) as being for the greater good even though both events cause him a great deal of pain. The power of time travel is too much for the machinations of two ordinary people concerned primarily with familial conflict and notions of heroism. Peter and Hiro may well be true time travelers, in the sense that they require only self-motivation to displace themselves chronologically, but they travel with the burdensome companion of their own character traits and each time stop reveals a little more about them as they save the world one personal step at a time.

Works Cited

Campbell, Joseph. *The Hero with a Thousand Faces*, commemorative ed. Princeton: Princeton University Press, 2004.
Ellis, John. *Visible Fictions*. New York: Routledge, 1982.
Fiske, John, and John Hartly. *Reading Television*. London: Routledge, 1994.
Genette, Gerard. *Narrative Discourse*. Oxford: Blackwell, 1980.
Johnson, Catherine. *Telefantasy*. London: BFI, 2005.
Lindelof, Damon. "Heroic Origins: An Interview with Tim Kring." *9th Wonders*, http://www.9thwonders.com/interviews/tim.php (accessed 28 Nov 2010).
McKee, Robert. *Story: Substance, Structure, Style and the Principles of Screenwriting*. London: Methuen, 1997.
Strackzynski, J. M. *The Complete Book of Scriptwriting*. London: Titam, 1996.
Vogler, Christopher. *The Writers Journey*. Los Angeles: Michael Wiese Production, 2007.

Filmography

The following lists represent the television shows and films discussed or cited in the text.

TELEVISION

Alias. ABC, 2001–2006.
Babylon 5. PTEN, 1994–1997; TNT, 1998.
Battlestar Galactica. NBC, 1978–1979.
———. Syfy, 2004–2009.
The Big Bang Theory. CBS, 2007–present.
Bones. Fox, 2005–present.
Buffy the Vampire Slayer. WB, 1997–2001; UPN, 2001–2003.
Chuck. NBC, 2007–present.
Dark Angel. Fox, 2000–2002.
Desperate Housewives. ABC, 2004–present.
Dexter. Showtime, 2006–present.
Doctor Who. BBC, 1963–1989; 2005–present.
Dollhouse. Fox, 2009–2010.
The Dukes of Hazzard. CBS, 1979–1985.
ER. NBC, 1994–2004.
Father Knows Best. CBS, 1954–1960.
Firefly. Fox, 2002.
Fringe. Fox, 2008–present.
Harsh Realm. Fox, 1999–2000.
Heroes. NBC, 2006–2010.
Heroes Unmasked. BBC, 2007–2008.
The Invaders. ABC, 1967–1968.
Life on Mars. BBC, 2006–2007.
Lost. ABC, 2004–2010.
Mad Men. AMC, 2007–present.
Misfits. E4, 2009–present.
Mutant X. Syndicated, 2001–2004.
The Office. NBC, 2005–present.
Primeval. ITV, 2007–present.
Psych. USA Network, 2006–present.
Quantum Leap. NBC, 1989–1993.
Reaper. The CW, 2007–2009.
Saturday Night Live. NBC, 1975–present.
The Simpsons. Fox, 1989–present.
Smallville. The WB, 2001–2006; the CW, 2006–present.
Spooks. BBC, 2002–present.
Star Trek. NBC, OnTV/Showtime, 1966–1969.
Star Trek: The Next Generation. Syndicated, 1987–1994.
Stargate SG-1. Showtime, 1997–2002; Syfy, 2002–2006.
30 Rock. NBC, 2006–present.
Torchwood. BBC, 2006–present.
Total Recall 2070. 1999.
24. Fox, 2001–2010.
The X-Files. Fox, 1993–2002.

FILMS

Adventures of Captain Marvel. Dir. John English and William Witney. USA: Republic Pictures, 1941.
American Beauty. Dir. Sam Mendes. USA: Dreamworks Pictures, 1999.
Armageddon. Dir. Michael Bay. USA: Touchstone Pictures, 1998.
Batman and Robin. Dir. Joel Schumacher. USA: Warner Bros. Pictures, 1997.
Batman Begins. Dir. Christopher Nolan. USA: Warner Bros. Pictures, 2005.
Battle: Los Angeles. Dir. Jonathan Liebesman. USA: Columbia Pictures, 2011.
Buck Rogers (cinema serial). Dir. Ford Beebe, Saul A. Goodkind. USA: Universal Pictures, 1939.
Carrie. Dir. Brian De Palma. USA: United Artists, 1976.

Children of Men. Dir. Alfonso Cuarón. USA: Universal Pictures/Strike Entertainment, 2006.
Cloverfield. Dir. Matt Reeves. USA: Paramount Pictures, 2008.
Dante's Peak. Dir. Roger Donaldson. USA: Universal Pictures, 1997.
The Day After Tomorrow. Dir. Roland Emmerich. USA: Twentieth-Century–Fox, 2004.
The Day the Earth Stood Still. Dir. Robert Wise. USA: Twentieth Century–Fox, 1951.
Deep Impact. Dir. Mimi Leder. USA: Paramount Pictures/Dreamworks, 1998.
Dick Tracy. Dir. Warren Beatty. USA: Touchstone Pictures, 1990.
Fight Club. Dir. David Fincher. USA: Twentieth-Century–Fox, 1999.
Flash Gordon (cinema serial). Dir. Frederick Stephani, Ford Beebe, Robert Hill, Ray Taylor. USA: King Feature Production/Universal Pictures, 1936–1940.
The Fly. Dir. David Cronenberg. USA: Twentieth-Century–Fox, 1986.
Forbidden Planet. Dir. Fred M Wilcox. USA: MGM, 1956.
Godzilla. Dir. Roland Emmerich. USA: Tristar Pictures, 1998.
Halloween. Dir. John Carpenter. USA: Compass International Pictures, 1978.
Hulk. Dir Ang Lee. USA: Universal Pictures, 2003.
The Incredibles. Dir. Brad Bird. USA: Pixar/Walt Disney Pictures, 2004.
Independence Day. Dir. Roland Emmerich. USA: Twentieth-Century–Fox. 1996.
Le jetée. Dir. Chris Marker. 1962.
Jurassic Park. Dir. Steven Spielberg. USA: Universal Pictures. 1993.
The Last Samurai. Dir. Edward Zwick. USA: Warner Bros. Pictures, 2003.
The Matrix. Dir. Andy & Larry Wachowski. USA: Warner Bros. Pictures, 1999.
A Nightmare on Elm Street. Dir. Wes Craven. USA: New Line Pictures, 1984.
Nightmare on Elm Street (remake). Dir. Samuel Bayer. USA: New Line Cinema, 2010.
Nightmare on Elm Street 4: The Dream Master. Dir. Renny Harlin. USA: New Line Cinema, 1988.
Poseidon. Dir. Wolfgang Peterson. USA: Warner Bros. Pictures, 2006.
Psycho. Dir. Alfred Hitchcock. USA: Paramount Pictures, 1960.
Romeo + Juliet. Dir. Baz Luhrmann. USA: Twentieth-Century–Fox, 1996.
Se7en. Dir. David Fincher. USA: New Line Cinema, 1995.
Skyline. Dir. Brothers Strause. USA: Universal Pictures, 2010.
Solaris. Dir. Andrei Tarkovsky. USA: Visual Programme Systems, 1972.
Solaris (remake). Dir. Steven Soderbergh. USA: Twentieth-Century–Fox, 2002.
Spiderman. Dir. Sam Raimi. USA: Columbia Pictures. 2002.
Star Trek: The Motion Picture. Dir. Robert Wise. USA: Paramount Pictures, 1979.
Star Wars: Episode IV: A New Hope. Dir. George Lucas. USA: Twentieth-Century–Fox, 1977.
Superman Returns. Dir. Bryan Singer. USA: Warner Bros. Pictures, 2006.
12 Monkeys. Dir. Terry Gilliam. USA: Universal Pictures, 1995.
Twister. Dir. Jan De Bont. USA: Warner Bros. Pictures/Universal Pictures, 1996.
2001: A Space Odyssey. Dir. Stanley Kubrick. USA: MGM, 1968.
2012. Dir. Roland Emmerich. USA: Columbia Pictures, 2009.
Le Voyage dans la Lune. Dir. Georges Méliès. USA: Star Film, 1902.
Watchmen. Dir. Zack Snyder. USA: Warner Bros. Pictures/Paramount Pictures, 2009.
X-Men. Dir. Bryan Singer. USA: Twentieth-Century–Fox, 2000.
X-2. Dir. Bryan Singer. USA: Twentieth-Century–Fox, 2003.

About the Contributors

Kristin M. **Barton** is an assistant professor of communication at Dalton State College in Dalton, Georgia. He graduated from Florida State University in 2007 with a PhD in communication. His previous work has examined the effects of watching reality TV shows such as *Survivor* and *American Idol*. He lives with his wife Gina and their pets Mingo and Dogg.

Stan **Beeler** is professor of English at the University of Northern British Columbia, Canada. His areas of interest include film and television studies, popular culture, and comparative literature. His publications include *Reading Stargate SG-1* (I.B. Tauris, 2006), *Investigating Charmed: The Magic Power of TV* (I.B. Tauris, 2007), and *Dance Drugs and Escape: The Club Scene in Literature Film and Television Since the Late 1980s* (McFarland, 2007).

Sérgio Dias **Branco** is auxiliary professor of film studies at the University of Coimbra, Portugal, and an invited member of the film analysis group of the University of Oxford, "The Magnifying Class." He has taught film and television at the New University of Lisbon and at the University of Kent, where he was awarded a PhD in film studies. The research work on the aesthetics of film, television, and video that he develops has been presented at Yale University and the University of Glasgow, among others. His writings have been published in refereed journals such as *Refractory* and *Scope*.

Torsten **Caeners** studied English and American literature and culture as well as computational linguistics at the University of Duisburg–Essen, Germany (1998–2004). He finished his studies in October 2004 with an MA thesis on the Augustan poet Dr. William King and has been teaching at the Department of Anglophone Studies at the University of Duisburg–Essen ever since. In 2010, he was awarded his PhD for his dissertation on the application of poetry to psychotherapeutic treatment. Apart from serving as the coordinator for the BA program Cultural Studies and Business Administration ("Kulturwirt"), he spends his time watching (and thinking about) TV shows and similar cultural phenomena.

Bronwen **Calvert** is an associate lecturer with the Open University in the North of England and subject area leader in literature at the North East Centre for Lifelong Learning in Newcastle upon Tyne. She researches on aspects of embodiment in science fiction and fantasy narratives, currently with a focus on the "cult" action heroine. Recent publications include a case study of *Battlestar Galactica* in *The Cult TV Book* (I.B. Taurus, 2010) and "Cyberpunk Echoes in the Dollhouse" in the online journal *Slayage*; she has work forthcoming on *Angel* and *Supernatural*.

About the Contributors

Kenneth **Chan** is assistant professor of film studies at the University of Northern Colorado. His book *Remade in Hollywood: The Global Chinese Presence in Transnational Cinemas* was published by Hong Kong University Press in 2009. Chan's essays have also appeared in scholarly journals such as *Cinema Journal, Tulsa Studies in Women's Literature, Discourse* and *Camera Obscura*. He is also a member of the editorial board of the *Journal of Chinese Cinemas* and volunteers as the chair of the International Advisory Board of the Asian Film Archive, Singapore.

Laura **Hilton** is in the final stages of her PhD at the University of Birmingham, where she also completed her BA and MA degrees. Her doctoral research questions representations of the Gothic double in the contemporary graphic novel and focuses on the work of Neil Gaiman, Frank Miller, and Alan Moore. She founded and co-edited the first two issues of *The Birmingham Journal of Literature and Language* (*BJLL*) and has articles forthcoming in *Gothic Science Fiction, Alan Moore and the Gothic Tradition* and *Comment Rêver la Science-Fiction à Present?* She has presented her work at several national and international conferences and her wider research interests include nineteenth-, twentieth- and twenty-first-century literature, comic book and graphic novel studies, and Gothic fiction.

David **Hipple** holds a first degree in English from the University of St. Andrews, an MA in education from the Open University, and an MA in science fiction from the University of Reading. His PhD dissertation on critical approaches to British and American screen science fiction was also completed at Reading, where he now teaches an occasional honors option on science fiction film. He has published work and given conference papers on numerous science fiction films and TV series, and is currently working on a study of the BBC's *Dominick Hide* teleplays as science-fiction drama in the mainstream. Other current research interests include HP Lovecraft on screen and radio, the development and theory of role-playing games, music and sound in screen science fiction, and the intersection of narrative techniques in graphic novels and screen drama.

Lorna **Jowett** is a senior lecturer in film and television studies at the University of Northampton, United Kingdom, where she teaches some of her favorite things, including horror, science fiction, contemporary television, and fiction, sometimes all at once. She received her PhD in American literature from Durham University, United Kingdom. She has published widely on horror and the fantastic, with much of her research dealing directly with genre and its operations in fiction, television, and film. Author of the monograph *Sex and the Slayer: A Gender Studies Primer for the Buffy Fan*, published by Wesleyan University Press in 2005, and a member of the editorial board of *Slayage*: *The Journal of the Whedon Studies Association*, her recent publications include work on representation, aesthetics, and form in shows such as *Angel, Battlestar Galactica, Firefly, Serenity, The Shield* and *The Wire*.

Lynnette **Porter** teaches humanities and communication courses at Embry-Riddle Aeronautical University in Daytona Beach, Florida. She writes books about television and film, including *Tarnished Heroes, Charming Villains, and Modern Monsters: Science Fiction Television in Shades of Gray on 21st Century Television* (McFarland, 2010), *LOST's Buried Treasures* (Sourcebooks, 2010), and *Unsung Heroes of* The Lord of the Rings: *From the Page to the Screen* (Praeger, 2005). She often writes about science-fiction television series such as *Heroes, LOST, Battlestar Galactica, Torchwood,* and *Doctor Who* and is a regular contributor to PopMatters. She frequently talks about science-fiction television at academic and fan conventions and is a member of the Popular Culture Association and the Tolkien Society.

Kevin Lee **Robinson** is a lecturer in scriptwriting and video production at the University of Northampton. Recently he has completed a series of scripts commissioned to raise awareness of youth homelessness and help to rewrite part of the national specification for the teaching of moving image production and scriptwriting. As well as lecturing in the area, he is an examiner, verifier, and moderator for media production. His research focus is British television science fiction writing and this was the subject of his recent article "Inhuman Nature" for *12point* (formerly scriptwriter magazine).

Julia **Round** lectures in the Media School at Bournemouth University, United Kingdom, and has previously taught at St. Martin's College, London, and Bristol University. She edits the academic journal *Studies in Comics* (Intellect Books) and is a member of Bournemouth University's Narrative Research Group and the International Society for the Study of Narrative. She has published and presented work internationally on cross-media adaptation, television and discourse analysis, the application of literary terminology to comics, the "graphic novel" redefinition, and the presence of Gothic and fantastic motifs and themes in this medium. She is working on a monograph entitled *Ghosts in the Gutter*, a discussion of the literary gothic in comics and modern fantasy cultures, to be published by McFarland. Further details at www.julia round.com.

David **Simmons** is a lecturer in film and television studies at the University of Northampton. He has written and published material on a wide range of issues related to twentieth-century popular fiction and culture including the sixties' countercultural movement, H.P. Lovecraft, the American horror film and contemporary genre television (including *Heroes, South Park, Spartacus: Blood and Sand,* and *Supernatural*). He is editing a collection on contemporary canonical British and U.S. novels.

Index

"Acceptance" 21, 26, 48, 128
The American Dream 31, 130, 131, 132, 136, 138, 140, 141
American Film Institute 1
Ando-cycle 21, 56
Ando Masahashi 20, 21, 25, 36, 43, 45, 47–48, 52, 56, 57, 63, 78, 102, 104, 106, 122, 149, 150, 151, 152, 158, 164
"Angels and Monsters" 25, 26, 27, 89
audience 1, 2–3, 4, 5, 6, 9, 13, 22, 24, 28, 30, 31, 32–33, 34, 36–40, 43–45, 49, 51, 52, 65, 68, 69, 70, 71–75, 78, 91, 93, 94, 95, 97, 100, 101, 103–106, 130, 132, 138, 139, 140, 141, 144, 149, 156–157, 165

Batman 19, 51, 53, 54–55, 56, 59, 61, 63, 64, 65, 71, 78, 79, 87, 89, 116
BBC 1, 65
Bennet, Claire 2, 4, 5, 7, 8, 9–10, 11–15, 16–18, 22, 23, 26, 27, 28, 30, 32–39, 42, 43, 45, 51, 54, 55, 56–57, 58, 64–65, 99, 112–113, 121, 124–129, 132, 136–137, 138, 142, 148, 164
Bennet, Noah *see* HRG
"Better Halves" 38, 122, 124, 126
The Big Bang Theory 41
Bishop, Elle 73, 114, 126
Bittorent 3
Bones 35
"Brave New World" 17, 18, 26, 28, 124, 126, 128, 153
"Brother's Keeper" 126, 128
Buffy the Vampire Slayer 2, 22, 29, 41, 44, 64, 125
"Building 26" 24, 128
"The Butterfly Effect" 24, 26, 27, 114

"Cautionary Tales" 126, 127, 167
Chuck 35, 41, 44, 76
"A Clear and Present Danger" 21, 24
"Cold Snap" 23, 24, 52, 89, 124
"Collision" 80, 82, 85, 103, 126
comics/graphic novels 2, 4, 5, 19, 28, 43, 44, 51–65, 67, 69–77, 78, 87, 89, 110, 113–115, 116, 117
The Company 2, 8, 10–17, 20, 28, 73–74, 87, 88, 112, 120, 121, 123, 125, 134, 148, 150, 153, 160
"Company Man" 7, 8, 9, 16, 112, 125

"Distractions" 122
"Don't Look Back" 43, 45, 82, 85, 113
"Dual" 26, 27, 124
"Dying of the Light" 73

"The Eclipse: Part 1" 23
"The Eclipse: Part 2" 47
"Eris Quod Sum" 126
"Exposed" 23

"Fallout" 38, 45, 86, 123
family 4, 7–15, 17, 30–39, 44, 49, 55, 57, 58, 72, 83, 86, 87, 88, 120, 122–126, 128, 129, 132, 133, 136–138, 141, 142, 147, 154
fan/fandom 1, 2, 3, 4, 7, 8, 9, 41–50, 63, 65, 66–67, 73, 76, 90, 93, 95, 100, 104, 121, 152
The Fantastic Four 57, 58, 61, 78
"Fight or Flight" 88, 123
Firefly 101
"Five Years Gone" 20, 99, 106, 120
"The Fix" 123
"Four Months Ago..." 48, 122
"Four Months Later..." 46, 75, 120, 152

gender 4, 5, 22, 29, 43, 124, 127, 129, 146, 149
"Genesis" 7, 25, 32, 43, 44, 68, 80, 85, 126, 127, 151
"Godsend" 46, 151

The Haitian 20, 35, 73, 74, 75, 114, 149
Halloween 33, 64
"The Hard Part" 8, 36, 124
Heroes Unmasked 52, 65, 91, 92, 93, 100, 103, 104, 105, 106

175

"Hiros" 9, 103, 105, 122, 127
Hitchcock, Alfred 36, 127
"Homecoming" 13, 38, 80, 84, 86, 122, 125
"How to Stop an Exploding Man" 9, 27, 46, 87, 123, 163
HRG/Noah Bennet 4, 7–18, 26, 30, 34, 35, 36, 44, 52–53, 54–55, 56–57, 63, 74, 75, 92, 107, 112, 124, 125–126, 127–128, 135, 136, 166
"Hysterical Blindness" 36

"I Am Become Death" 27, 88, 122, 166
"I Am Sylar" 164
The Incredibles 57, 119
"Ink" 26
"Into Asylum" 37
"An Invisible Thread" 27

Jenkins, Henry 42, 45 47, 49, 50, 53, 65, 101, 108

Kensei, Takezo 46–47, 74, 77, 127, 151, 152–153, 160–161, 162
"Kindred" 46, 88
Kring, Tim 2, 3, 6, 42, 44, 52, 55, 57, 63, 65, 91, 92, 93, 94, 96, 100, 108, 121, 125, 126, 129, 149, 155, 165, 167

"Landslide" 86–87, 99, 124, 152
Lee, Stan 57, 58, 78
Linderman, Daniel 82, 86, 92, 98–99, 120, 124, 133, 148, 152
"The Line" 46, 88
"Lizards" 113, 126
Lost 2, 41, 66, 122, 148, 156

The Matrix 51, 102, 109
Mendez, Isaac 20, 45, 47, 51, 58, 67, 78, 99–100, 102, 106
Misfits 19
Monroe, Adam 46, 47, 73, 74, 127, 153, 160, 162

Nakamura, Hiro 6, 7, 25, 30, 42, 47, 62, 68, 72, 112, 121, 144, 145, 148, 149–154, 158, 159, 160
NBC 1, 3, 5, 8, 18, 36, 40, 66, 69, 71, 76, 77, 78, 92, 107, 108, 117, 130, 144, 155
9th Wonders 45, 65, 67, 78, 113, 167
Nolan, Christopher 116
"Nothing to Hide" 38, 80, 83, 84, 86, 121, 128

Oka, Masi 1, 30, 42, 45, 103, 106, 112, 144, 150, 158
"Once Upon a Time in Texas" 53, 128

"One Giant Leap" 102
"Orientation" 24, 25, 48, 153
"Our Father" 161, 167
"Out of Time" 47, 88, 162, 164, 167

Parkman, Matt 25, 30, 51, 52, 60, 63, 75, 99, 112, 121, 122, 132, 148, 150
"Pass/Fail" 125, 154
Petrelli, Angela 11, 32, 44, 58, 74, 114, 124, 125, 128, 134, 160
Petrelli, Nathan 7, 11, 12, 15, 20, 22, 25, 26, 27, 35, 46, 51, 52, 57, 60–61, 63, 64, 80, 85, 88, 99, 105, 112, 121, 124, 125, 128, 133, 134, 135, 148
Petrelli, Peter 4, 7, 11, 20, 21, 22, 23, 25, 26, 27, 28, 30, 35, 46, 51, 52, 53, 54, 55, 57, 60, 61, 62, 63, 65, 68, 69, 79, 99, 103, 106, 107, 115, 116, 121, 125, 129, 132, 138, 158, 159, 160, 161, 162, 163, 165–167
"Powerless" 46, 74, 88, 123, 126
Primatech 2, 10, 27, 59, 62, 92, 108, 135, 160

Quantum Leap 43, 64
Quinto, Zachary 36, 114, 151, 164

Reaper 41
"Run!" 98

Sale, Tim 53, 67
Sanders, Micah 4, 20, 21, 24, 30, 32, 38, 39, 51, 56, 63, 75, 80, 81, 82, 83, 84, 85, 86, 87, 88, 89, 122, 124
Sanders, Niki 5, 7, 9, 20, 21, 23, 38–39, 60, 71, 78–89, 112–124, 125, 126, 127, 129
"The Second Coming" 20, 21, 27, 88, 162
"Seven Minutes to Midnight" 13
"Shadowboxing" 49, 116
"Six Months Ago" 39, 83, 84, 88, 122, 123, 124, 151
Smallville 19, 44
special effects 5, 80, 101, 102, 144, 147, 164
spectacle 2, 19, 67, 90, 92, 94–95, 101, 102, 104, 107, 110, 111, 123, 127, 147, 148, 156–157, 162, 164
Spiderman 55, 58
Star Trek 41, 43, 45, 47, 51, 66, 96, 101, 102, 108, 156, 157
Star Wars 43, 47, 51, 90, 94, 95, 96, 97, 101, 102, 108
Sullivan, Samuel 11, 12, 32, 36, 49, 52, 57–58, 63, 64, 120, 124, 126, 137–138, 140–142, 144, 153
Superman 19, 22, 47, 51, 53, 54, 55, 59, 60, 79, 89, 148, 167
Suresh, Mohinder 20, 22, 23, 26, 27, 28, 30, 54, 55, 70, 91, 98, 103, 106, 114, 115, 120, 127, 149

Sylar 7, 8, 9, 11, 13, 17, 21, 25, 26, 27, 28, 35, 36–37, 39, 45, 46, 51, 53, 54, 55, 56, 58, 60, 61, 62, 63, 64, 65, 79, 87, 98, 106, 114, 121, 122, 124, 129, 132, 134, 138–140, 151, 152, 164, 166

"Tabula Rasa" 48, 49
telefantasy 2, 164, 167
time travel 6, 151, 156–167
"Truth and Consequences" 127
"Turn and Face the Strange" 22, 150
Twain, Mark 157

"Unexpected" 75
"Upon This Rock" 153

Walker, Molly 55, 123, 148
"The Wall" 8, 12
Watchmen 2, 19, 28, 59, 78, 89, 109, 119
webisode 2, 63, 66, 92
Whedon, Joss 64, 101
Writer's Guild of America 1

The X-Files 2, 41, 44
X-Men 2, 19, 29, 43, 45, 78, 100, 104, 116, 164